ROGER
THE AUTOBIOGRAPHY

ROGER MILLWARD MBE
WITH
MIKE STERRIKER

FOREWORD BY COLIN HUTTON

RIVERHEAD
PUBLISHING

BIBLIOGRAPHY
Rothmans Rugby League Yearbooks
by Raymond Fletcher and David Howes
Hull Kingston Rovers - A Centenary History
by Michael E. Ulyatt
The Rugby League Challenge Cup
by Les Hoole
The Hull Daily Mail
Yorkshire Post Newspapers
Hull: A Divided City
by Michael E. Ulyatt
Photographs courtesy of:
Roger Millward, Hull Daily Mail,
Andrew Varley Picture Agency and Eddie Rolmanis

© Copyright 2005 Roger Millward MBE and Mike Sterriker
First published in Great Britain in 2005 by Riverhead Publishing
Second edition printed 2006

A CIP catalogue record for this book is
available from the British Library

ISBN 0-9550237-0-X

Typeset in 11 on 13pt Palatino by
Riverhead Publishing
44-46 High Street, Hull, East Yorkshire. HU1 1PS

Printed by
Fretwells Limited, Oslo Road, Kingston Upon Hull, HU7 0YN.

CONTENTS

DEDICATION

This book is dedicated to my late mum and dad, Ivy and Bill.
To my brother Roy, his wife Phyllis and his family.
And to my wife Carol, my daughter Kay,
son-in-law John and grandson Charlie.
It is also for the supporters of 'the greatest game' everywhere
but especially those of Castleford, Hull Kingston Rovers and Cronulla.
You made every day of my time in rugby league very special.
I'll never forget you.

ACKNOWLEDGEMENTS

I'd like to thank Mike Sterriker for his help and enthusiasm in writing this
book. He listened to my story for many hours and spent many more
researching other details that I couldn't hope to remember.
I'd also like to thank all the players, officials, supporters and friends who
contributed to this publication with their stories and personal memories.
A sincere thank you to you all.

COVER DESIGN: RIVERHEAD DESIGN, HULL
COVER PICTURES:
Front: Roger celebrates after Great Britain's 18-14 victory
against Australia at Bradford in 1978
Back: Great Britain versus Australia, 1978
Hull Kingston Rovers - First Division Champions, 1978-79
Roger's induction to the Hall of Fame, at Old Trafford 2000
Roger and Carol

FOREWORD

It is a great honour to be invited to write the foreword to this autobiography by Roger Millward.

Whenever and wherever the game of rugby league football is discussed, Roger's name will be at the forefront of any talk about the all-time greats of our game.

It was my privilege to be involved at first hand in the majority of Roger's career and I am certain his story will bring back some very special memories.

Roger's involvement at Hull Kingston Rovers is something very special, as is the friendship our two families have enjoyed for so many years.

I'm sure that this book will make fascinating reading and be a great success, not only in this country but in Australia and New Zealand, where he captivated the fans with his performances on tour and during his time with Cronulla.

Colin Hutton.

FIRST AND LAST
Top: Scoring in my first test appearance against the Australians at Headingley in 1967
Below: Lining up with some of the Great Britain squad at the Sydney Cricket Ground on
my last tour of Australia in 1979. That's me on the left and Brian is on the right

INTRODUCTION
A
RUGBY LEAGUE
GENIUS...

BY MIKE STERRIKER

Even as a boy there was nothing I enjoyed more than having a lie-in on a weekend. But on Saturday May 9 1964 I was up at the crack of dawn. It was the first time I remember actually seeing and not just hearing the milkman making his noisy deliveries. It was barely daylight as I put my scarf on and sat down to wait patiently on the settee by the front window.

I waited. And I waited. My pal from school was due to pick me up at seven o'clock. But when the grandfather clock in the living room struck eight, I realised there was little point in waiting any longer. We were going to see Rovers' first ever appearance at Wembley. But I never got there! Because although the trip had all been arranged - unfortunately the 'friend' who I'd planned it with and who was supposed to collect me for a great day out to London - forgot to tell his dad!

'It's the sort of thing that happens when young lads try to arrange things - but don't worry, you'll get other chances to go to Wembley,' said my mum. But her words of consolation did nothing to lessen the disappointment.

My 'friend' and his dad enjoyed a fantastic day at Wembley whilst I remained in Hull. When kick-off time finally arrived I watched the match through tear filled eyes on 'Grandstand' - in black and white! It was an experience that could have easily put me off rugby league forever - especially as Rovers lost!

But it didn't - at least not for long! During the following season, after a few unsuccessful attempts, my dad and 'Uncle Arthur' finally coaxed me to Craven Park. Arthur wasn't actually my real Uncle but a friend who my dad worked with. And following their constant invitations I finally decided to give Rovers another chance on a cold Saturday afternoon in November when there was nothing better to do.

I was an impressionable ten-year-old - and after just one visit, like many thousands of others - I was instantly hooked. For the next forty years, Craven Park, the old and then the new version, became my second home. I've been going there ever since. And I did get another chance to see my beloved Rovers at the twin-towers but it wasn't until sixteen years later. In 1980 they battled their way to the final again and faced their arch rivals,

Hull FC in the first ever all Hull Wembley Challenge Cup Final. I had no intention of missing out a second time...

The sixteen years between those two unforgettable Wembley Cup finals coincided with the playing career of the greatest player to ever play for Rovers. I was lucky enough to follow every minute of it.

I watched Rovers - and Roger Millward - play hundreds of times. I've seen them win in every way possible - from producing a breathtaking performance that overwhelmed the opposition, to securing the narrowest of victories with a late drop-goal or a last minute try. They won Premierships and League Championships. They contested Cup Finals and took on Australian touring teams - and emerged victorious from both! And I've also witnessed them suffer every type of defeat - some very humiliating, some unbelievably one-sided, some heartbreakingly close - and many highly contentious!

My first view of the precocious talent called Roger Millward was watching him playing in the ATV series of Under 17 Inter-Town matches. As far as I was concerned there was no better way of enjoying a cold Sunday afternoon than curling up on the sofa as the tiny black and white television lit up the living room and the winter gloom descended outside. For me, anything involving Rugby league was a must-see programme. And when the camera zoomed in, it invariably focused on a young halfback as he mesmerised the opposition, before scampering over the line for yet another try. It was Roger. He was sixteen years old, the diminutive star of the show - and obviously already destined for greatness...

Only a few weeks after my early morning disappointment and Rovers' defeat at Wembley against Widnes, Roger made his professional debut - with Castleford. His career took off at a meteoric pace. Less than two months later he broke into the first team, vying for the halfback spots with Internationals Alan Hardisty and Keith Hepworth. And his own International debut followed during the following season, his only full campaign with the Wheldon Road club.

In the summer of 1966, the Castleford directors amazingly decided Roger was 'surplus to requirements'. Rovers moved swiftly and signed him on August 7 for £6,000. It proved to be the best deal in the club's history...

Roger's impact at Craven Park was equally impressive. In his first season Rovers finished second in the league, their highest position for over fifty years. One of the season's toughest games of that campaign was at Wheldon Road at the end of October, the first time Roger had returned to face his old club. Hundreds of Rovers' fans poured into Castleford that night to see the match, I was one of them.

Roger later said, 'Castleford and Rugby League are the same thing.' I'm sure every one of those fans would probably agree! It's a nice enough place - but not many people would describe it as a very remarkable town.

When I first visited it as a youngster on that cold, wintry Friday evening in 1966 to watch Roger's return, I certainly didn't. At the time, as far as I was concerned, it was famous for only two things - rugby league and the place where Roger came from! On first inspection, the only other thing that might have changed my assessment was the tremendous number of public houses there seemed to be. And the fact that everyone who lived there appeared to suffer from a severe case of jaundice! The fact that Hull still had 'white' streetlights - and Castleford had amber ones, no surprise there, I suppose - could have been the reason for the apparent outbreak of yellow fever! Whatever it was, it was more than a bit worrying for a young lad not yet in his teens...

Walking the relatively short distance from the train station to the Wheldon Road ground, it always stuck in my mind that I counted no fewer than fourteen pubs on the way. The actual number I confess may have been exaggerated over the ensuing years. But whatever the exact amount was it was considerable for just one street, in what was 'only a relatively small mining town' in west Yorkshire. That impressively large number probably stayed indented in my memory because of my age. Because although most of the older members of the group stopped off at the various 'watering holes' along the way, at such a tender age I was only able to view their warm, inviting interiors from the cold street outside.

First impressions can be very memorable especially when you're young. And I witnessed more unforgettable scenes before the evening was over. Rovers won that night at Wheldon Road, a win that took them to the top of the league...

As a youngster I'd started my rugby league travels with short trips to the Boulevard, moved on to savour the delights of the A63 with slightly longer journeys to places like Castleford, Featherstone, Leeds and Wakefield. Before broadening my horizons still further with epic treks over the Pennines to 'unknown' destinations including Oldham, Leigh, Widnes and Rochdale!

Even in those early days when I watched Roger play, I knew I was watching an exceptional talent. He could do everything! And I'm still convinced to this day that I undoubtedly witnessed the emergence of the most complete player who ever played 'the greatest game'...

Roger was a unique sportsman. The type of player you have the privilege to see only once in a life time. He weighed only ten stone-ten pounds, and was a mere five feet, four inches tall. And if anyone had suggested that he'd go on to become one of the finest players of all time in what is regarded as the toughest team sport in the world, most people would probably either have laughed in their face or suggested they seek immediate help! But that's exactly what the diminutive Roger achieved. And his name will probably remain in the record books forever.

Roger had everything. He could score tries, kick goals, was an unbelievably accomplished defender and a devastating attacker. He possessed the type of wizardry that left opponents mesmerized and floundering helplessly in his wake. Quite simply Roger was a truly gifted player who could do things on a rugby field that no other player, before or after him could emulate.

He possessed self-confidence, arrogance and a total belief in his own ability. He was a player who constantly produced the unexpected. That breathtaking break, that indefinable touch of class, that flash of sporting genius which left the onlooker aghast with admiration.

Roger was the undoubted star of the last team to beat the Aussies down under, and return to Britain with the Ashes.

He finished his career with a unique record that nobody is likely to equal. It was argued that the only thing he lacked was size, but even this was never a drawback to him. More often than not he changed what could have been an apparent disadvantage into a benefit. Pound for pound, he was without doubt one of the most technically gifted and most effective tacklers the game has ever seen. He continuously brought gasps of approval from the crowds all over the world as his copybook tackling brought forwards twice his size crashing to the floor. Whilst in attack his small stature was another undoubted bonus, enabling him to weave and dodge his way through the tightest defences. He was a rugby league genius and arguably the most elusive attacker to ever wear a British jersey.

Whether Roger received the acclaim he undoubtedly deserved in Britain will always remain a matter for the fans to debate in the pubs and clubs of east Hull. I'm sure that if he'd been born in Sydney instead of in Castleford he'd have been worshipped as a true great of the sport. In fact it could be argued that because rugby league is Australia's national sport he probably received more acclaim and got ten times the amount of accolades there than he ever did in his native Britain...

Roger wasn't only my boyhood hero - over the next quarter of a century he became an important part of many thousands of Rovers' fans lives.

After following your hero's career, writing a book about him may sound like embarking on the ultimate labour of love. And although collaborating with Roger to produce this autobiography was in many ways exactly that - a thoroughly enjoyable task - at times it was also hard to imagine attempting anything more difficult! The main problem about writing about Roger was there were very few negative things to say about him to balance the overwhelming amount of positive ones. And simply trying to discover anything about him that wasn't perfect or very nearly, was more difficult than finding the proverbial needle in a haystack.

Many people had asked why there had never been an autobiography before? After all it's now twenty-five years since Roger played his last match - and fourteen since he finished his reign as the most successful coach in Hull Kingston Rovers' history.

During his career he became one of the most written about players in the history of Rugby League, but never before has he put pen to paper himself. The reason for this I soon discovered was mainly down to his unbelievable modesty. He's unquestionably one of the finest players the game has ever seen - but he never really believed his story was worth telling. He didn't regard the unique achievements that he enjoyed, both as a player and coach as worthy of appearing in print.

Fortunately, along with some members of his close family, including his wife, Carol, and his Mum, Ivy, I was able to convince him he was wrong. It wasn't an easy task. But I'm sure when you put this book down, you'll agree we were right to persevere in persuading him to tell his remarkable story. Roger's record-breaking exploits and endless list of achievements are legendary. He was only sent off once in his entire career - and even that dismissal, in a 'friendly' was of course 'the other player's fault!' The referee that day was a certain Fred Lindop, an official who cropped up with alarming regularity during Roger's career - and didn't always provide him with the best of memories. Roger was seldom in trouble with the authorities, was popular with his teammates, worshipped by the fans and even admired and respected by the opposition - well - most of them. Nobody it seemed had a bad word to say against him. So why I decided should I bother to look for anything that didn't fit into that image, if it didn't exist? And why should people regard the lack of any faults as something missing from Roger's unique story? After all, aren't we British always being blamed for not blowing our own trumpet loud enough?

Wasn't it about time the trend of looking for the negatives ended? So that a true portrait of arguably the finest player ever to wear the red, white and blue of Great Britain and the red and white of Hull Kingston Rovers could be painted. I thought so!

That's not to say Roger was always whiter than white. He wasn't! But if you're hoping to read about a player who lived on the edge, deliberately broke the rules or flouted authority, you may as well put this book back on the shelf now!

This book is about an ordinary lad from Yorkshire, who possessed an extraordinary talent. It's about an individual who used that gift to become one of the greatest rugby league players - not just of his era - but of all time. It's about a sporting genius. Most of all it's about a winner...

For those who followed Roger's career as I did, I'm sure the following pages will provide you with an informative and nostalgic trip down memory lane. And for those of you who didn't, I hope you'll enjoy an insight into a unique, sporting career that the world will undoubtedly never see again...

Nearly twenty years after those televised Under 17 matches, the picture on the television screen had changed to a colour one. But Roger - following a sensational career - was still the star.

In 1980 he led Hull Kingston Rovers out at Wembley to play local rivals, Hull, in the Challenge Cup Final. The last piece of the Millward jigsaw was finally in place. But even as he achieved his ultimate dream, the highs and lows that punctuated his career threatened to bring it to a tragic and abrupt end. Apart from the first thirteen minutes, Roger played the entire match with a broken jaw. The game proved to be his last ever first team appearance. The final chapter of a unique sportsman had been written. This is his story...

FACING THE CAMERA
The first time I faced the camera - pictured with my mum Ivy, and my dad, Bill.

SCHOOLDAYS
The Castleford Boys Modern School team 1959-60

CHAPTER ONE
I JUST WANTED TO BE ME...

THE DREAMS OF A CASTLEFORD LAD

The late summer evening light was fading rapidly. I knew it was now or never. I made a break, side-stepped two defenders and raced over in the corner to score the winning try. The opposing fullback had tried in vain to take me into touch five yards from the line. But my pace took me past his despairing dive and he was left clutching nothing but the cool, night air. My teammates cheered enthusiastically and gathered around to add their congratulations with the customary pat on the back.

'How do you always manage to be in exactly the right place every time?' asked Pete.

'I don't know,' I replied, shrugging my shoulders, 'It just happens.'

But there was no final whistle to this game! No applause from thousands of jubilant fans. And no cup for the winners. The only reason the match had finished at all was that it was now too dark to play on any longer...

We picked up our jumpers and jackets that had formed the touchline and made our way out of Ferry Fryston Woods, laughing and joking as we went. The large clearing between the trees made a perfect rugby pitch. There, we could be Great Britain taking on the Australians - Castleford clashing with Leeds in the Wembley Cup Final - or anyone else we wanted to be! But for now, another night's rugby was over. All that was left for a bunch of rugby-mad teenagers was the short walk home, supper and bed!

Later on, as I did most nights, I told mum and dad about how I'd won the game. And I thought one day I'll score another winning try - one that will mean something! Where there will be a final whistle - and thousands of jubilant fans - and a massive trophy to parade around a packed stadium. I'll be playing against the Aussies in the deciding test match. Or I'll be at Wembley starring in the Challenge Cup Final!

It was the summer of 1961. And at thirteen years of age those were just dreams. But I always thought if you didn't have any dreams - how could they ever come true?

Castleford had always been my home. I was born and bred there. I'd entered the world on September 16 1947 in Bridge Street, one of the main streets off Wheldon Lane - less than a stone's throw from the Castleford

Rugby League ground, Wheldon Road.

My mum, Ivy, lived in Castleford, in Princess Street, virtually next door to the ground. When I was young, she worked at the local offshoot of Rowntree Mackintosh. They called it 'Bellamys' in those days - it was also down Wheldon Lane - and was later taken over by Nestle. My mum was always my biggest fan. I suppose she had to be to wash the muddy jerseys, shorts and socks I brought home week after week. The pitches we played on weren't exactly up to bowling-green standard, particularly when January and February came round. She was also one of the main driving forces in ensuring this book eventually saw the light of day. Many of the pictures, facts and figures are from her collection of scrapbooks and photographs that she accumulated during my career. Like any proud mum, she often encouraged me to tell my story in print. And I'm sure she'd be delighted her collection has finally been put to such good use. Until recently mum was a well-known face in the 'Early Bath' pub opposite Wheldon Road or 'The Jungle' as it's known now.

My dad, William, came from a little place called Hanley, near Stoke on Trent in Staffordshire. He started out working in 'the Potteries' but after moving to Yorkshire, finished down the mines - he was a 'ripper' down the pit.

Dad was a pretty good soccer player in his younger days and played for a short while for Rotherham United. He also played amateur rugby league for the 'Wheldale Hotel'.

My uncle Frank, Frank Lockwood, played professional rugby league for York in the 1950s. He was a stand-off and I remember going with my granny to watch him when they played at home. Annie and I would catch the train in Castleford and then walk from the station in York to the ground, Clarence Street. It was a great adventure for me. Travelling on a noisy steam train was always a lot more exciting than going by car or bus - and definitely better than the uninspiring diesels we have today. I'd only be about five or six years old at the time but I remember it like it was yesterday. Annie was one of a very large family. She had a dozen children, including uncle Frank, and uncle Walt, Brian's dad. We'll hear a great deal more about my cousin Brian of course later.

My one brother, Roy, is seven years older than I am. He worked as a steel erector and was actually on the site when they built the cooling towers at Ferrybridge. He played a little bit of professional rugby league at Bramley. But he also finished up down the pits.

Apart from going to watch my uncle Frank, I can also remember watching Castleford from five or six years of age. I've always been a Cas' supporter and still go and watch them now whenever I can.

I remember being at a match at Wheldon Road when they played the 1955 New Zealand tourists and one of the Castleford lads collapsed on the pitch and sadly later died in hospital. He was a 'Wheldon Laner' named Dennis Norton, a young prop-forward who had a lot to offer and his whole life in front of him. The tourists won the match - and again a few weeks later when they returned to play a second match to help raise funds for Dennis' dependants. The scores of course were totally insignificant to everyone. The tragedy put everything into perspective. Sport may have seemed everything to lads like me at that age. But when something like that happened, rugby and everything else that you thought of as being important, paled into insignificance. That was in the mid-fifties when I was only eight years old - but no matter how old you are, things like that stay with you for ever.

I also remember when I was still at Grammar School, which was rugby union orientated and the Australian Rugby League tourists were here on the 1963 tour. They were due to play against Castleford on the Wednesday afternoon and because we were at school it looked like we were going to miss the game. I couldn't miss the opportunity of having the Australians playing at Wheldon Road and not being able to see them, so I took the Monday off. My plan was to stay off school 'ill' so I could go to the match on the Wednesday. Staying off on just the Wednesday would have been too obvious, I thought, and there'd be less chance of 'them' suspecting anything if I had a few days away.

However on the Tuesday I got to know that we were being allowed the afternoon off from school on the Wednesday anyway, so we could go to the match, it was brilliant. A lot of lads, it seemed, went back to school on that Wednesday morning. There wasn't just me who had taken time off, we had all had the same idea! We all thought it was very funny of course and even had the last laugh as well, when Castleford won the match, 13-12 after Mike Smith scored a try in the last minute. It was a fantastic day and one that always stayed in my mind.

Castleford and Featherstone Rovers were the only two club sides to beat the Australians that year. In fact it was the Aussies' most successful tour to date, winning the first two tests, to take the Ashes for the first time since the 1911-12 season. The tourists ran up a record score, 50-12 in the Second Test at Swinton when Britain were reduced to eleven men due to injuries - all of which made Castleford's achievement more memorable. There were players in the Castleford team like Colin Battye, Denzil Webster on the wing, Albert Lunn at fullback and John Sheridan who I actually later played with, they were all superb players.

People often say that your schooldays are the happiest days of your life. I wouldn't agree with that sentiment totally because although I enjoyed my schooldays, I was just as happy when I'd left full-time education. My first school was Wheldon Lane Junior School, which I attended until I was eleven. After that, there were two senior schools that you could go to. If you passed your 'eleven plus' you went to Castleford Grammar School - and if you didn't pass, you went to Castleford Boys Secondary Modern School. Well I didn't pass my exams at my first attempt so I went to the secondary modern for a year. But a year later I did pass and went on to the Grammar School and was there from 1960 to 1964. But there were no GCE's at the end of my stay, I can assure you. And that was a drawback, which I found out to my cost afterwards, when I went to become an electrician and it took me another eight years to get my HNC honours.

At school I didn't get any qualifications at all. I loved P.E. and I liked Maths but apart from those two subjects, there wasn't anything else that particularly interested me. I don't remember how I got on the road to becoming an electrician, it just happened. I was probably sensible for once. I realised I wasn't going to get any G.C.E.s so I might as well start thinking about what I wanted to do when I left school - and how I'd achieve it. Most of my pals were going to be electricians or fitters. It was a very good, five-year apprenticeship at the time. First you did a full year at College, then you got day release, building up to a class one certificate in City and Guilds - and then you could go on to HNC and HNC honours, which was a hell of a good qualification for becoming an electrician. Castleford of course was a huge mining community then, with a very large number of pits surrounding the town - and that's the way I jumped...

My best pals at Wheldon Lane Juniors were Carl Dyson, Mick Redfearn and Brian Lovick. We were inseparable. Mr Turner and Mr Bellwood took us for sport and I suppose you'd have to say they introduced me to the game of rugby league. I know Mr Bellwood is still very interested in sport. And even today, I often see him in the 'Early Bath' enjoying the Super League coverage on a Friday night.

At senior school Mr Whittaker at Castleford Secondary Modern and Mr Hughes at Castleford Grammar School were my next influences. None of the four were professional coaches but their love of the game and enthusiasm rubbed off on me throughout my schooldays.

When I was very small, I loved playing at 'cowboys', the same as any kid. I had a cowboy suit, a cowboy hat, a pair of cowboy boots and of course two guns in holsters that came nearly down to my knees. Compared to some of the other kids I was probably regarded as a bit shy when I was young, but I'd certainly say I was 'one of the lads' at school. I had some very good friends, especially during my time at Grammar School. Kids like Roger Worth, Geoff Rutherforth and Michael Parrish. We were all great mates and always together. They were certainly good times, and those lads were good friends - and no matter what happened, we always looked after each other. We would always be out on the field, playing rugby, football or cricket. That's all we seemed to do on a night. From coming home from school, we used to throw our bags in the house and go out to play touch rugby in the street. The only problem with that pastime was that we occasionally had to stop the game and wait until the bus went by. Luckily there weren't that many cars in those days, otherwise it's doubtless whether we would ever have reached half-time, let alone completed any of our matches. But when we heard the bus we'd all stand still, it was sort of an unwritten law of the game. It must have looked like the match had been put on 'freeze-frame' - but it gave us a few seconds to plan our next move! Later on the Council workmen made life even more difficult for us by planting some trees on either side of the road. And before they got used to the new obstacles some of the lesser skilled lads would constantly run into them. But it toughened 'em up, I suppose.

Once we'd started at secondary school we progressed to a much more suitable venue. Every evening we'd all make a beeline to play in the woods at Ferry Fryston. In the middle of the woods there was a clearing which made a perfect rugby pitch. And every evening - we didn't even have to arrange to meet, we'd just turn up and there'd be about twenty kids there wanting to play rugby all night - or at least until it got too dark to see what we were doing. Basically that's all we did - there weren't that many other distractions in those days. Things like television were still to make an impact. But at that age all we wanted to do was go out and play sport.

Peter Astbury was one of the lads who played with us in the woods - he went on to play at Castleford in the Under 17s and then signed for Leeds.

As a teenager for years I used to play two matches every Saturday. In the morning I'd play for the school team and in the afternoon for Castleford Under 17s nursery team. I was also a pretty useful soccer player, as an under 14 player I regularly stole the limelight scoring 34 goals in 10 games, including 8 in one match.

Castleford may have been far removed from London's glamorous West End, or the attractions some of the other big cities had to offer, but it was a great little place to live when you got to know it. And I got to know it much better when I got to sixteen and started going out on the town - with my Beatles suit on! The other fashion that proved ideal for me at the time was the 'Cuban Heels'. In the sixties they'd had winkle-pickers first, and we laughed at them but then they brought out 'Caribbean Heels'. The Beatles used to wear them, chunky shoes with a big heel. What could be better as far as I was concerned, I thought? It was the only time I was ever five feet eight - but unfortunately everybody else was six feet two - because they'd bought a bloody pair as well!

Every Saturday night I'd go 'out on the town' with my mates from the Castleford Under 17s. 'The Engineers', 'The Feathers' and the renowned 'Kiosk' were our regular haunts. We were too young to drink any alcohol of course and had to be content with lemonade and orange juice - will anyone actually believe that?

I love music and always have. And for me, at sixteen, there was nothing to beat the Beatles and the Rolling Stones! Nowadays I'd have to admit to a far more varied taste in music. There are some very good groups around now but I think the sixties are still the best. I can listen to classical music especially in the car. I wouldn't say I'm a great lover of Jazz but I do like some Country & Western - such as the Eagles and Kenny Rogers - and I always thought that Queen and Freddie Mercury in particular, were fantastic artists. I don't think you can get much more diverse than that collection...

My dad used to watch me in every game I played. He wasn't like some of the dads you see today who stand there shouting and bawling - they didn't in those days. But he stood and watched all the same and took note of what I did, right and wrong, and then had a quiet word with me afterwards. And that's how I think it should be. I can't do with people pushing kids into things. Kids will be what they want to be. It's no use pushing a youngster into a game of rugby league if he doesn't really want to be there - it's a hard enough game to be involved in without that. But I never needed any coaxing from my dad or anyone else. Ever since the first rugby league game that I played for Wheldon Lane Junior School - I played on the wing and I was eight year's old - I always wanted to be a professional rugby league player. And I always wanted to play at halfback. Stand-off was a great position to play, it was the position for me. And even though some people called it 'suicide corner', when I made a break, there was no feeling in the world like it!

Playing rugby was always just a natural progression for me - an integral part of my life. It's simply what had to happen. I didn't think about it - I didn't plan it - it was something that just had to be. I'd go to school and play. I'd come home on a night and play. That's just the way I thought in those days. I can't ever remember saying to myself 'I'm going to be a professional rugby player,' I honestly can't ever remember saying such a thing. I just enjoyed what I did, turning out and playing rugby league. Everything else after that, as they say, would be a bonus. But I didn't ever get to a point and have to think is playing rugby what I want to do? It was just something I always knew would happen - it was where I wanted to be. And the older I got, there were certain roads I had to travel down to get there. The first road at that time was to get into the Castleford Under 17s team. They had a massive reputation at the time because they were a hell of a side who had won trophies for the last three or four years and were very rarely beaten. There were some great players in the side - and that was my first challenge - to become one of them.

The first problem I had was that although all my old mates from the Secondary modern were going down to train with the Under 17s, I was playing rugby union at the Grammar School at the time. But I took part in a trial match, got a place and that was it. It just went from there. And there were some good players in that team. The main thing for me at the time was to get into the side and stay there. I could think about what would happen next, after that!

You'd always picked up things from watching matches. In the late fifties I saw Alex Murphy for the first time. St Helens came across to play Castleford in the Challenge Cup and at half-time Castleford were winning 10-0. But a bit of magic from St Helens inspired by Alex and Saints won 18-10.

The next time I played with my mates I would want to be just like Alex, but as with most kids of my age, that was a constantly changing aspiration. I would want to be a certain player one day, and someone different the next. But most of all I suppose, I just wanted to be me...

There were a lot of things that happened to me when I was a youngster. But probably the one thing that sticks in my mind the most was when I was thirteen and I broke my leg playing rugby at school. My 'mate' Pete Astbury, 'Razza' did it - and as usual there were no half measures with me. No simple break! No hairline fracture for me! I had a double fracture! I broke both my tibia and fibula and was in pot for thirteen weeks. And not just a little pot either, this one went from my ankle, right up to the top of my thigh. But the injury never made me think about what a dangerous sport I was getting myself into. I never once thought about the dangers. And Pete is still a good family friend to this day.

The incident did have its' funny side though because it happened in the period when I was transferring from Secondary Modern to Castleford Grammar. I broke my leg playing for Castleford Boys Modern at rugby league and still had the pot on when I transferred to the Grammar School. But the injury didn't stop me playing sport. And I remember getting more than a few rollickings from the teachers when they saw me playing football in the playground at lunchtime - with a full-length pot on my leg.

At Grammar school we played rugby union in the first term and then soccer in the second. This was basically because our facilities weren't particularly good and we only had one sports field. I just loved playing all sports at that time and was soon picked for the school soccer team at 'inside left'. I suppose the pace I had helped me and I'd just got a knack for scoring goals. I recall I did surprise some of the sports masters by scoring so many goals. And it was rumoured that scouts from some professional clubs had been to watch me on various occasions. But that was before I started with the Castleford Under 17s and I joined them when I was only fourteen. If I'd been offered the choice in those days there was only one game I wanted to play.

I've often been asked if I realised how much better I used to be than the other kids that I played with, even when I was still very young. And how much potential I had to become even better. It is of course a tricky question to answer without appearing conceited. But in my own mind I did know. And certainly at this stage of my life it is something I'm not going to deny. When we went to play rugby after school in the woods for example, I would only be twelve or thirteen and some of the lads I played against were sixteen - but it was easy for me. I appreciated the fact even then and obviously it made me feel that I had something special.

And fortunately I always had great people around me to bring that talent out of me. I've always been very lucky in that respect starting at Wheldon Lane with a superb chap called Laurie Turner. When I moved on to Secondary Modern School, the encouragement continued from Mr Whittaker. And at Grammar School, I received a great amount of help from a Geography teacher, Mr Hughes, who was also the coach of the rugby union team - so I had important influences all through my schooldays. They brought me down to earth a few times. But I don't think that was needed very often because I've always been level headed and always respected people.

I loved playing all sports. Apart from rugby and soccer I also represented the school at Athletics and cross-country. I loved athletics and I loved cricket. There was nothing better on a hot summer's afternoon than being wicket keeper! At that age, to me that's what life was all about - sport!

Mick Muffit, the Under 17's coach was the next big influence on my career... My first success with the Under 17's was in the 1963/64 season when we won the ABC TV Inter Town Cup. The games or at least the second half of them were televised live on television on Sunday afternoons. That was quite a coup for rugby league in those days - and it certainly did a great deal to promote the game. It also made me a household name - well, at least in Yorkshire and Lancashire, where the programmes were transmitted.

The thing that I've always found amazing, and still do today, is the number of people who say they remember watching them. The amount of people who used to watch that programme and the amount of interest it created was phenomenal. But the stupid thing about it was the programme only lasted for one season. Bill Fallowfield used to be the commentator and everyone, of a certain age at least, remembers it!

We beat the Hull & District League in the Inter-Town Knock-Out Cup Final at Wheldon Road on Sunday 24 November, 1963. I remember the line-up as if it was yesterday - Howard Bibb, Bill Francis, Phil Evans, Mick Redfearn, Wilfred Newton, Me, Carl Dyson, Edward Parker, Anthony Miller, Graham Isherwood, Michael Broom, Barry Lockwood and Anthony Pell. A number of that side went on to enjoy successful professional careers. And one in particular, Bill Francis, would play a significant part in one the most heart-breaking defeats I ever suffered. But that setback happened much later in my career...

Back in the 1963-64 season I could do little wrong. Although the following Sunday I tasted defeat when I was drafted into the Castleford Under 19s side for their televised final against Wakefield. We led at one stage 5-2 but were then badly disrupted when our winger, Major broke his jaw and our loose-forward Hamer had to be pulled out of the pack. I managed a try but we were well beaten in the end by 20 points to 8. I soon realised that losing, and more importantly how you dealt with losing, was also an important part of maturing as a rugby league player. I also realised very quickly that it was definitely something I didn't want to make a habit of.

Happily, back with the Under 17s things soon improved again. Only a few weeks after the win over Hull we played Widnes District League on Sunday January 12 1964 in the Television Trophy Final at Headingley, Leeds. Widnes were the Lancashire winners of the Inter-Town Cup and a match against Castleford would decide the overall winners. And fortunately that proved to be us!

The Castleford lads were in full control from the start and led 13-0 at halftime. Mick Redfearn, Bill Francis and yours truly scored tries and I also kicked two goals. After the break Bill and I did even better, adding two more tries each to both finish with hat-tricks. It wasn't the last time Bill and I played together in a successful side. On March 1 1964 we were both selected for the Yorkshire Under 17s to face Cumberland at Doncaster. Bill played on the right wing and scored five tries whilst I played at stand-off and had to be content with three. Yorkshire ran out easy winners 45-5 and not surprisingly I suppose it was reported that we were both attracting a fair amount of interest from a number of senior clubs.

Before our games as teammates, I'd actually played against Bill. The first time was when I was playing rugby union for Castleford Grammar School and he was playing for Normanton. I think it's probably an encounter he'd prefer to forget. I remember leaving him helpless after I'd tackled him and his jersey had come right over his head. He couldn't see a thing until he managed to get up and pull it down again. By that time though the game was continuing over fifty yards away. We would both have been fifteen years old. There's always been a friendly sort of rivalry between Bill and I ever since that initial tussle.

Originally he was a Featherstone lad. But he never signed for a Yorkshire club. He signed for Wigan and went to live in Lancashire straight after his final season at Grammar School. He got an apprenticeship and everything there. He was one of the first kids I knew that as soon as he reached the age of sixteen - he'd gone.

Two other players who played with me in the successful Under 17's team were my cousins, Barry and Brian Lockwood. Brian signed for Castleford just ahead of me and I'll always remember we were soon in direct competition with each other. One particular Saturday, Keith Hepworth was sidelined due to an injury and Castleford were picking the first team and had to choose a scrum-half for the day to replace 'Heppy'. It was to be either Brian or me. He was a loose forward then but he got the nod. And I think it was down to my size - there was still a thing about me being a bit on the small side...

I often played two matches a day when I was a teenager. I'd play for the school team in the morning and then play for the Under 17s in the afternoon. The only position I ever played in for the under 17's was stand-off. I played on the wing later on but that was for the Castleford first team.

After the Under 17s matches I always enjoyed a hot bath and a joke with the other lads, especially when we'd won. It wasn't so much fun when we'd lost, but fortunately that didn't happen too often. We didn't of course get paid for playing but we still always went all out to win.

The other thing I remember about playing for the under 17's had nothing to do with anything that happened on the field. It was the Chinese meals we got afterwards. The coaches used to take us to the Chinese Restaurant in Castleford and as you can imagine an awful lot of chow mien, chop suey and chicken curry and chips soon disappeared when twenty-odd ravenous under seventeen-year-olds descended to satisfy twenty-odd healthy appetites. After the meal was the bit I didn't like, though - the worst ordeal of all as far as I was concerned. I'd always been nervous before a game - even when I'd played with a few old socks for a ball in the street with my schoolmates. Captaining the under 17s didn't help that! In fact it meant I was also nervous after the match as well! As the captain of the side it was my duty to make an after dinner speech. I'd rather have faced a pack of burly forwards any day!

The changing facilities at Castleford were good, as it was a professional ground. But that wasn't always the case. At some places we played, conditions were far from ideal. Some of the junior grounds could be a bit 'primitive' to say the least. In the 1960s hardly any of the grounds we played at had showers - we had to get scrubbed clean in communal baths - something which certainly wouldn't be allowed today of course.

I recall one game we played at Heworth, the changing rooms were about a mile away from the pitch. At least it seemed that distance when you had to walk there and back in your rugby boots through everything including muddy fields and allotments! The 'old chaps' we passed on the way never batted an eyelid as they planted their spuds or stoked their bonfires. We could only assume our appearance was either a regular sight for the busy gardeners or that they simply weren't very interested in rugby.

On one occasion when we played against Endike in Hull the changing rooms were OK - but the spectators I remember were so close to the pitch, they often got involved in the match. One particular woman, obviously an avid Endike supporter, was so keen to help her team that she pushed her pram, complete with sleeping baby, out onto the pitch and stopped our winger in full flight, abruptly ending his run down the wing. Fortunately her defensive efforts didn't alter the final result - we still won!

The Castleford Boys Modern School team 1960

The Castleford 'A' team which won the Yorkshire Senior Competition Championship for the second time in three years in 1965

CHAPTER TWO
BARLEY MOW & BILLY BOSTON

MY EARLY DAYS AT WHELDON ROAD

When I look back on it now, the start of my career at Castleford was nothing short of amazing. I remember my debuts for Castleford 'A' and fortunately for all the right reasons. I say debuts because like birthdays in the case of a certain member of the Royal Family I'd meet a few years later, I had two. I'd actually turned out for the 'A' team in a match at Batley at the end of the 1963/64 season. That game took place before I'd signed-on however, so I played at stand-off under the accustomed pseudonym for rugby league trialists of 'A. N. Other'.

It was a very painful introduction - the first time I wore a pair of shoulder pads. But as I hurt my shoulder quite badly - it was very rare that I wore them again. They undoubtedly help some people but definitely not everyone. The match was my first 'A' team game for Castleford at Dewsbury. The coach of the 'A' team at that time was a smashing bloke called George Clinton. He was the Deputy Mechanical Engineer at the pit at Glasshoughton. Everything and everyone seemed to be connected to the pit in those days. Most of the lads used to work there. I remember I still went to work on the Monday morning. I was only sixteen and had started work at the pit only a few weeks earlier. I certainly didn't want to have any time off!

My cousin Brian, was in the team at loose-forward. We won the game 14-10 and although my first accolades as a Castleford 'A' player remain treasured to this day, I still have to smile at the fact I had to use an alias, when of course virtually everyone in the ground knew who I was. The newspaper report contained the following paragraph:

'A feature of the game was a classical display by a trialist stand-off who paved the way for a first half try by Baker and then beat four men superbly soon after half-time to score himself. He rounded off his debut with a forty-yard penalty.'

Not a bad start for a lad with no name, I thought.

My official debut however was at the start of the following 1964/65 season. It was a game against Bramley 'A' at Barley Mow. Names like Barley Mow, and Mount Pleasant, where the aforementioned Batley played, and still do

25

today, always sounded like inviting venues to play professional sport. I can assure you, with no disrespect to fans and officials at either of those clubs - on a cold, wet and windy winter's afternoon they were anything but!

I wasn't allowed to sign on as a professional until my seventeenth birthday in September, so before that played my next few matches on amateur forms. I could then be named in the match reports. So I always think of the game at Barley Mow on August 22 1964 as where my 'professional' career officially started.

It was a Saturday, this after all was long before the advent of Sunday matches and also way before many teams had floodlights - so virtually all games took place on Saturday afternoons - with kick-off usually scheduled for 2.30pm to ensure the action was completed before darkness fell.

In my very first game I remember already being a marked man, or at least that's what the local newspaper suggested afterwards. The 'attention' was something that I would naturally have to contend with for the rest of my career - but it was nothing new, I'd been used to it for as long as I could remember!

'Elusive, he often left opponents empty handed as Bramley's hopes of slowing him up by 'heavy' tackling were unsuccessful.' read the match report. But I didn't care about things like that. I was playing for Castleford 'A'. I'd scored a try in my very first professional rugby league game that day and we'd won 4-28. I was already on the next rung of the ladder. And the second match was even better...

On August 29 Wakefield Trinity 'A' were the visitors to Wheldon Road and we played brilliantly and beat them 24-8. It was my home debut and I celebrated in style by scoring my first professional hat-trick. More accolades of course followed:

'For the second week running the star of the match was 16 years-old, Roger Millward, who thrilled the many thousands of TV watchers on Sunday afternoons last season with the Castleford & District Under 17 side. There was a crowd of around 1,000 at Wheldon Road, more than some first team games the previous Saturday and no doubt the type of football played by these youngsters is well worth watching and should continue to draw the supporters.

There is an abundance of talent at Wheldon Road these days and practically all so youthful that it would be possible quite easily to run an Under 19 professional team - with a few reserves to spare.'

Those first two wins gave me a tremendous start to my career but seven days later I was brought down to earth with a bump.

In my third match we lost 31-18 at Hunslet 'A' following a below par performance. Fortunately I managed to score a first half try to keep my scoring sequence going and the game proved only a minor setback.

The next game saw us back at our best with a 35-0 home victory against Batley. I had my best match so far that day, scoring four tries - and I remember them all. The first three came in a nine minute spell early in the first half and the fourth, seven minutes from time, after I intercepted a pass eighty-five metres from the Batley line. Bell 2, Mick Williams, Maurice

Williams and Baker scored the other tries and Ron Willett and I also kicked two goals each.

Not surprisingly the reports were once again favourable:

'The 'A' team were having a scoring spree at the expense of Batley 'A' in their 35-0 victory. Once again it was Roger Millward who had the crowd roaring with delight and approval with four more tries, having scored in all four games played to date and taking his tally to nine. One particular effort on Saturday was a try from an interception inside his own 25, and no one could get anywhere near him in his dash to the Batley line. Just for good measure he also popped over two goals in the second half.'

When I signed for Castleford on my seventeenth birthday in September 1964, Len Garbutt was the secretary, Harry Street was the coach and the Directors included people like Bill Broxup and Ronnie Simpson. Mick Muffit, the Under 17s coach and Len Garbutt invited me to sign on. I just wanted to get on with it. I was so keen to sign, I never thought about the fee, money didn't come into it.

Just before I signed, Leeds had also expressed that they'd like to sign me and had offered me £1,500 on the table. Castleford offered me £200 and I took that. I was a very silly lad at times. But that's all that bothered me then, I'd been watching them since I was five years old, and all I wanted was to play for Castleford. And don't forget, apart from the money, there was another 'minor' factor that should have made me think twice about putting pen to paper. Internationals Keith Hepworth and Alan Hardisty, were already there, and I wasn't even guaranteed to get a place in the team ahead of those two. But that never entered my head either. I just wanted to sign for Castleford. To get the club badge on my blazer and walk round the town as a Castleford player!

Once I'd signed, things just happened to me from the word go. I had good quality football players around me. The 'A' team had got to be such a tremendous side at that time that we regularly used to get over 2,000 spectators coming to watch us.

The side was a superb blend of young players who'd come up from the under 17's mixed with some experienced first- teamers, working their way back to full fitness after injury. When it was all put together there was some really good football played - it was really enjoyable. I learnt lots in that team at the time because there were so many experienced players around, you couldn't fail to pick up things to help your game. And you had to learn quickly or you could soon find yourself in a lot of bother.

In the early days I was a good trainer, but let's get it straight from the start - the older I got, the worse a trainer I became.

I was also a quick learner, you had to be, otherwise somebody would soon catch you out. On the field, you also had to have good mates around you. When you came into the professional game you had to have people looking out for you. I realise I was very lucky in that respect. And I'm sure my size probably helped me a little bit as well - people tended to look after me just a little bit more. But it was off the field where your so-called mates could catch you out...

I remember the first night I went to training. There was a tremendous bunch of lads down at Wheldon Road when I started. And some very 'funny' lads as well. People like Johnny Ward, Johnny Walker and Bill Bryant, they'd already made the first team but they looked after the young ones as well, at least most of the time...

When I arrived at the ground, Johnny Ward and Johnny Walker came over to chat to me. They could see there was something wrong and Johnny Ward said, 'What's up young 'un?'

I said that I had a bit of a hamstring problem.

Johnny immediately suggested,

'Go and see the physio, old Billy Rhodes, he'll look after you.'

Billy was what you'd describe as a real 'old-timer', and I took Johnny's advice, and went straight into the 'physio' room and jumped on the table.

Billy glanced at me and repeated the question,

'What's up with you lad?'

I think I've got a bit of hamstring trouble, I replied, hoping for a little help and advice now I'd joined the professional ranks, I think it needs a bit of a rub. I got neither help nor advice!

'Now listen young 'un.' said Billy. 'Good 'uns' don't need it, and bad 'uns' aren't worth it - now get out!'

And that was it. My first 'consultation' with the 'medical team' had come to an abrupt end! The lads had set me up and I'd gone and got my come-uppence. It was things like that I unfortunately remember - and how naive I was at the time to fall for such tricks...

I suppose I didn't really start thinking about the game and what I wanted to achieve in rugby league until after I'd signed on. But once I had, I thought about the game very carefully - and put my life into some sort of perspective. After signing on the first thing that I wanted to do was obviously get into the 'A' team. From there progress and consolidate a place in the first team, and then go on to play for Yorkshire, the Under 21's, Great Britain - and beyond my dreams, go on tour. That was the plan but that only started after I'd signed. So my first job was to work hard and become a regular member of the 'A' team - and make the most of any opportunities I received to play in the first team. Thankfully I didn't have to wait long!

I made my first team debut at Dewsbury on October 3 1964. It was the beginning of a whirlwind start to my professional career. Only twelve months later I made my England Under 24s debut and was chosen for the Great Britain team. And although I had to sit out my first two Internationals from the 'comfort' of the bench, it proved to be third time lucky when I made my debut against France on March 5 1966 at Wigan. Before those International call-ups however, there was a great deal I had to achieve first at Wheldon Road...

That started with my full Castleford debut at Crown Flatt - only a fortnight after my seventeenth birthday!

The thing I remember most about the game was how nervous I was before the kick-off. And then once the match was underway, how I encountered my first 'bit of trouble' with a referee over the scrums. It was a tough match and a very close one, because Dewsbury at that time weren't a bad team - but we managed to win.

A physical encounter at Dewsbury wouldn't have been my ideal choice for my first team debut but I look back on the victory now with a certain amount of satisfaction. I also think that without breaking any pots, I played all right that day.

I was one of four players who made their Castleford debuts that afternoon. Trevor Waring and David Appleyard, two other youngsters from the 'A' team were with me. And Abe Terry, who we'd signed from Featherstone also started his first game for the club - but only lasted ten minutes before coming off with a broken nose.

The other thing that stuck with me about the match was listening to the 'big' fellas on the park - and it was a totally different language again to what I'd been used to. I'd learned a 'language' in the Under 17s and a different 'language' in the 'A' team and all of a sudden I was playing with the big boys - and I knew it didn't get any better than that! But it was different. It was a half a yard quicker here - and a half a yard quicker there. And it was that difference in the pace of the play, which I was trying to pick up all the time.

There were plenty of other things I had to get used to as well. Like the old 'nine hole' at Dewsbury, which I naturally found out all about during my debut there. The 'nine hole' as it was infamously known was a big delve in one corner of the pitch and once you were pinned down in that area of the field it was virtually impossible to get out of it.

Dewsbury would continuously kick the ball down into that area - and we were left to ponder, why the hell can't we get out of here? Especially when we knew it had been there for years and years. In the end, once I'd experienced it a number of times, I could use it to our advantage, both as a player and a coach.

Dewsbury wasn't the only pitch with testing characteristics. I soon found out that winning at a few other grounds could be equally tricky. Apart from the opposing players, you also had the unique slopes of places like Batley and Featherstone to contend with.

After the victory our prop forward, Maurice Williams, put his arm around me and we walked off the field together. It was a fantastic feeling to have triumphed in my first senior match. I felt like I'd won the Cup final! But I had to keep my feet on the ground. One thing that helped me do that was the fact I wasn't being chosen for the first team every week. I was still down the half-back pecking order, behind players like Alan Hardisty and Keith Hepworth. I had to fight for a place in the first team and remain patient about not playing regular first team football. But I wasn't too unhappy about that. After all I was still extremely young and there was still a lot for me to learn. And the 'A' team was one of the best sides in the competition - I had no doubt I'd learn it playing with them.

My next career milestone, my first team home debut, followed less than two months later. As you can imagine it was a momentous occasion for me to play for my hometown team, in front of a crowd of supporters that I'd been a part of only a year or so earlier. Saturday, December 5 1964 was another afternoon of more 'firsts' for me. I couldn't have wished for better opposition, Wigan! I couldn't have hoped for a better result - we won 17-0! I only played because Chuck was on International duty in France. But I scored my first senior try that day early in the second half. It was truly incredible. John Taylor, who was playing in only his third match for Castleford since his arrival from Hull Kingston Rovers, scored another of our five tries. He formed a tremendous second-row partnership with Bill Bryant that day. But little did I realise at the time, that his signing was to have possible repercussions on my own career a little further down the line...

Our performance against Wigan was largely recognised as our best of the season. It was also the first time I recall Eddie Waring writing about me.

'With a powerful pack led by 'Big Bill' Bryant and a pair of 'little smashers' Millward and Hepworth at halfback, Castleford were devastating,' wrote Eddie.

'Slender as a sapling, but tough, he swerved and side stepped in thrilling style. He showed a football brain and even when tackled had an uncanny knack of letting the ball go to a supporting colleague,' enthused Bill Bowes. The accolades were just a couple of the countless compliments that followed our impressive performance and could have created serious problems for some players. But I like to think I was more intelligent than to let them have a detrimental effect on me. We've all seen young sports stars ruined by the pressures created by too much hype in the early stages of their careers.

Reading those reports might easily have left me feeling that I'd already 'made the grade'. That there was little left for me to achieve - that I was the finished article - a seventeen-year-old who had already reached the top! Fortunately they didn't! I can't deny I appreciated the acclaim, who wouldn't have? But I'd already set myself much greater goals.

I didn't allow the hype to become a problem, quite the opposite in fact. I realised some time later that I'd subconsciously actually used the praise for my own benefit. It had helped me to clarify the fact that I was a player with tremendous potential. But only that. To get where I wanted to be, I had to remain focussed, keep my feet on the ground and continue to learn from the coaches and players around me. Then I could only improve even more...

Eddie in most people's eyes, is the man who christened me 'Roger the Dodger' when commentating for the BBC during my early appearances for Castleford. I've got no reason to dispute the fact, but of course just about every other newspaper and TV reporter soon used it, so there was always a question mark against who actually said it first. But I'm happy to think it was Eddie.

He did as much as anyone to promote my career especially in the early days, with his unique style of commentating. He was undoubtedly one of my earliest admirers and although for obvious reasons I didn't get to hear hardly any of his commentaries, I was regularly informed he usually had nothing but good things to say about my exploits. He also regularly put pen to paper to write about me in the Sunday Mirror.

The name 'Roger the dodger' of course stuck with me throughout my career and caused regular comments. Even during my early days at Castleford, I recall reporter Arthur Haddock suggesting that my parents must have been clairvoyant - to have had such an accurate premonition of me becoming a rugby star with a dodging style - in order to give me such an apt Christian name as Roger.

My only full season at Castleford - 1965-66 - was when my career really took off! 'Chuck' Hardisty had of course been the Great Britain stand-off at the time but he was out injured. It was the opportunity I'd been waiting for.

I started playing in the number six jersey for Castleford, made a series of first team appearances, and was almost immediately picked for Great Britain. And things just snowballed from there. It was unbelievable. I just kept climbing. Going up and up - rather like the start of a roller coaster ride. And there was no sign of that particular roller coaster going over the top. I just sat back and enjoyed every minute of it. It was a season packed with fantastic matches for both club and country...

The first league match played under the new Wheldon Road floodlights was Castleford against Wigan on Friday September 24 1965. I remember it was a great occasion but unfortunately the game didn't supply the spectacle that the history-making game deserved. Castleford versus Wigan matches were usually very competitive and highly skilled encounters. That game though, certainly wasn't one that many of the players or the fans will remember much about. But it was a game I recall well, because although we lost 9-12, I scored all my teams' points that night, with a try and three goals. Three days later on Monday September 27 an evening game brought me more than a touch of deja-vu! I went one better than the Wigan game and scored all ten of Castleford's points - but we lost again!

It was another important match - the Yorkshire Cup Semi-Final at Parkside. Hunslet were a pretty formidable outfit at the time. At the end of the previous season they'd taken part in the Challenge Cup Final against Wigan. The Wembley showpiece, which the Lancashire side won 20-16, was regarded as one of the best seen at the twin towers for many years. And Hunslet showed they were still formidable opposition when they beat us 17-10. I scored two tries and kicked two goals, both from the touchline - but still finished on the losing side. Derek Edwards and Keith Hepworth were our halfbacks - I played on the wing - and was probably a lot safer away from the 'action' going on in the middle of the pitch. I've a photograph that shows if Alan Preece, the Hunslet off-half, had connected with me that day, I'd have probably landed somewhere behind the main stand. Alan was always a tough little nut, but a nice lad all the same.

There's another thing that sticks with me about that night. Although we'd been beaten, Carol's family was from Hunslet and after the team bus had gone, Carol and Walter, Carol's dad and I walked into Hunslet and went into 'The Anchor', Jeff Stephenson's pub. We had a few beers in there and then caught the bus home. That's how different it was in those days.

The next game I played in was another clash with Wigan, this time at Central Park - and televised on 'Grandstand'. John Sheridan and John

Taylor played that afternoon - and I remember John Sheridan's contribution in particular. He must have been thirty-four or thirty-five years old and in the twilight of his career. But he'd actually played for the 'A' team the night before and then ended up propping for the first team at Wigan, the following afternoon. I also remember it was the first time I played against one of the all-time 'greats' of rugby league, Billy Boston. He was on the wing for Wigan - fortunately I was playing scrum-half. Billy was already a legend and someone I'd watched as a wide-eyed youngster. Incredibly, now I was playing against him. And more incredibly, we won 10-8.

I remember Billy and I did meet at least once during the match though. It was at a scrum about five yards from the touch-line and Frankie Parr was the opposite number seven. These were the days when scrum-halves had to fight for the ball at every scrum - and Frankie and I certainly did! We finished up having a bit of a 'set-to' and rolling about on the floor. Billy strolled quietly over and got hold of us both. Without uttering a word, he separated us and then simply stared at the pair of us as if to say, come on - let's get on with the game!

It was a typical winter's afternoon, neither light nor dark and there was a big crowd at Central Park that day. Wigan had started well that season and it was one of the few wins Castleford had ever had there. It was certainly regarded as a major shock for us to win at Wigan. The match had been a closely fought affair throughout and the scores were actually tied at 8-all at half-time. The only points of the second half came from my late penalty - it was a memorable kick - and produced a memorable victory.

Things were very different nine days later when I faced 'foreign' opposition for the first time. Castleford played against the New Zealand tourists on October 6 1965. I was supposed to be kicking goals that night but it was a case of hero to villain as I missed a few - and we lost 6-7. It was a foggy, Wednesday night at Wheldon Road but I couldn't even blame the poor visibility for my below-par performance. In just over a week my kicking ability had won us a famous victory - but had then denied us another.

After the game both the teams and a number of invited guests went to the 'Kiosk' for a reception. The 'Kiosk' was a dancehall in Castleford - you wouldn't describe it as a nightclub - The Lord Mayor was there and everything. But needless to say I didn't feel much like celebrating.

The International selectors can't have been as disappointed as I was with my display against the Kiwis. Less than a month after my eighteenth birthday I was selected for the England Under 24s to face France and then for the full Great Britain side to face New Zealand in the Second Test at Odsal. What was slightly worrying though was that the two games were only three days apart!

Whenever you played against France they always did the unorthodox. You practised things and worked on moves before the game but they were always totally flamboyant and always tried the unexpected - nothing they did looked planned. My England Under 24 debut against them at Oldham on Wednesday, October 20 1965 was no exception. It was a filthy evening, typical Lancashire weather. Terry Major, the Hull Kingston Rovers' centre, played that night, in fact he was the captain of the side. I later played many games for Rovers alongside Terry. And I'll tell you later of one match in particular when we appeared together at Workington. It was a game that didn't last very long as far as I was concerned.

This however was the first time I'd ever played International football. But I knew what to expect against France. Everything was always somehow different against the French - everything seemed 'backwards way round'. And that was certainly the case that night. It also proved to be a very tough game because they were a good side then.

There were a lot of names on both sides that cropped up again and again throughout my career, Terry was one of them. I recall he was very careful in the lead up to the match. Two Hull K.R. players had been picked to captain representative sides the season before, and both had missed out through injury. Harry Poole had withdrawn after being chosen to captain Great Britain against France and Alan Burwell missed out after being named skipper for the first ever Under 24 match against the French. Terry didn't intend on being the third.

He succeeded partly - but his luck only held out for forty minutes. Because although he did manage to start the game, the injury bug struck again and he had to pull out at half-time with a leg injury.

At that stage we were 5-2 behind. I'd kicked a penalty and then led an English revival in what turned out to be a very ill tempered second half. The French hooker Patrick Mazard, prop forward, Jean-Claude Sogorb and Dewsbury's Brian Taylor were all sent off. I scored a try after kicking ahead from a penalty and winning the race to touch down. I also converted another try scored by our left winger, Bob Wear and kicked a late penalty to seal a 12-5 win. It was far from being a classic match - but that didn't matter. I'd got my first representative game under my belt - we'd won - and that's what it was all about for me...

The second of my two Internationals followed less than seventy-two hours later. Between the two games I remember an interview by Bill Fryer which appeared in 'The Sun' on the eve of the Odsal Test. I'd only just turned eighteen don't forget and wasn't perhaps the most talkative person he'd ever met. He wrote that he'd expected to meet 'a mini-Tarbuck'. His reasoning was because 'after all little Roger Millward looks the chirpiest chappie to step on to the Rugby League stage since the great Alex Murphy. In his newly studded boots, his head just emerging from the longer grass, he bobs up and down in a perpetual look-out for the ball, he jinks, he dribbles, he bounces through a game - everything in fact, bar a song-and-dance act. I have to report that the only person in Rugby League land unaware of the heretofore is Roger Millward.'

What he actually found, he related was: 'A joker? Not a bit of it. Rather a serious lad, a quiet lad, a shy lad, a both-feet-on-the-ground lad.'

'He's a lad who's not going to put all his eggs into the Rugby League basket, no matter how much he is eulogised.' he continued. 'That I suggest, shows how unaffected he is by the praise. A very small headed prodigy, this. His exercise book was as neat and tidy as his fringe, his suit, his nicely polished shoes, and his hands - those hands that may well launch a thousand tries. Yet this precocious 18 year-old infant, not 18 months out of school, after only twelve senior games for Castleford, played for England's Under 24 team against France on Wednesday, scored nine of the 12 points, and is substitute for the Great Britain team against New Zealand tomorrow.'

I can't say that I agreed with all of Bill Fryer's findings but that was how he saw me. And as he had himself pointed out, whatever these reporters wrote wasn't going to have any affect on me. Was it?

The following day, October 23 was my Great Britain debut. Although we won 15-9 to clinch the series 2-0, it turned out to be a bit of an anti-climax for me. After all the build-up and all the hype I didn't even get onto the pitch. I'd been named in the Great Britain squad to face the Kiwis but only as a substitute. 'Chuck' Hardisty played at stand-off. And at that time you could only go on as a substitute up to half-time. After that you just had to sit on the bench and watch. I remember the rule very well because that's exactly what I did! In fact I did it twice in a fortnight as I also sat on the substitute's bench for the 9-9 drawn Third Test at Wigan.

I would have got £500 if I'd got onto that field in either game! I remember in the match at Odsal 'Chuck' got a knock just before half-time and I thought this is it! But he stayed on - so I didn't get the opportunity to take part in the match at all.

I'll give 'Chuck' his due though, he stood up for me when we went to see the board on the following Tuesday night at training.

'He's been picked for Great Britain - he wants his £500' pleaded Chuck.

But the directors were not having any of it. They said because I hadn't played, I couldn't have the money. So although I'd been selected but hadn't actually got on the field they wouldn't pay me my £500. I couldn't believe it! But it was of course all in my contract, in very small print. I got £200 when I signed on, £300 when I played for Yorkshire and £500 when I played for Great Britain. And that was the key.

I hadn't just to be picked - I had to play! I'll never forget it. I had to wait until I got to Rovers to pick that money up! Walking away from training that night, empty handed, ended a very busy week for me...

CHAPTER THREE
TWO'S COMPANY, THREE'S A CROWD

LEAVING CASTLEFORD

A few weeks later that disappointment was completely forgotten. On Tuesday December 14, I was part of the side that won the BBC2 Floodlit Trophy. It was the first major competition the club had won since Castleford skipper, Arthur Atkinson lifted the Challenge Cup following his side's 11-8 victory against Huddersfield at Wembley in 1935.

The previous season's Eastern Division Cup had been a welcome addition to the under-used Wheldon Road trophy cabinet. But that success wasn't comparable to the prestige that the televised Trophy win brought to the club. Castleford had been one of the first clubs to install floodlights and soon reaped the benefits. They were one of only eight teams who were eligible to enter the inaugural Floodlit competition. The other sides who competed for the trophy were Leeds, Leigh, Rochdale, St. Helens, Salford, Swinton and Wigan.

In the qualifying rounds we'd first drawn with Leeds at home 7-7. We could have won the game but for some very poor goal-kicking. Ron Willett missed two shots from relatively simple positions and then I pulled another attempt wide from in front of the posts. It was another game where I realised how crucial the art of goal-kicking could prove to be.

We then went on to beat Oldham 4-6 and Widnes in the semi-final 9-12, both away from home, to book our place in the final. The win against the Chemics was our eleventh successive victory. Another victory in our next league game at Bramley gave us a twelve consecutive match-winning run, our best ever! But the Saints who had beaten us in two league matches already that season had gone into the final as firm favourites having completed a run of fifteen games without defeat. But in our first major final for over thirty years we beat the mighty St Helens, 4-0 at Knowsley Road.

I confess I don't remember too much about it however. The games were played on Tuesday evenings and my main memory of the final was one of Johnny Ward smacking the legendary Alex Murphy across the chops. I don't think John had a lot of time for Alex. But then again John didn't have a lot of time for quite a few people back then.

The big surprise about that game again concerned goal-kicking - and the

Top: The Castleford Town team

Middle: Out on the town with my mates

Bottom: Pictured in my early days at Castleford with teammate, Ian Stenton

importance of being able to take your chances when they come along. Saints' usually brilliant goalkicker, Len Killeen missed all his shots at goal and we won 4-0 thanks to two penalties by Ron Willett...

I hoped a New Year might bring me a change of luck. I'd watched two test matches against the Kiwis from the sidelines at the end of 1965 so when I was selected again as a substitute for Great Britain against France at Perpignan on Sunday January 16 1966, I hoped it might prove third time lucky. But again I had to be content with spending a couple of 'enjoyable hours' sitting on the bench alongside Bill Bryant. And again I didn't actually get a chance to play in the match.

Bill, a giant, second-row forward and I, a rather smaller in stature halfback, were described by columnist Jack McNamara as we strolled through the streets of Perpignan as 'one of the most incongruous sights of the weekend.' He went on to say that I 'barely reached Bill's middle shirt button.'

They were the sort of remarks I'd enjoyed all through my youth. My size was never a problem for me.

I was always grateful to players like Bill who gave me a lot of protection during matches. Bill on the other hand would usually insist that he wasn't a 'minder' and that I could look after myself. But the fact many of the other players in the British squad joked that I was the first rugby league international to 'still sleep in a cot', I think suggested which one of our descriptions was nearer to the truth.

For this game however I didn't require any protection because I didn't actually spend one second on the pitch. It was a game we should have won, but one which sadly slipped away from us. We'd led 13-12 with only sixteen minutes left but we eventually lost 18-13. Alex Murphy, rated as the world's best scrum-half at the time, captained Britain that day but his 'Jeckyll and Hyde' display left the selectors with a bit of a headache, deciding whether he'd even make the 1966 summer tour of Australia.

'This could have been Alex's finest hour. Instead it became one of his most miserable,' proclaimed the Monday morning headlines. Alex had led the side superbly for most of the game before his two late indiscretions cost us the match...

Alex, one of my boyhood idols, was my halfback partner, when I finally made my International bow less than two months later. The date was March 5 1966, the opposition - France, the venue - Central Park, Wigan. It was the only cap I got whilst at Castleford. But I remember there was a minor hitch at the ground that meant I nearly didn't get it at all!

When I arrived at the players' entrance, the doorman refused to let me in! He thought I looked too young and too small to be playing in a rugby league international! The situation could have turned into my worst nightmare had Eddie Waring not appeared and told the doorman in no uncertain terms, that I was who I said I was. And that I was definitely playing for Great Britain.

Moments later, I ran out onto the pitch - alongside 'Murph' for my debut. And at such a young age, the feeling, I have to admit, was a little surreal. I'd grown up watching players like Alex and there were a few others in that

Top left: Boarding the bus with Trevor Waring (top) and David Appleyard (right) for my Castleford debut at Dewsbury

Above: Leaving the field with Maurice Williams after my debut win

Top right: Floodlit success - Alan Hardisty lifts the BBC2 Floodlit Trophy with Peter Small and in the foreground

Left: Training with first team at Wheldon Road

side I'd watched as a youngster, like Ken Gowers and John Stopford of Swinton, Geoff Shelton of Hunslet and Cliff Watson of St Helens.

But of course there was no fairytale beginning to my international career, when we lost 4-8. And I recall the papers said that the defeat had not only provided a harsh and costly lesson for me - but had virtually ended my chances of making the 1966 Lions' squad to tour Australia.

Five years later, I actually captained Alex in a test match at Castleford. That was against the Kiwis on October 16 1971 when unfortunately we lost again 14-17. I never seemed to have much luck playing alongside Alex!

A lot of people had expected me to be chosen for my first trip to Australia in 1966. And some respected judges reasoned why I shouldn't have been. But I suppose it was that dismal performance by Great Britain against France that ultimately decided I wouldn't be going down under - at least not just yet! And in the end those opinions didn't count as the selectors opted for 'Chuck' Hardisty and Willie Aspinall instead of me.

At that stage of my career I of course read everything that the newspapers had to say about me. And anything I missed I was sure my mum would tell me about! Sports reporter, Jack McNamara, thought I might have made the trip. 'With rugby league crying out for personalities Roger Millward may prove to be one of the great entertainers,' he wrote. 'He must stand a fair chance of touring Australia and New Zealand with Great Britain this summer - they will love him Down Under.'

Arthur Haddock, who had watched the build-up of seven previous tours suggested there were very few 1966 'certs'. He thought the players who were likely to get a unanimous vote were Ken Gowers and John Stopford of Swinton, Berwyn Jones of Wakefield, Geoff Shelton of Hunslet, John Mantle of St Helens, Dave Robinson of Swinton and me. Unfortunately Arthur didn't select the party but out of his seven 'certs', six were duly chosen for the trip. And yes, you've guessed it, the odd one out was me!

And former Great Britain skipper Alan Prescott wrote a very complimentary article about me, hinting he thought I'd be a success in Australia...

'I applaud the choice of Castleford's Roger Millward as stand-off half' he wrote. 'I hear whispers about him being too small, but this is rubbish. This boy is tough and has a big heart and is such an exciting player that I'm sure he'll make the International grade - they like cheeky players down under.'

Frank Dyson, the Oldham coach was equally forthright about my possible tour selection, after being named for my debut against France.

'It may sound a little contradictory,' he said, 'but although Millward is the obvious selection for the stand-off position, I don't think he should be picked with a view to the Australian tour. Millward is only 18, and this is his first full season in the game. He is a brilliant player, I'm not denying that. And after being international substitute - he was the obvious choice after Wigan's Cliff Hill hadn't really shone in Perpignan a few weeks ago. But I do think he is being rushed along too fast and this may have a serious effect on his career. The Australians have some big, robust forwards and if they drop on him fairly often he is going to be sick of football, halfway through the tour. I have seen players put back two or three years by being rushed along too fast, and I hope this doesn't happen to Millward, who really is one of the brightest young players we have had in the game for the last few years.'

Frank's concerns were very much appreciated, although at the time I did think he might have sounded a little over-protective - a little too 'let's wrap him in cotton wool' ish. After all this was a Lions' tour we were talking about! It appeared opinions about my inclusion were definitely divided.

As it turned out, Frank and Alan both got their wish. I wasn't chosen for the 1966 tour and although Alex was, it wasn't as skipper or even at halfback. He was chosen in the centre, a position he'd been playing for his club, St Helens. And the shocks didn't end there.

The selectors showed their dissatisfaction with recent international performances by leaving no fewer than seventeen players who had taken part in them, out of the touring party. And perhaps the biggest surprise of all was the choice of captain.

That distinction went to Leeds' Harry Poole, who had never played for Great Britain before and received the news of his selection as he celebrated his thirty-first birthday! Harry was a player who I already knew and respected - and a man who only ten years later would sadly provide me with one of the most tragic moments of my entire life!

Never in my wildest dreams did I imagine things would happen so quickly. It was unbelievable. There I was after less than two seasons since signing on. I'd already played 'A' team football, first team football, international football, starting with the England Under 24s and had now made my full Great Britain debut.

It was just a continuous progression, the roller coaster still just kept going up and up - and to that point at least, there had been no dips! They would come along sooner or later, I knew that. But for now, things couldn't have been any better...

Alan Hardisty and Keith Hepworth have been two of my best mates throughout my entire career. I've always got on marvellously well with them. We've often been asked if we always got on. The answer was always the same, Yes! We never had any disagreements. And jealousy, backstabbing and envious thoughts were never parts of our relationship! We always got on and simply never had the arguments or problems that people imagine we must have had.

The amount of times I've been asked the same question is unbelievable. But it doesn't bother me. With me the question was always, 'What about Hardisty and Hepworth?' And with those two it was vice versa, 'What about Millward and Hepworth?' they asked 'Chuck' and 'What about Hardisty and Millward?' they asked 'Heppy'. People must have thought there was a continuing problem but it was never like that at all. None of us have ever looked at it that way. I suppose they thought if they asked the question often enough, one day they might get a different answer - the one they wanted to hear! The one that would make a more interesting story!

After all 'two's company and three's a crowd' they say - but that adage was never true about 'Chuck', 'Heppy' and I. Not as far as we were concerned at least. Whether I think about us - when I was first starting out - or further on in 1970 - it was always Hardisty, Hepworth and Millward. With admittedly, later on, a few other names thrown in for good measure like Barry Seabourne and Mick Shoebottom.

The only problem that emerged about the three of us was one that the Castleford directors had to deal with. Could they afford to have a trio of players regarded as arguably the top three halfbacks in British rugby league on their books at the same time?

With that question in mind, someone at Castleford had to make a decision. And the decision which was made - and it was fair enough - was that they decided that I could leave!

And it was no good arguing about it once the decision had been made - it was rather like a referee - he wasn't going to change his mind.

But there was never the slightest bit of jealousy between the three of us. I can honestly say I never had any problems whatsoever with 'Chuck' and 'Heppy'. They've always been fantastic! When 'Heppy' was injured I'd play scrum-half and when Chuck was injured or on International duty I'd play stand-off. I was the one that could play scrum-half, stand-off or on the wing - so I was happy just to be in the side.

I thought that 'Chuck' and 'Heppy' were both marvellous players. And you couldn't help but learn things from both of them, things that you could wrap up and have as a part of your own game. I was very lucky to join a team with people like that. When you saw them doing things it obviously rubbed off on you. Keith's defensive game was brilliant - he was a marvellous tackler. I've seen him bring blokes of six feet six down with no problem at all - although it was a bit different from how I used to do it. Alan's backing-up was second to none - and his little 'chip throughs' - you were picking up hints every time you watched them. You're gathering information all the time when you're a sportsman - and if you're not, you want to get out of it.

I remember watching St Helens play a few years before I signed on, and there was a lad called Abe Terry playing for them. And when I made my first team debut for Castleford at Dewsbury he was playing for us.

Needless to say, when you later turn out and play alongside players who have impressed you when you'd watched them from the terraces as a kid, like Abe and Chuck and Heppy, that was reward in itself. And there were plenty of other great players there at the time. I remember a lad who played fullback called Derek Edwards. He wasn't much bigger than I was but at that time he was second to none.

Castleford also had a great pack of forwards, three of whom deserve a special mention. My first 'minder' Bill Bryant - he was a tremendous, old-fashioned hard-working forward. Johnny Ward, one of the best footballers I've seen. He was a hell of a player - very creative, with a superb off-load - and as hard as nails. And Johnny Walker in the second-row, his cover tackling was outstanding.

I never played with Malcolm Reilly at club level because he came on the scene a couple of years after I was at Wheldon Road. But it was a pleasure to play with him at International level - another Castleford lad. They were all great players. Castleford was a great club - and although my days there were numbered, I'd luckily been a part of it...

The last match I played for Castleford was on the wing - coincidentally against Hull Kingston Rovers in the Championship Play-off at Wheldon Road - and Rovers won. I was injured towards the end of that game, I tore my medial ligament and I was off work for five or six weeks. During that time things went round and round at an ever increasing rate, and I finished up at Rovers...

I'd only just returned to work when it came to the summer holidays. At that time the pit used to shut down for the first two weeks in August. That was when everybody took their holidays. I was going away to Blackpool that year with a mate from the pit called Terry Sissons. We were going for the second week. My mum and dad were already over there. One day, I was painting the window frames at home in Kendal Drive, when two cars pulled up outside. Ronnie Simpson and Bill Broxup got out. And I thought, what the hell do they want?

I didn't have to wait long to find out, as they came straight up to the house and knocked on the door. I let them in but then we all just stood there in the living room, staring at each other. Ronnie finally broke the silence, and I'll never forget his words, all he said was:

'There's been a club in for thee. Chuck's had a good tour, we think you should go.'

And that was it! That was how I was told I was being transferred! I asked which club it was that was after my services and he replied it was Hull K.R. Rovers had put out a few feelers about me the previous season and had been told that should I become available, they'd be given the first chance to sign me. That opportunity had now arrived.

Fair enough, I said, and inquired what was going to happen next? Ronnie said that Rovers were coming to see me, to which I replied that I was going on holiday the following week. Ronnie asked if I was going to Albert Road, which was Ken and Barry's place in Blackpool. I replied that I was. Ken Westmorland and Barry Blueman were ardent Castleford fans and used to come over from Blackpool every other week to watch all our matches.

'We'll get them to come across there.' insisted Ronnie.

And they did. Whilst I was at Ken's, Hull K.R. contacted him and he passed on the message that they'd like to come and talk to me. They came to the hotel, I think there was about six of them. But Wilf Spaven, the Hull K.R. chairman wasn't with them. He was over in Australia, he was the Tour Manager with Great Britain. And Colin Hutton wasn't with them either. The group included Percy Johnson, Frank Parkinson, Fred Alford and Ron Chester. The deal was struck there and then. The whole thing had only taken four days from the start to the finish. That was it!

The fee of £6,000 had been agreed - and after only forty first team games for Castleford - I was a Hull K. R. player...

CHAPTER FOUR
NEW FRIENDS & FORGOTTEN DRINKS

Whatever the reasons were for my transfer from Castleford to Hull KR will probably never be fully known. But I think it's safe to say that like the majority of transfers that take place in professional sport - the reason for the move was down to just one thing - money!

Even with international halfbacks, Alan Hardisty and Keith Hepworth on their books, surely any club with ambition would have wanted to keep young, talented players with potential in their ranks. At least any club that could afford to would have.

Why I was transferred from Castleford was a simple question to answer. The only reason that made any sense for my move to Craven Park, was purely to balance the books.

Was it all down to the signing by Castleford of John Taylor as many people suggested? Perhaps! He'd been Rovers' most expensive export when he moved to Wheldon Road during the 1964-5 season - coincidentally for £6,000. He was a seasoned International and the type of forward who was obviously at the top of Castleford's wanted list. Were Castleford just selling me in order to pay off what they owed Hull K.R.?

Whatever the reasons were I didn't let them bother me. Once I'd been told I was leaving, that was it as far as I was concerned. And looking back of course it was the best thing that could have happened to me.

The deal not only changed the course of the two clubs involved, Castleford and Rovers, but arguably also the history of rugby league over the next twenty-five years. You can only guess about how my career would have progressed if I had stayed at Castleford. Would I have forced my way into the Castleford team? Would I have been selected for the Great Britain side ahead of 'Chuck' Hardisty?

And would I have even been playing therefore when I enjoyed one of my greatest successes, winning the 1970 Ashes with Great Britain. The questions are endless, the answers will never be known - fate decided all that on a summer Sunday afternoon in Blackpool...

I signed for Hull K.R. on Sunday August 7 1966 for £6,000. It was the biggest fee Rovers had parted with since they signed Bill Holliday from

Whitehaven and Frank Foster from Workington Town a year and a half earlier. But most Rovers' fans agreed it was probably the best business deal the club ever made.

The story of the impending transfer of a teenage rugby league player may not have made the headlines - apart from in Hull and Castleford - because of a big sporting weekend elsewhere in the world.

The day before, the Great Britain team with 'Chuck' Hardisty and Tommy Bishop at halfback and Harry Poole, captaining the side in the second-row, won the first test against New Zealand 8-25 in Auckland. And on the same night Cassius Clay, now wishing to be known as Muhammad Ali, defended his World Heavyweight Boxing title against Britain's Brian London at the Earls Court Arena in London.

But eight days later I'd already forgotten about those events as I made my Rovers' debut on August 15 at Hunslet. The game was played on a Monday evening with a 7p.m. kick-off. I started at stand-off with Mike Stephenson partnering me at scrum-half. Happily, it was another winning debut for me, by the convincing margin of twenty-eight points to eleven. There wasn't a great deal more to enthuse about, although I did make the break to set up a first half try for winger, Mike Blackmore. But I also remember I didn't even finish the match. I retired at half-time with a knee injury. In fact I have to confess, I didn't finish either of my first two games in Rovers' colours!

My second match was at Derwent Park against Workington the following Saturday. We went up on the Friday and stayed at Cockermouth at 'The Globe'. My first Rovers' room-mate was Joby Shaw. I remember there was a band on in the bar downstairs and we were almost straight above it, trying to get to sleep. The hotel had some of those old warming pans on the wall and every time the band struck up the pans would start vibrating - it sounded like Rolf Harris on his didgeridoo - and just about as annoying! It was like that for what seemed to be hours but we finally got to sleep.

I'm pretty sure it was the first time I'd played at Workington because I don't remember ever playing there with Castleford. Terry Major scored our only try that day but we lost 15-5. We seldom seemed to do well in Cumbria.

I don't remember very much about the game, except that my dad actually made the long trip to watch me in his old Zephyr. He must have regarded it as a wasted journey however because I was only on the field for ten minutes! By that time, I was flat out and they'd carried me off to the dressing-room with concussion. When I came round I couldn't remember a thing about what had happened. All I know is that I went into a tackle and the next thing I knew was when I woke up, somewhere in west Yorkshire on our journey home. Apparently it had been my new teammate, Terry Major, who had accidentally hit me. Everyone said it was an absolute 'beauty' but I didn't take that as any consolation whatsoever!

I'd then regained consciousness in the dressing room - but I didn't remember anything about that either. The first thing I could remember was waking up on the outskirts of Leeds. Johnny Williams, our physio, was the first face I saw. He had given me some paracetamol or something - you were never quite sure what you'd been given in those days. And a couple of the lads repeated the story. That I'd gone in to tackle a Workington player, Terry had come in from the other side to hit the same guy - had missed - and hit me instead. It was a hell of a hit by all accounts, but he always could throw a good punch, could Terry...

When I'd first arrived at Craven Park, Colin Hutton was the coach. Now, what can you say about Colin? I know I could write a book about him! He has certainly been one of the biggest influences throughout my career. Over the years many people have described us as having more of a father and son relationship, rather than one of a coach and player, or mentor and pupil - and I wouldn't disagree with that assessment. I was only eighteen when I arrived at Rovers and he started looking after me from that moment on. He never stopped really - even when things had gone full circle and I became coach. He was always there to talk to and he and his wife Marjorie, are two people for whom I have always had total respect.

His contribution to Hull Kingston Rovers and to the game of rugby league is incredible. How he and Johnny Whiteley, at the other side of the city, haven't been recognised in a more tangible way, I'll never know!

It's been one of life's privileges knowing Colin, Marjorie and their daughter, Susan. They've provided my family and I with the type of friendship you don't find very often. And the good times I've spent 'looking after his pub', they're all marvellous memories that I'll never forget.

Colin is a very knowledgeable man and a brilliant conversationalist. He's also a great councillor and so easy to talk to. But things haven't always been perfect between us. It hasn't always been smooth sailing. We've had our disagreements, like anybody else. But being able to have an argument and put your feelings across truthfully, so you're both aware of each other's opinions is vital to any meaningful relationship. You're then in a much better position to work together and solve any differences you may have. That's what real friendship is all about! And that's the type of friendship Colin and I have always shared...

The very first training session I went to was just after the time I'd spent out of action with my medial ligament injury. I hadn't trained. I hadn't done anything. In fact I was in pretty poor condition, I bet I'd put a stone in weight on.

So the first thing they did to me when I got to Craven Park was that Colin got me a 'sweat suit'. There's no doubt it was very effective and I soon got rid of the weight!

Once I was back to a relatively decent level of fitness, it was then time to reassess things again. This was my life now, I thought. I'm in Hull, I've got a job to do with this team - and I'm going to make sure I do it well.

Fortunately, when I looked around at the make-up of that side, I realised it was a great side - and it was a pleasure to play in it. And it was a pleasure for the next two years or so, before a few players started leaving and the club had more than its' fair share of money problems.

There were a few ups and downs that we faced along the way in the late sixties and early seventies, before we dragged ourselves back up to what we became in the end. But that didn't concern me then! When I started out and we were training, my usual thought would be, by hell, these lads could play a bit!

We used to train over on the opposite side of Holderness Road from Rovers' ground, in East Park. And further along Holderness Road, either at Hull Brunswick's ground or on a piece of land that Rovers owned down Winchester Avenue.

At the time it was thought the land might ultimately provide the site for Rovers' new stadium. But because of the prohibitive costs involved that idea never materialised and the land was later sold.

When I arrived for my next training session I was with Cyril Kellett and Frank Fox. I got to know them first. They used to pick me up in Castleford and we'd travel over for training and home games together. At training, I looked around and saw players like Bill Holliday, Frank Foster, Terry Major, Brian Tyson, Peter Flanagan and Chris Young - the list was endless - it was an impressive line-up. And for a kid from out of town all a bit awe-inspiring! But there was also a tremendous team spirit there. I think that was partly due to the fact that there was a good balance of local players and others who had come to live in Hull, like Frank Foster and Bill Holliday.

They were great players and I got on well with all of them. Brian, Frank, Bill, Terry and Brian Mennell, they all looked after me. I dropped on my feet there! I'll always say that until my dying day. It turned out to be a fantastic move for me because I don't think I would have done anything in the game like I have done, if I hadn't gone to Rovers...

Frank and I had a little ritual that started almost as soon as I arrived at the club. I've no doubt it was a pre-match habit that would be very much frowned on today. Before every home match we used to take it in turn to buy a miniature bottle of brandy and a bottle of 'Lucozade' from the supporters' club. We took them into the changing rooms to share before kick-off. One game he would go and get it and the next, I would. It was an easy thing to remember, or so I thought.

This particular day I was in the dressing room getting changed and I was down to my vest and shorts. It was my turn to get the drinks but for some reason I'd completely forgotten. I soon remembered them however when I caught sight of an irate looking Frank, staring at me.

'Where is it,' he asked. I didn't even ask him where's what? I just ran! I knew by the look on his face I'd better get them quickly, otherwise I'd get a thump. And Frank's punches hurt! I remember running straight out of the changing rooms and dashing into the packed supporters club. I wasn't exactly dressed for the occasion. When I got back following a embarrassingly long wait at the bar, all Frank said was,

'Thank you Marra.'

Needless to say, I never forgot again...

It was one of those rituals that once we'd started doing it we just didn't stop. Not that we were superstitious but you do tend to stick to doing things in the same way if you think it's helped things to run smoothly previously. It's a load of rubbish of course really - but you do it all the same...

'Flash' Flanagan I always thought of as an exceptional footballer. It was obvious how he'd got his nickname. You'd play matches with him when you'd be defending on your own line. Next, there'd be a break and a length of the field move - and he'd finish up scoring under the posts after following the wingers and centres. He just had that uncanny knack of being in the right place at the right time.

I'd only been at the club a week or two when I realised there was a lot of very hard work ahead of me. Because when I looked around and saw players like Mick Stephenson and Alan Burwell, they made me sit up and take note. Alan had been in two minds about playing again after missing a lot of matches during the previous season, due to his studies in Bradford. Happily he decided he would resume his career and I for one was delighted. He may have been a rival for a starting place in the team but Alan was an unbelievable player who I just couldn't wait to play alongside. He scored many crucial tries for both Rovers and Great Britain in the ensuing years. But for now I had a new challenge and something to aim at. And I was determined that if I was going to come all this way to play rugby league football, I had to fully apply myself and make a success of it!

But to be quite honest, I had been a little puzzled about why Rovers had signed me at all! I'd played against Rovers with Castleford and I'd seen what talented players both Alan and Mike were. Then all of a sudden, one August afternoon Rovers came and signed me on. And I must admit I thought to myself more than once - why? Because there were two kids already at the club who could definitely play this game.

But that I decided had been Rovers' choice. They had wanted to sign me. What I had to do was to knuckle down and make sure I did things properly. And when I went to training I had to be competitive. I had to respect people. Most of all I had to respect players like Alan and Mike. Because they were the players who were playing in my position. They had my shirt!

The week after I'd been signed, Mike scored a hat-trick of tries in Rovers' 27-2 Eva Hardaker Cup win against Hull at the Boulevard. I knew he wouldn't be giving the shirt up easily. But if Rovers were taking me over to Hull, I wasn't going there to play 'A' team football. And I wasn't going there to play scrum-half or on the wing. I was going to play stand-off and that was that!

On the field, the difference from being at Castleford to going to Rovers was a huge transformation for me, a real eye-opener! But off the field I already felt at home. The nature of the people in Hull was very similar to the nature of the people I'd lived with all my life. In Castleford, we were a mining community, whilst Hull was a fishing community - and there wasn't a lot of difference between us I don't think.

Within the first few weeks of my first season at Rovers we won the Yorkshire Cup! And from not being in many big club games, all of a sudden I seemed to be playing in them every week...

The fact that I failed to complete my first two matches was definitely something that worried me for a while. I was a young man who had just moved to a new club and I couldn't help but wonder, what on earth were people going to think of me? Luckily though I avoided any further problems for quite a while after that. Better things were just around the corner.

My third match was on August 22. It was my home debut and Batley provided the opposition. We struggled during the first half but Arthur Bunting was brought on at the break and he transformed the game. We scored five tries after the interval including my first for the club and went on to win 28-6. The match heralded the start of an incredible run of seventeen consecutive victories, which didn't end until the last week of November! The run included four Yorkshire Cup-ties, the last one seeing Rovers lift the trophy for the first time for thirty-seven years.

The First Round of the Yorkshire Cup provided me with my first experience of something I'd already heard a lot about from the other lads, a Hull and Rovers derby match! We won the see-saw game 24-20 with a late try by Arthur Bunting finally settling a stirring encounter. I'd been warned about the unique and intense atmosphere the matches created. The attendance was only a little over 8,000 but it sounded more like 80,000 at times. The Boulevard was an awesome place to be that afternoon. I knew that there'd be many more Hull derbies for me to enjoy in the future. They were and still are very special occasions.

The Second Round was another away tie. Hunslet were the opposition on Wednesday, September 14. They had reached the final the previous season and were expected to present us with a stern test at Parkside. But the match provided us with another great win 29-3 and gave me a very special memory - my first hat trick for Rovers.

The Semi Final against Huddersfield followed twelve days later - another evening kick-off, this time a Monday - but for once at Craven Park, watched by a crowd of over 10,500. I scored two tries to help us into the final but I recall the game, especially the first half, was dominated by the forwards for long periods. Our pack had the ball in their hands for seventeen consecutive minutes and then Huddersfield had possession for another thirteen minutes. It was an interesting statistic to emerge from the game, especially as the introduction of the 'four tackle rule' was only a few weeks away.

Bill Holliday, Peter Flanagan and Arthur Bunting were our other try-scorers and Cyril Kellett kicked six goals. We won the match 27-7 to book our place in the final against Featherstone.

Before that Headingley showpiece however, we had another three league games to play. The first was a comprehensive 31-8 home victory against Doncaster. But the other two matches were rather more interesting!

On October 1 we travelled to Post Office Road for a Cup Final rehearsal against Featherstone. And returned with a confidence boosting 20-6 win.

A week later came one of the matches I'd been looking forward to - my first clash against Castleford. It turned out to be another memorable afternoon, especially as we won. I scored two more tries and Chris Young got one. But Castleford equalled our try-scoring exploits and the 19-13 victory was mainly down to Cyril Kellett who landed another five crucial kicks. Cyril was one of the most reliable goal-kickers I've ever played with. He saved us more times than I care to remember.

I'd only been at the club for just over two months but the time had just flown by. And incredibly I'd already played in thirteen games. Every one seemed important in one way or another. We'd got to the Yorkshire Cup Final and were vying for top spot in the league with Leeds. It had been an amazing start for me. One that was very difficult to believe for a lad who'd only just turned nineteen. But there was no time to dwell on it, I was to play my first Cup Final with Rovers the following Saturday...

Seven days later, our captain Frank Foster lifted the Yorkshire Cup at Headingley after we crushed Featherstone 25-12. I didn't get on the scoresheet that day but our five tries against Featherstone's two emphasised our superiority. I already knew I'd joined a very good team the day I arrived at Rovers, but that victory confirmed it.

And with players of the calibre of Frank Foster, Bill Holliday, Peter Flanagan, Brian Tyson and Terry Major in the pack and backs such as Chris Young and Alan Burwell, I was confident we'd be winning a lot more trophies in the months to follow.

Cyril again chipped in with five more goals to complete our victory that was more or less sealed by half time, when we led 17-2. He won the 'White Rose' trophy for the game's outstanding player.

Apart from the Floodlit Cup win with Castleford, winning the Yorkshire Cup with Rovers was my first major trophy as a professional. The match went pretty much to plan. It was a typical autumn Saturday in Leeds - pretty chilly! I remember coming back to Hull. It wasn't the warmest evening of the year and when we arrived back and were greeted by the fans in George Street, believe it or not - we were on an open top bus!

Carol and I were courting at the time and along with the other out of town players and their wives and girlfriends, we stayed at the New Manchester Hotel, near North Bridge. I remember the celebrations went on long into the night...

Lifting the Yorkshire Cup was only the beginning of a tremendous campaign for Rovers. And I like to think it was no coincidence that my first season at Craven Park also proved to be a very successful one for the club.

We played in some big games that season. But not surprisingly, three of the other games I recall the most vividly from that season were all against my former club, Castleford. The first time I returned to Wheldon Road to play for Rovers against Castleford was on a chilly Friday night at the end of October. It turned out to be a very memorable return - we not only won the game 15-9 but Rovers went to the top of the league.

The next meeting with Castleford turned out to be a truly massive encounter in more ways than one. The following February the two clubs were drawn against each other in the second round of the Challenge Cup at Craven Park.

15,830 fans packed into the ground on Saturday, February 25 for the game which ended in a nine-all draw. Mike Blackmore scored our try and Cyril Kellett kicked three goals. And ironically none other than John Taylor scored Castleford's try with 'Chuck' Hardisty landing two goals and Ron

Willett, one.

On the Sunday morning, I received a phonecall to say the whole team was going to the east coast for a few days to prepare for the replay. We stayed at the 'Expanse' in Bridlington and trained up there and then on the Wednesday came down to Castleford by coach for the game.

It was utter chaos at Wheldon Road that day. They had to put the kick-off back for forty-five minutes to get the crowd in. The official attendance was given as 22,582. But thousands more were in the ground having scaled the stadium walls - and thousands more still were left outside. Castleford's average attendance that season was around 5,000. But the size of the Wednesday afternoon crowd, which was boosted further by the large number of fans who'd skipped work that day, was probably nearer the 30,000 mark.

I remember the whole thing was a very strange experience for me. It had never happened like that before because with me being 'an out of town player' when I'd played against Castleford before I used to travel to the ground by car. But this was the first time I'd ever arrived on a coach - it virtually went past the end of our road.

It was a marvellous atmosphere but unfortunately from our point of view the wrong result - my old team beat my new one 13-6. Alan Hardisty, Jack Austin and Peter Small scored their tries, with Ron Willett kicking two goals. We only managed three goals, two penalties by Cyril Kellett and a drop goal from Frank Foster.

On the day we had no complaints, they were the better side. And I honestly thought they would have gone on to Wembley that year. But Featherstone, who then went on to beat Barrow in the final, knocked them out in the next round. And Brian Wrigglesworth, who'd been signed by Rovers just after me but was then transferred back to Featherstone, ended up playing fullback in their 17-12 Wembley win.

We also finished the season in style when we battled our way to the semi-final of the Championship Play-Offs.

I scored a try in our 17-15 home win against Barrow in first Round. And two in our 36-10 home victory against Swinton in the second round. 13,000 watched the Craven Park semi-final, hoping we could make another Cup Final. But we lost to Wakefield Trinity 6-18.

It was a season to look back on with a great deal of satisfaction however. We'd achieved our highest league finish for forty years, second, and also had the league's best defensive record for the first time in the clubs' history. We'd won the Mackeson Trophy for being the league's top scorers with 888 points including 178 tries, both club records. And we'd also achieved a run of seventeen games without defeat. Cyril Kellett and Dave Elliott had shared a successful benefit season, and the former had broken his own goal-kicking record with 145. I'd scored 25 tries and Chris Young had finished as top try-scorer with 34 equaling Graham Paul's post war record. It had been a sensational start for me, I couldn't have dreamed of a much better one...

CHAPTER FIVE
THE BEST GAME I'VE EVER SEEN

For me the following season was equally memorable - with even more achievements.

As well as the two Test matches against the Australians in 1970 that became highlights of my entire career, there was an earlier meeting against the Kangaroos, which I remember with almost as much affection. My first ever encounter with the men from down under undoubtedly provided me with the best memory of my second season at Rovers.

The date was October 7 1967 - the day we enjoyed a fantastic victory against the Aussie tourists at Craven Park. It was a great day for me. I again received the accolades having had an influential part in the win by scoring a hat-trick of tries to celebrate my Great Britain selection for the first test against the Aussies. But it was also a marvellous day for the club. And provided me with a memory of what I still regard today as one of the best team performances I ever took part in throughout my career. It was also the day that I realised I'd well and truly arrived on the International scene.

It was a truly great game - and a truly amazing performance. We simply couldn't put a foot wrong that day...

My situation at the time was perfectly clear. I'd only made one appearance for Great Britain whilst at Castleford. I'd then been transferred to Rovers and now found myself settled in a team that was going well. So naturally there was only one thing on my mind during the week running up to our clash with the Aussies at Craven Park. Who would the selectors pick at stand-off for Great Britain to face the Australians in the Test Series to follow? Would I be chosen ahead of Alan Hardisty and Mick Shoebottom? The answer came two days before Rovers' clash against the Australians.

I was named along with Chris Young, Bill Holliday and Peter Flanagan in the side for the first test! Having four members of a test side was an unprecedented achievement for Rovers. And we celebrated the occasion in devastating fashion, producing a breathtaking performance to win a fantastic match that everyone who witnessed it, declared simply as, 'The best game I've ever seen.'

Rovers 27 Australia 15 - it was an unbelievable scoreline! Chris

Above: The Rovers' side which won
the Eva Hardaker Cup at the Boulevard in 1967
Below: The Yorkshire Cup winning
squad from 1966-67

unfortunately didn't get many opportunities to show what a quality finisher he was - but Bill, Flash and I were all influential in what was acknowledged as one of the finest team displays ever seen at Craven Park. With the Yorkshire Cup Final against Hull to come on the following Saturday some people imagined we might have taken the game against the tourists lightly. They were all wrong! As kick-off time approached I knew it was going to be a very special afternoon. The conditions were perfect - bright sunshine and hardly a cloud in the sky. Craven Park was packed to the rafters, with fifteen thousand expectant fans ready to cheer every move, creating a fantastic atmosphere. And from the first whistle to the last, the match simply oozed with skilful, exciting football. Something that couldn't be said about a lot of Anglo-Australian clashes I'd seen.

The game wasn't without its' moments of controversy though, far from it. This was an Aussie touring team desperate for victory, let's not forget. One such moment, which I remember very well, was a 'tackle' I suffered from Aussie forward, John Sattler in the first half. It was described later as 'outrageous' in the local press. I think I could have thought of a few different adjectives for it! Sattler received a caution from referee, Mr Hunt, but what made it worse for me was Cyril then missed the resulting penalty. That was the first Australian side I'd played against and for the game to develop as it did was just an unbelievable experience. It turned into a bit of a see-saw game. First we got in front, then they nudged ahead. Next, a converted try by Alan Burwell put us 14-10 up at half-time. But then John McDonald scored and they led 15-14 at one stage, midway through the second half.

McDonald scored all his team's points that afternoon with three tries and three goals, but still ended up on the losing side. Because in the last quarter we blitzed them! I scored my second and third tries of the match, Johnny Moore got another, Cyril added two conversions, and it finished 27-15!

That performance confirmed my selection for the first test at Headingley. It also led Johnny Raper, one of the greatest Australian forwards of all time, who had been captain for the day, to describe Rovers as the best club side he had ever played against during his four tours of Britain...

A week after we'd beaten the Aussies, we played Hull in the Yorkshire Cup Final at Headingley. The weather couldn't have been any more different from our sun-drenched clash with the Aussies. It rained continuously during the morning and throughout the match. But even that couldn't dampen the enthusiasm of the 16,719 crowd that braved the dismal conditions to watch the first all-Hull final for forty-seven years.

I know we started as clear favourites. We'd beaten Hull twice already that season. But it was a tough, dour match. A typical derby that obviously nobody wanted to lose. And one that ended, as many derbies did, with a real 'nail-biting' finish.

The main thing I remember about that game was that Frank Foster was on the bench. Frank had been sidelined since August with a hand injury that ended up needing two operations. The final was his first game back. During Frank's absence, Johnny Moore had taken over the captaincy and he lifted

A Rovers' line-up from my first season at Craven Park, 1966-67 when we finished second in the league, our highest position for fifty years
Back row: Phil Lowe, Bill Holliday, Frank Fox, John Moore, Terry Major, Chris Young, Mike Stephenson. Front row: Alan Burwell, Peter Flanagan, Frank Foster, Roger Millward, David Wainwright, Stan Flannery.

The 1967 Great Britain Squad

the Cup that afternoon, after our narrow 8-7 victory over our neighbours from the Boulevard.

The match started pretty badly for us. Hull's scrum-half, Chris Davidson, who had an outstanding game and finished up with the man of the match award, scored an early try before we'd even touched the ball. But then I scored a crucial try when I intercepted a loose Hull pass and rounded their fullback Arthur Keegan on a forty yard run to the corner. Penalties by John Maloney and Cyril Kellett completed the first half scoring and left the game 5-5 at half-time.

Frank appeared at the beginning of the second-half as a substitute for John Hickson. But Hull nudged their way in front with a drop goal by Davidson. And they led 7-5 until the last few minutes, when Alan Burwell scored the winning try, running over in the left corner off a long pass by Terry Major. Cyril couldn't add the difficult conversion but in the end it didn't matter. We held out for the closing seconds and the Cup returned to Craven Park for the second successive year. The test matches against the Australians followed...

The first test at Headingley couldn't have gone much better. Chris Young scored a great sixty-yard try. I scored Britain's match-winning try and kicked three goals. And the British forwards, including Peter Flanagan and Bill Holliday were described as 'brilliant' - with Bill, who captained the side as 'outstanding'. We won 16-11 and were regarded as strong favourites to regain the Ashes. But the second test at the White City in London was a different story.

The build-up to the match went well enough with another record-breaking number of Rovers' players picked for the side. We had no fewer than five players in the Great Britain line-up, Frank Foster joining the Rovers' quartet from the first Test. The match could have been an unforgettable occasion - after all it's not every day that you have five players in the National team with the opportunity to clinch the Ashes! But when the day of the match arrived things went rapidly down hill.

It all started for us with a bang - literally, when we were involved in a car-crash on the way down to London. We were all travelling in Bill's car. I recall my dad had taken me to Bawtry and the others had picked me up there. We had the crash at Huntingdon, and for the last part of the journey we had to take the train. Not surprisingly, we arrived at our hotel at Crystal Palace late!

Bill's car was a right mess, a complete right off. And the second test unfortunately could be described in the same way! We lost 11-17 and the series was decided by the third test at Swinton.

That was a match that I don't think should have even been played! It was early December, the ground was frozen rock hard, and we were beaten again 11-3. The Ashes had gone and with an injured shoulder for my pains, my year was over!

I didn't play again until New Year's Day, when watched by a crowd of 9,000, I scored three tries in our 26-5 home win against Featherstone...

Like most players I always hated losing, no matter who I was playing against or whatever the stakes were. After being so close to winning the Ashes, losing the second and third tests were particularly humbling experiences for me. But equally there was nothing to be gained by dwelling on a defeat for long. You had to learn from experiences like those, put things into perspective and look forward to your next opportunity.

After the second test match in particular, I remember thinking that being in London and playing International rugby for my country - and losing - had been a sobering experience for me. But I also recall, only a couple of hours later, going out with the rest of the team after the match certainly wasn't. The clubs and bars of the West End were a million miles from the back streets of Castleford. And some of the people I mixed with, I'd only previously seen on television or in magazines. After the Second Test for example, I met Georgie Fame and Alan Price. They'd been at the White City supporting Great Britain.

Georgie was born in Leigh and was a big friend of Colin Clarke, the Wigan and Great Britain forward. And back in 1967 he and Alan were massive pop-stars! Georgie had thirteen chart hits including three number ones. The first two were 'Yeh, Yeh' in 1964 and the second 'Get Away' in 1966. In December 1967, just after we met him in London, his third chart-topper, 'The Ballad Of Bonnie And Clyde' entered the charts.

A number of the Great Britain lads, including me, went out with them for a drink after the game. Rugby league stars were all but anonymous walking around London in those days. But of course Georgie and Alan were definitely not! They were recognised everywhere we went. They were both very 'big' at the time and Georgie, I suppose you would have to say, is still doing very well now.

Alan had started out with his pal from the north east, Eric Burdon, as a member of the Animals. But he also went on to have a string of solo hits throughout the sixties and seventies, including 'The House That Jack Built', 'Don't Stop The Carnival' and 'Jarrow Song'. But the one I always remember the most - although I never quite knew why, was the infectious, 'Simon Smith and His Amazing Dancing Bear'. They seemed to play that record constantly in 1967, wherever you went. Later on in 1971, Georgie and Alan joined forces for another hit entitled 'Rosetta' that reached number 11. I had only just celebrated my twentieth birthday and remember thinking that mixing with 'pop-stars' in trendy London pubs seemed a far cry from a Saturday night out in Castleford! It was a different world. I was going to say, those were the days... but that of course was by Mary Hopkin!

But even after those disappointments I could again look back on another season of achievements. We finished third in the League and reached the Championship Final. In fact going into the final we'd put a couple of good runs together and were favourites to win. But like the previous season however, Wakefield once again wrecked our hopes when they beat us 17-10 at Headingley in front of 22,000 fans.

There was no doubting that Trinity were the best team on the day and we couldn't grumble with the result. I recall I came up against another great player that day, Harold Poynton.

Wakefield had featured in another 'first' earlier in the season. They'd been the opposition when Rovers' new floodlights, costing over £18,000 were used for the first time on September 29. We won the match 25-3. And four days later we won our next league game at Oldham 9-7. The significance of the second result was that it was the first time we'd ever won at the Watersheddings since the two sides first met in 1900!

Rovers' achievements were rewarded at the turnstiles with an average home crowd that year of 9,545.

On a personal note, I won the ABC Top Try Scorer for the season with 38, which was a record for a stand-off. I was particularly pleased with that achievement because it had after all only been my second season at Rovers. My total of 38 tries beat the 35 scored by Frank Myler, then of Widnes, in the 1958-59 season. The tries were made up of: Rovers' Cup and League games - 27, Yorkshire - 3, Great Britain - 3, Rovers v Australia - 3, BBC2 Cup Competition - 2

I have particularly fond memories of the 36th try that set the new record, which I scored in the league match at Craven Park against York on March 8. Alan Burwell had actually crossed the try-line and could have easily scored himself. But instead he waited for me to join him and then passed the ball, allowing me to score one of the simplest tries I've ever scored. It was a great gesture from a great player.

I was also again Rovers' top try scorer with 32 and finished as top points scorer as well, having kicked 38 goals, after been entrusted with the goal-kicking duties following Cyril Kellett's transfer to Featherstone in January.

At the end of the season I won the club's Supporters Player of the Year Award for the first time. I received it on four other occasions and they were all a great honour and meant a lot to me. Whatever club you're at it's nice to know that the people at that club think a lot about you. When I was both a player and then later a coach, I used to think a great deal about how the players should all be seen as representatives of the club. They were all a part of a team and whilst representing the club should dress and behave as such - and should be willing to mix with and talk to the supporters.

Just because you play the game shouldn't mean you don't talk to people. After all, the fans are part and parcel of your life and probably the most important part of any sport! When you think about it, how could any professional sportsman have a successful career without them?

I was lucky enough to be selected for eleven representative games during that season and on the following summer's tour. Apart from the three tests I played for Great Britain against the Australians, I also played in two more against France. And appeared for Yorkshire against Cumberland, Lancashire and Australia.

Matches against Australia in Sydney, France in Auckland and New Zealand in Sydney followed on the World Cup Tour during May and June. They were hectic times but everything that I'd dreamed of as a boy...

MY FIRST TOUR

Top: The Great
Britain players
meet comedian,
Dave Allen

Middle:
The 1968
World Cup
Squad

Bottom: That's
me on the right
with some of the
lads

CHAPTER SIX
HONG KONG &
A BOYHOOD HERO
THE 1968 WORLD CUP

We were all very disappointed at how the 1968 World Cup turned out because I think going into that tour everyone was extremely confident about our chances of success.

You'd have to say it was probably one of the best-prepared touring teams to leave these shores. We'd played about half a dozen warm-up matches against English club sides even before they picked the touring team. But when we got there, it just didn't happen. I recall we played Australia in the first game. And I remember being in training going up to the match and the Australian press thought we were kidding because it appeared a lot of the British players couldn't even handle the ball very well.

It was a different shaped ball that we had to play with out there - it was more pointed - but some of the media guys just thought we were trying it on. If only that had been the case - the fact was simply that we genuinely couldn't pass or catch the ball properly at first.

The first match was against the Aussies on the Sydney Cricket Ground and we were well-beaten 25-10. We never really performed. However the match that knocked us out of the competition was the next game when we played France in Auckland and they beat us 7-2. And with Australia beating New Zealand, the Aussies and France were already through to the Final after only the first two rounds.

We were already out of it and although we then beat New Zealand pretty easily on the Sydney Cricket Ground it was the game at Carlow Park in Auckland that had ended our hopes. It was a poor match, it had rained a lot during the week and it was always a bad pitch to play on - always very heavy when it was wet. And really that was the end of the tour - at least as far as the chance of winning anything was concerned!

We just never seemed to fire at all on that tour and nobody played to anything like their potential. One of the problems was there weren't many ex-tourists in the party. And the people who'd played well at home in the domestic competition that season just didn't perform when we got out there. We didn't really gel as a team. We'd expected to be in the final but in the end finished up watching it from the stands. And the obvious theories of what had gone wrong inevitably followed.

The highlight of the tour, if you can call it that, was undoubtedly when we stopped off at Hong Kong on the way home. BOAC went on strike for a week so we all got an unplanned extra few days holiday in Hong Kong, which was an incredible place at the time. The Vietnam War was still on and there were American soldiers everywhere! There was a constant buzz about the place - it was something very different and a fantastic place to visit...

Rugby league has always been a game that's never been afraid to alter its' rules. And long before we left for Australia, there was a suggestion the British team in particular, were heading for another competition packed with controversy. Australia, New Zealand, France and Great Britain all played their domestic competitions under slightly varying rules. You didn't have to be a brain surgeon to see that when the four sides met, even under the scrutiny of a 'neutral' referee, problems were likely to occur.

Even before the first game kicked off, the British Team manager, Bill Fallowfield had to play down the concern over referees' rule interpretation. He said any rule variations would not affect the side - but naturally all teams wanted to know what the referee expected of them.

Another disadvantage Britain had to contend with was playing under two different referees during the series. New Zealand referee, John Percival took charge of Britain's opening match against the Australians. Aussie referee Col Pearce was in the middle for their games against both France and New Zealand. And if Britain progressed to the final, Percival would again take charge. The Australians on the other hand would have all their games officiated by Percival. It may have seemed a minor point but it was a problem for us that was certainly emphasized as soon as a ball was kicked...

The trip to Australia for the 1968 World Cup was my first tour. I was still only twenty years old and the youngest player in the nineteen strong touring party. But I was in good company as three Rovers' teammates, Alan Burwell, Peter Flanagan and Chris Young were also selected for the trip which left for the southern hemisphere on May 8.

The squad suffered a major setback almost immediately after arriving in Australia, when a doctor was called to the team hotel to treat 'Flash' Flanagan, who was suffering with stomach pains. He was ruled out of the first test match against Australia in Sydney, with what was reportedly feared to be a duodenal ulcer. His place in the front row went to Leigh's hooker, Kevin Ashcroft. Happily 'Flash' recovered soon after, his illness actually being put down to a serious bout of food poisoning.

Chris Young was another of the Rovers' quartet who missed out that day, when Ian Brooke from Wakefield Trinity was named on the right wing. Brooke along with Hull winger Clive Sullivan, making his World Cup debut, each scored spectacular tries for the Lions and Bev Risman added two goals. But apart from those successes, our defence of the World Championship on May 25 couldn't have got off to a much worse start.

Aborigine fullback, Eric Simms was the star of the match. He'd been brought into the Australian team mainly for his goal-kicking ability. And when New Zealand referee, John Percival handed him a glut of penalty opportunities, the Australian certainly showed his inclusion had been an inspired decision. Simms was playing in his first test and he finished it with eight goals, many the result of Percival constantly pulling-up our players with off-side decisions, which frequently turned into 'doubles' when the lads disputed them. The decisions were the main thing that the British side criticised after the game. But although the Aussies only scored one more try than we did, ultimately it was Simms' phenomenal kicking that was the main factor that put Britain out of the game. In the end we were well beaten 25-10, in front of a 62,000 crowd at the Sydney Cricket Ground. In the other game France, inspired by Jean Capdouze beat New Zealand 15-10. Australia were made favourites after their win against us but both games had shown there was little to choose between the four sides. If we could have beaten France and then New Zealand in our other two matches we could have gone on to have another crack at the Aussies in the final.

But those hopes disappeared the following weekend when we lost 7-2 to France. The only points we managed was a penalty by Bev Risman after ten minutes and we were still ahead at half-time. But the French played much better after the break and drew level on three-quarter time when their scrum-half, Roger Garrigues dropped a goal. A late try by France's new cap, Ledru, converted by Capdouze ended our World Cup bid almost before it had started. With Australia crushing New Zealand 31-12, the Aussies and the French had already assured their places in the final - and an end to the long sequence of Australia v Britain World Cup Finals.

We only had our pride to play for in the final test against the Kiwis on June 8. Chris Young was left out again which meant he travelled half way around the world but didn't play at all on the tour. Colin Hutton, our coach at Rovers was also the Great Britain coach. He was adamant we should show everyone what we were capable of.

'We are out to redeem - the players are ready to show just how good they are,' Colin said. And to a certain extent we did salvage a little of our lost pride, although the whole performance in what was after all, a 'dead rubber' was a big anti-climax. We beat New Zealand convincingly enough, 38-14. Clive Sullivan scored a hat-trick of tries and my Rovers' colleague Alan Burwell scored a superb long-range try. But third in the table was definitely not where we'd planned to finish!

Australia beat France easily in their third game of the tournament, 37-4 and then defeated them again 20-2 in the final.

Our disappointing tour finished with four games against club sides. First we beat Toowoomba, 28-10. I scored two tries and two goals and Alan Burwell also scored a try. We then beat Queensland 33-18 in Brisbane and I scored a try. But the star of the victory was Clive Sullivan who finished the match with four touchdowns. Clive had become one of the main British successes of the tour and scored two more tries in our penultimate game, when we defeated North Queensland 25-2 at Townsville. Our final game against NorthWest Queensland ended with another win, 33-5. Again Clive and I both crossed for tries. The match was played at Mount Isa and the crowd of around 2,000 was the biggest seen there for over four years.

But the trip finished with further problems when our journey home and arrival back in the U.K. had to be postponed from the Friday to the following Monday, owing to a BOAC pilots' dispute.

I recall I met Dave Allen whilst he was in Sydney. Like us he was on tour but I imagine he was enjoying his a lot more than we were enjoying ours. Dave Allen was probably the most successful comedian of that era and had a weekly television show on BBC1 on a Saturday evening, although it was later moved to a mid-week spot. I also met one of my boyhood heroes, Bobby Charlton. He'd gone out there to do some football coaching but he came to the Sydney Cricket Ground to see us play and we had a few beers with him afterwards. Bobby had always been one of my idols from being a kid. I'd have only been about ten or eleven, a very impressionable age, when the Munich Air Disaster happened and Manchester United of course were a big team at that time as well, even if they were from the wrong side of the Pennines. For that reason alone, I can't say I was ever a great United fan but I always admired Bobby as a player. And it was a big thrill when I finally got the opportunity to meet him. He's always been a fantastic sportsman and was a great guy to talk to!

I met another England footballer a few years later, but in totally different circumstances. It was whilst I was being treated by a physiotherapist called Mr Blackburn. The remarkable thing about Mr Blackburn was that he was totally blind. He worked at the Pontefract Hospital but he also had a treatment and massage room at the back of his home. He treated hundreds of people there ranging from ordinary members of the public to professional sportsmen.

I remember going to his house one evening after tea. There were three booths in one room and he used to go around from booth to booth treating each of the patients in turn. I went in and was told to make myself comfortable on the bed in the left-hand booth. I was due to play for Great Britain ten days later. On the bed in the middle booth was Billy Bremner. He was a Scottish International soccer player and was due to turn out for his country again the following week. And on the third bed in the right-hand booth was England International, Terry Cooper.

All we did for most of the session as he got to each one of us in turn, was to yell out. Mr Blackburn was brilliant with his hands but you have to appreciate we were all in a lot of pain. As he treated us, we'd each shout out, 'Arrrgh!' It must have sounded hilarious but probably also quite disconcerting to the other patients in the waiting room.

He'd then go round to the next bed and another slightly different 'Arrrgh!' broke the silence. It was so funny to think that Billy, Terry and I, three International sportsmen, all hopeful of representing our countries within a few days - were there in the back room of a house in Knottingley - with one blind fella responsible for ensuring we all did.

You usually went through some pain when you went to see Mr Blackburn - but I'm pleased to say he did get all three of us fit in time - he was a brilliant man with his hands!

CHAPTER SEVEN
WHAT THE HELL AM I DOING HERE?

If I'd ever thought about the dangers I faced - or the injuries that I might sustain playing rugby league - I'd probably never have played the game again. But it was something that I'd grown up with - so things like that never bothered me. I knew what I could and couldn't do. And I knew which players to look out for, who not to go near - and where to position myself. But I can honestly say I've never ran out onto a rugby pitch and been frightened of anybody on that field. If I had been, I would just simply have got out of rugby league for good!

There were always certain players who came at me but that I regarded as part and parcel of the game. And in a way that was a compliment because they obviously regarded me as the threat, the player who could affect their chances of winning. And later on in the professional game, the player who could be the difference between them taking winning or losing pay home that day. So from the first game I played, I was constantly learning about how to stay out of trouble. But as far as I was concerned, that was as much about me being able to avoid any problems, as the opposition doing anything to prevent me from playing to the best of my ability.

I know for a fact that some players have gone out on to the field with just one thing on their mind - and that was to put me out of the game. That wasn't just when I was sixteen or seventeen - that was all the way through my career. It was all about my experience from then on. I had to be better at staying out of trouble, than the opposition were of getting near enough to me to cause any.

It didn't always work of course. I've been caught plenty of times. And there were certainly occasions when I thought, what the hell am I doing here? I've had some good clouts - but I'd say I got out of trouble about 95% or more of the time...

There's a photograph that I always have to smile at of Jim Mills, the former Widnes and Great Britain prop forward and I. Jim looks about two feet taller than I do. And there's a good reason for that - he was! It was the same with the Aussies, they were all massive blokes as well. But you didn't think about size when you were out on the pitch.

When I was playing at Rovers, especially in the early days, we'd often play our home matches on a Friday night. And as I still lived in Castleford and still knew a lot of the Castleford lads, I'd often go down to watch their match the following day. I usually stood just behind the fencing and watched the game - and cringed at some of the tackles. And I must admit, I'd often think to myself, how on earth do I play this game?

But whenever I was in the dressing room getting changed and as soon as that whistle went, it never bothered me! I'd just think, come on, let's get on with the job.

I know for a fact 'taking players out' has always gone on. It's happened on many occasions in the past - when it's been said on the field - as somebody's been targeted. 'He's got to go - he's the dangerman' or 'let's make sure he knows he's been playing today.'

Whatever the terminology was, it amounted to the same thing - and we all knew what that was!

It always went on and it always will do, it still goes on today. But that's life in rugby league. And you've got to love this game to play it, because it's bloody hard once you get out on that pitch.

There's no place to hide on that field and your fellow professionals all know if you 'fancy it' or you don't. When I watch the game on the television now, as an ex-professional player, I can easily tell who 'fancies it' and who doesn't. Just by looking at them, by the body language as they call it today, I can tell, I know who wants it and who doesn't.

My biggest attributes in my opinion were my ability to read the game - and my defence. Rugby League had to be understood to be played properly. And my experience at halfback had made me not only ultra alert but better than most at predicting how play would develop.

I have always been a marked man and had I not been able to find plenty of ways to get past big forwards, I would have been hammered out of the game years before. And defending was never a problem to me, no matter what size the opposition was. I always said, the day I had doubts about tackling any man, big or small, would be my last in rugby league football.

I used to love tackling. It's an art that never receives the recognition it deserves. After all, a tackle that stops a try, can be the difference between winning or losing a match, just the same as scoring one can.

And there's one tackle I'll always remember above the thousands I must have made in over seventeen years of first class rugby. It happened during a game against Leeds at Headingley. Leeds had a scrum very close to the halfway line. They worked the blind side and Barry Seabourne put John Atkinson away down the wing. John was a superb winger and definitely one of the fastest around. I came across the back of our pack and with a full length dive, took him around the ankles and we both rolled over and over and into touch. John just got up, tapped me on the head and said, 'Well done, mate.'

Now that was the sort of thing that I remember because to me that was what rugby league was all about. Although I must add that it was a side of the game that you didn't always see!

I always said that I was very lucky to be 'a complete footballer'. I don't mean that in a conceited way but just that nothing ever frightened me about playing, whether it was tackling or any other aspect of the game. They were simply parts of the job of being a rugby league player.

I don't recall how I perfected my tackling technique, I suppose it was just down to a lot of practising whilst I was growing up. Even when you were just playing for fun with the other kids, if you were on their side and you were letting people through by not tackling, they'd soon let you know!

And you always had your bigger mates around you who showed you how to do things. The penny soon dropped and you soon found out the easiest and the safest way to do it.

Kicking goals I think also came naturally, although when I look back, I also spent hours and hours practising that too. A mate and I used to go down to Fryston Park, where the rugby posts were always up. He'd go to one side of the goal and I'd go to the other and we'd spend hours and hours either drop kicking or place kicking. It was just something we loved doing. So all that practice that went in then, which I never thought of as practice at the time stood me in good stead when I came into the 'big' game.

It just seemed to be natural to me and I never had any nerves about goal kicking. It was an ability I always had - I could put a ball down and kick a goal. I was lucky but I'll admit there was also a lot of hard work that went in, but at the time we didn't think of it as practising, we were just having fun. But yes, the saying is certainly true, the harder you work at something, the luckier you seem to get.

I wish kids today could be the same and just enjoy playing the game. But unfortunately I see kids at training sessions now - maybe only under 9s or even under 8s - and they're doing press-ups and laps and things! I'd just throw them a ball and let them enjoy themselves, let them be happy, that's how we learnt. There's enough competition, conditioning and training for them to follow later in life, without them starting when they are only eight and nine years old!

I remember going to a kids' presentation evening not very long ago, when I stood up for over an hour and presented everyone with a prize. And really it didn't warrant that. Those kids needed some more gear to practise with - that's what I'd rather have used the money on. Let the kids enjoy themselves, that's what we did, we played in that wood until we were thirteen or fourteen. The kids of today, they're wearing shoulder pads at under 8s, it's crazy!

I just think we should relax a little, let them enjoy themselves, and teach them the finer points of the game later on in life. It's a hard game is this, kids have to enjoy it to play it...

Top: John Stephens and I between
Colin Hutton and Bill Fallowfield
during England's match in
Toulouse, 1970

Below: The Great Britain
Touring Team 1974

CHAPTER EIGHT
WEDDING BELLS & A CHRISTMAS DISASTER

When I got back from the 1968 World Cup tour, the team at Rovers was described as being in a 'transitional' stage. I suppose that was a polite way of saying - it was breaking up! And I feared my third season at Craven Park wouldn't be as enjoyable as my first two. I was right!

At the start of the campaign things were far from perfect. I cut my holiday in Skegness short in order that I could return to play in the opening league game against Leigh at Craven Park. Frank Foster had just recovered from an appendicitis operation and captained the side at loose-forward. But Alex Murphy, Leigh's player-coach, a man suffering from a heart condition that had reportedly threatened to end his career not long before, led his side to a 15-27 victory that night. I was the first to admit I'd been far from my best. I'd played over sixty matches in four different countries in the previous twelve months and I felt jaded. Not surprisingly Rovers rested me for the match against the Cup-holders Leeds, seven days later.

Another defeat followed however as an under-strength Rovers side lost 10-17, albeit with the aid of a hotly disputed try by Barry Seabourne.

The season was only a month old when I faced an important 'match' of a totally different kind - my wedding to Carol.

I'd first met Carol at the 'Fryston Club' in 1964. The romantically named setting was a big Miners' and Working Men's club which had been built on land alongside the rugby and soccer pitches, just down the road from where I lived. I met her again a short time later when we were both on holiday in Blackpool. She was there with some of her friends and I was there with a group of mine.

I was still only sixteen years old - and it was the first time any of us had been away on our own - without our parents. We all stayed at Ken and Barry's in Albert Road. We'd all booked in for the same week. At that time you had to take your holidays during the first two weeks in August, you couldn't just have them when you wanted. It was difficult, especially then, because with pre-season training and then starting the new season, if you didn't have those two weeks, you didn't get a holiday! It was as simple as that. So you had to take them because the pits shut down and that included the maintenance staff, electricians - everybody.

I was in Blackpool with five of my pals, including Mick Redfearn. He along with my cousin Brian Lockwood, went on to play in both the victorious Castleford Wembley Cup Final sides of 1969 when they beat Salford 11-6 and 1970 when they beat Wigan 7-2. Carol was there with a group of her friends. We more or less started going out together immediately after that holiday and were engaged in 1966. We were married at Kippax Church on September 21 1968 - a week after my twenty-first birthday. And we were very lucky. September 21 was a Saturday - the only free weekend in the league programme. Immediately after the wedding we set off to Blackpool for our honeymoon, to the same hotel. But I had to be back to play for Yorkshire against Lancashire at Craven Park on the following Wednesday, so the honeymoon only lasted for three days. Carol probably didn't agree but for me it was worth coming back early. We beat Lancashire by ten points to five - to add to our previous win against Cumberland - and so became County Champions for the first time since 1964.

My brother Roy was my best man. My best friends at that time were naturally mostly other players who I'd played with, like Peter Small, Clive Dickinson and Johnny Walker. They were all still Castleford players but were the lads I still went around with. We'd still go out regularly together on a Saturday night, even though I'd been at Rovers for two years by then of course.

When we were courting and when we were first married, Carol worked as a hairdresser. But since then she's worked as a 'Sales Rep' for numerous companies including 'Guinness' and 'Woodside Products'. The latter was known locally as 'knobs and knockers' - they sold those two items - and lots more throughout Yorkshire. And needless to say, all the lads used to have a good laugh with a multitude of jokes, most of them unprintable, about that particular company's goods. Carol's now gone full circle though, as she's currently back working in her friend's hairdressing salon, 'Jason's Of Kippax'.

Behind the scenes at the start of the season, Rovers looked set to dive into the transfer market, with a scrum-half the top of their wanted list. They were reported to be set to make a bid for Featherstone's Carl Dooler and then only days later, be ready to pay £8,000 for my International half-back partner from St Helens, Tommy Bishop.

The club's signings included Artie Beetson, regarded as the best front row forward in the world, Paul Rose and Terry Clawson.

Terry soon became one of my regular travelling partners. There were some tremendous characters in the game during the sixties - that's what made it such a great sport to be part of. I soon discovered Terry was one of them!

But I remember not long after his arrival at Craven Park he met his match when he tried to get the better of Johnny Williams...

Just after my arrival at the club, Johnny had christened me 'the mouse' because he said I was always so quiet and reserved. I'll let you draw your own conclusions about it, but let's just say it was a nickname that for one reason or another, didn't last for very long. John was a brilliant man though and we had a lot of laughs together. I remember one night when I picked Terry up - we were playing at Craven Park in a midweek game - and I knew he didn't want to play because he'd had a 'knock' the previous Saturday.

We drove over to Hull in the car together and as soon as we arrived at the ground, Terry got changed but then went straight to see Johnny and said, 'I'm injured John, I don't think I'll be able to play tonight.'

'Right.' said Johnny 'You'd better come in here then.' And he took him into the treatment room. The hot water tap in there was always absolutely scalding and John held a towel under the steaming water and then slapped it straight onto Terry's bare leg. He left it there for a few seconds and then peeled it off. You could see a patch of red skin already starting to rise on Terry's leg. And although he didn't make a sound, the look on Terry's face I would liken to that of a man enduring considerable torture.

Johnny then put the towel into a bucket of ice-cold water. Next, with one well-rehearsed movement he pulled the towel out of the bucket and slapped it firmly on Terry's leg again. The cold towel lay on the leg for the same amount of time as the hot one had, accompanied by the same worried look on Terry's face. It was quite a relief to me, when, as Johnny prepared to place the second 'scalding' hot one on the 'injured' leg, Terry shouted out, 'Hold everything, I'll play.'

It was brilliant. I couldn't stop laughing. Although at the time, Terry didn't seem to see the funny side of it! But he did play, in fact he not only played, he also won the 'man of the match' award that night.

Johnny was a truly marvellous man - and I rarely saw anyone get the better of him. He was a great 'physio', knew exactly what he was doing and just got on with the job. And more often than not he'd do things, get the result he wanted - and have a good laugh all at the same time.

Johnny looked after me on many occasions, although I'd estimate he also nearly drowned me at least three times as well. When that sponge full of water hit you square in the face, you could easily have nearly choked to death...

Although Terry and Artie arrived at the club, on the down side, Bill Holliday, Frank Foster and John Taylor all left. And not surprisingly, without players of that calibre, things slowly got worse and worse. I was concerned. My third season with Rovers looked destined to be a big anti-climax...

Things hit rock bottom when Artie had to return to Australia having played only twelve matches for us, after breaking his leg in the Christmas Day derby match against Hull at Craven Park.

I didn't play many games at the start of the season due to a spate of injuries but I did play eight games with Artie. And every one was a lot easier than playing against him. His injury certainly robbed us of a big asset. He improved with every game he played and in November won two consecutive home man of the match awards with two brilliant displays against Featherstone and Castleford.

Castleford were at the top of the league at the time and unbeaten in fourteen matches. It was described as the best game seen on Humberside so far that season. But it was a tragedy that Rovers' fans were robbed of seeing more of Artie following that Christmas Day disaster!

The year drew to a sad close with the memory of the two things that could have been the year's highlights - the World Cup and Rovers signing one of the top players in the world - both ending as major disappointments.

The frustration was perhaps only relative. And things maybe appeared far worse than they actually were because I was comparing them with our two previous years of success. There were after all a number of positives...

Phil Lowe emerged as a towering figure in more ways than one and ended the season as an ever-present in Rovers' team. I'd always appreciated how tough rugby league could be. And it was interesting to know that even the bigger lads who played the game - and they didn't come much bigger than Phil - felt the same as I did.

Injuries of course were all part of the game - something that you expected to happen sooner or later - although naturally you always hoped you'd be one of the lucky ones. But I remember Phil saying, not long after he'd started playing for Hull K R, that if you ever stopped to think about the dangers you faced on the pitch, then you'd never play the game again...

The main saving grace for me that season was that I continued to be selected for Yorkshire and played for my County against both Cumberland and Lancashire. But there was no denying it was the poorest season I'd experienced at Rovers by a long, long way. I only kicked 75 goals and crossed for 15 tries, three less than top try scorer, Mike Stephenson. I found it all very disappointing. Rovers were certainly on the slide. It was a slump that lasted into the early seventies. And it wasn't until 1972 when we saw the first signs of turning things around - but even then it was still hard work. The problem was fortunately easy to identify. To put it bluntly there were simply just too many players there at the same time that wouldn't have lived with the players who'd been there just before them.

The failing was an easy one to diagnose but far more difficult to find an answer to. Rovers had neither the money to buy their way out of trouble - nor many quality youngsters to bring into the side. But at the time a large percentage of the fans didn't recognise Rovers' problems. A lot of people thought that Rovers were a top side right through from the mid-sixties to the mid-eighties - but they weren't!

We only finished tenth out of thirty teams in 1969. And as the end of the decade approached, the club continued on its' downward spiral...

The problems continued during the 1969-70 season. We reached two major semi-finals, which helped to paper over the cracks, but unfortunately we lost them both. The Play-off semi against Leeds was lost 47-5 and the Challenge Cup Semi-Final against Wigan at Headingley, 19-8.

At the beginning of the season, Paul Rose became the youngest player to appear for the first team when he played against Leigh on September 27 1969 - aged only 16 years and 9 months. It was a significant debut in more ways than one. It not only showed that Rovers were having to 'blood' their young players far earlier than they would have a few years earlier, or later for that matter. But it also heralded, as Phil's emergence the previous year had done, the start of the 'new Rovers', which would become a force in the second half of the seventies - and beyond. Ten years later, both would be in their prime, seasoned Great Britain internationals and integral parts of the Robins' Cup and Championship winning sides. But for now, they had to contend with far more testing times.

For me it was another season when I received more than my share of honours. The first was a different type of honour and a quite unexpected one. In November 1969 I was chosen as the new Rovers' captain at the age of only twenty-two.

There were other players at the club, who were a lot more experienced than I was and who'd played the game a lot longer than I had. So I admit it came as a bit of a surprise when the club said they wanted me to skipper the team. But I accepted it straightaway and it proved to be a good move for me because it definitely made me think a lot more about the game.

I also played for England against Wales twice and France twice - and for Yorkshire against both Lancashire and Cumberland. I won the Players' No. 6 'Player Of The Year' award and was again Rovers' top points scorer with 99 goals and 21 tries. But the one achievement I craved more than any other though, still eluded me. Because although we reached the Challenge Cup Semi-Final that year, we fell at the last hurdle and the dream of appearing in a Wembley Cup Final had to be put on ice for at least another twelve months.

The Semi-Final against Wigan on March 21 was such a disappointing game for me. I'd been on tour. I'd played for Yorkshire and I was just one game away from fulfilling another ambition, to play at Wembley. It took me another ten years to get there. After the loss against Wigan, I thought the chance had gone to be honest. It was a major ambition of mine to play at Wembley. And although I achieved all my other ambitions, it was always something that was missing out of my life.

Bill Ashurst kicked us to death that day. He was a super player but a bit of an enigma - I don't think he ever really achieved his full potential. However that day he was the main difference between the two sides. Every kick he put in seemed to go fifty or sixty yards and bounce straight into touch.

I spoke to another Bill after the match, my old pal, Bill Francis. He'd played in the centre for Wigan against us that afternoon.

Bill and I had always remained great friends and kept in regular touch. We're still great friends today, in fact I saw him recently at the Lions' reunion. And although the semi-final defeat was a big disappointment to me, it was just nice that somebody like him had got to the cup final.

As far as I was concerned however, I couldn't help but think that I was six years into my career and Wembley had been there again for the taking but again we'd lost in a semi-final.

Having said that, I still couldn't put the semi-final defeat into the same category as some of the other matches we lost because to reach a semi- final is an achievement in itself. There were a lot of contributory factors to the defeat. I've gone over and over them in my mind on many occasions since. But I suppose no amount of analysis could tell me why we didn't get to

Wembley that year. It was simply down to a bad performance at Headingley that day - we just never really got going. And unfortunately Bill Ashurst did! Wigan beat us fairly easily in the end, 19-8. And Castleford beat Saints 6-3 in the other semi to book their second successive Wembley final. They'd beaten Salford the year before and went on to beat Wigan to record a rare Wembley 'double'.

I always thought of getting to Wembley as another rung of the ladder, rather like going on a tour, I suppose. It was another goal that players set themselves. And especially during the later part of my career, one that I thought I was never going to achieve. It was always nice to achieve my goals, get them under my belt and say, well at least I've done it. And then I could settle down and enjoy the rest of my life in football. But my goal of getting to Wembley was always there at the back of my mind. That I hadn't done it! And the seasons were running out. We could win the Yorkshire Cup but it was just that next step up that always seemed to elude us.

I remember way back in 1964 Rovers played Oldham in the Challenge Cup semi-final at Headingley, because I played in the curtain-raiser for Castleford Under 17s against Leeds. When we'd finished we came back out and watched some of the main game but I had to get on the bus and leave before the end. Rovers were losing before 'Flash' Flanagan dropped a goal to level it up and it went to another replay - and then another - before Rovers finally got through to Wembley. And I realised even then as a teenager, how difficult that last hurdle could be!

And against Wigan, it was another occasion when I thought, this is it - this is my time - but then it didn't work out for me. You set your goals as a kid, and my goals were to sign on as a professional, play for Yorkshire and then if I was very lucky and I happened to be playing well when the fourth year of the cycle came round, get picked to go on tour. And finally to play at Wembley. They were my main ambitions. I'd fulfilled two of them, playing at Wembley still stood out. It gets you thinking am I ever going to get there? And I'll tell you, the doubt got a lot bigger in the early seventies!

Our second semi-final defeat that season came in the Premiership Play-Offs. I didn't play due to a groin injury. In fact I recall we took a very under-strength side to Headingley that day - Johnny Moore, Gordon Young and Colin Cooper were also absent - and paid the price. Leeds at home were virtually unstoppable around that time and ran out 47-5 winners. It was a disappointing if somewhat expected end to the campaign. And although there were still a number of very good players at Craven Park, the decline continued...

But after all the ups and downs, the season ended on a definite high. I was chosen for Great Britain's Ashes Tour to Australia. It was a defining moment for me. The dream I'd had since I was a small boy was about to become reality. As I waited for our departure day the excitement and anticipation became unbearable. Flying to the opposite side of the world still seemed totally unreal. And little did I know then, the trip would prove to be not only an unbelievable episode in my life - but would also provide me with some of the most fantastic moments of my entire career...

CHAPTER NINE
THE
1970 ASHES
THE TRIP OF A LIFETIME

My second trip to Australia was in 1970. It couldn't have turned out much different to my first, the disappointing World Cup Tour, I'd experienced two years earlier. The time away from home was much longer, the tour had far more matches and of course the stakes were much higher. When I left Great Britain in 1970, to go half way around the world again, there was only one thing on my mind. Only one goal I had to achieve - to return home with the mythical 'Ashes'...

When I woke up on July 4 1970 the sun was already high in the Sydney sky. The temperature was also already rising - it was going to be a very hot day. I hadn't slept that well, I rarely did before a big game. I never felt like eating much either. The excitement and anticipation of the match I was about to play in was the only thing on my mind. I was always nervous before a game. It was something that I had to live with throughout my career. But whatever happened in the following few hours, I knew it was going to be a memorable day...

I was part of a British team that would make history in one way or another. It would be an unforgettable match whether we won or lost. If we won every British player and every British fan, would remember the day we won the Ashes in Australia, for the rest of their lives. And of course if we lost, we'd all recall the day when the opportunity to write another page in the rugby league history books was missed...

It was undoubtedly the greatest day of my playing career - so far - although ten years later there would be another occasion to rival even this! I'd played in some amazing matches in the first few years of my career but there was nothing to compare to the Ashes tour of 1970. And especially the third test at the Sydney Cricket Ground.

Victory in the second test was fantastic. But when we won the third to clinch the series and win the Ashes it was unbelievable!

We stayed in The Olympic Hotel on Moor Park Road, overlooking the Sydney Cricket Ground. I could look out of my window and there were people there at half past seven in the morning already queuing up to get in.

It was a hell of a feeling to think that they were all there to watch us.

It was a funny place where we stayed - it was more like a pub than anything else - with rooms upstairs. I'd doubt if you'd get it today. You had an International team staying there, who all congregated downstairs in the hotel and then walked to the Sydney Cricket Ground to play a crucial test match. But that was one of the things that made it so special. You walked through the crowd, mingling with supporters from both sides. It was a walk of about four or five hundred yards. But that walk helped to make the occasion even more memorable.

When I arrived in the ground it was even more amazing. To walk into the dressing rooms where a wall full of photographs of some of my childhood heroes looked down at me, gave me a fabulous feeling.

It's a fabulous place. It was old and decrepit in some places even then in many ways. But it was the history of the place. What had happened there made it almost a museum of sporting achievements. It was all encapsulated in that stadium. All depicted on those walls. And to think that most of the great cricketers and rugby league players of the past had sat in the same place as I was then. And then to actually turn out on the Cricket Ground was an experience in itself - but to win there was even better.

Being a Yorkshireman, my heroes included players such as Freddie Trueman and Brian Close. I loved them. But there were many others like Lancashire's Brian Statham. They were all of course the stars of my boyhood, my heroes from my schooldays when I used to follow cricket passionately. And to see some of the names and the old photographs of those players on the wall and to know I was now following in their footsteps was an incredible feeling...

Over the years most of Britain's 'finest moments' have been in Australia. Very few of our test teams failed to receive accolades for their performances. And certainly the major, historic victories have usually been achieved down-under and not in England. From the early days, when in 1914, we won the 'Rourke's Drift' test with only ten men, to the 1958 tour when despite suffering from a broken arm, Alan Prescott led eleven 'Brits' to victory in the Brisbane test. That team was probably the best that ever toured Australia and New Zealand, playing thirty matches and only losing two and drawing one. The 1932 tourists achieved the same number of losses and a draw but they played four fewer matches.

But why were these amazing feats usually achieved overseas? And why couldn't British teams repeat such great performances on home soil more often? The answer is an obvious but often overlooked factor - the amount of time a touring team has to gel. On a lengthy tour the players have the time to train together, perfect planned moves, build up team spirit - and bond together, rather like a club side would. At home this was never possible and teams would often take to the field, almost always far less well prepared than their opponents...

The first tour match was scheduled for May 22 only two days after we landed in Australia and less than a week after the Championship final at Odsal Stadium between Leeds and St Helens. The tour was due to finish on July 30 - over two months later - so we'd be back just in time to begin our preparation for another domestic season!

I had to laugh when I read the comparison made between our timetable and that of our early international counterparts. They enjoyed four or five weeks aboard ship, recuperating from their strenuous season before taking on the Aussies. How the game had changed. And how different again I suppose, it is for the players of today.

The format of the tour was intense. A squad of twenty-six players travelled over 30,000 miles and played twenty-three matches on a tour lasting just over two months. The itinerary included three test matches against Australia and three against New Zealand. For this it was predicted each player would earn the princely sum of £600.

Britain had lost the Ashes four years earlier. But the 1970 party contained eleven players, including yours truly of course, who had played in Australia before, either on the previous Ashes tour or in the 1968 World Cup. And we were all confident we could reclaim them. Jack Harding from Leigh was the Tour Manager and Hull's Johnny Whiteley was the coach.

Johnny played over four hundred matches for the 'black and whites' during the 1950s and 60s before becoming the club's coach in 1965. But when he flew out from Manchester Airport on May 20 however, it was as a 'free agent'. Johnny had been the coach at The Boulevard for five years. But he left for Australia without signing a new deal that would have tied him to the Airlie Birds and seen him back at the club on his return.

That situation obviously left the way open for Johnny to receive and consider offers from both Aussie clubs, as well as other British clubs, whilst he was away for over two months down under. But before he left I remember he made it clear he would be returning initially to Hull, whatever happened in Australia.

'I shall definitely come back to Hull,' he was quoted as saying. 'I have an entirely open mind on the situation and it is a question of waiting to see what turns up.' Johnny did exactly what he said he would of course, he has always been a man of his word and he did return to Hull. But it was Hull the city, not Hull the club...

There were plenty of other characters in that squad, a number of who had come from differing backgrounds and many with remarkable stories to tell... The Salford centre, Chris Hesketh for example was on his 'trip of a lifetime' after battling and beating polio as a boy. Exactly like me - and probably like most of the other lads in the squad I imagine, Chris had always dreamed of playing for his country and going on tour. But unlike us, he never thought there was any chance of achieving his ambitions after he contracted the disease at the age of seven. His chances had gone, or so he thought. It was almost two years later that he took the first, hesitant steps back to health.

But polio had left him very weak. His legs were spindly and he turned to rugby league to build up his strength. It did the trick - and that was why rugby was always more than just a game as far as he was concerned.

I remember Chris looking forward to another bonus when we got to Australia - to play against his brother-in-law, Bob Cane, who was a league star in Sydney.

Even though Chris achieved his dream to go on tour to Australia and play for Great Britain, more heartbreak was just around the corner. Whilst he was on tour, both Chris' father and grandfather died within a week of each other. But having agreed with his dad before he left Britain, what he would do should the worse happen whilst he was away, Chris stayed on tour.

He also went on the next tour in 1974 - as captain. He'd got all the skills and attributes required to tour and be a success. His attitude was brilliant. He was one of the most focused and determined players I've ever known. And probably a lot of that was down to that illness he'd had as a youngster. He played for Salford and then Wigan and whenever I played against him he always showed what a good player he was. He was a born winner - and hated losing! He was also just a very nice guy - but that was the thing about that tour - there were twenty-six players on that tour and they were all brilliant individuals. But they were also a team in every sense of the word. You could go out with any of them, anywhere, any time, there were no cliques. I'm sure with the team spirit being what it was, the lads would all have helped Chris get through his troubles.

The Great Britain captain was St Helens' Frank Myler. When he was only sixteen, Frank was a talented golfer and had the opportunity to become an assistant to the club professional at a course near his home in Widnes. Unfortunately his parents couldn't afford the money it would have taken and happily Frank never regretted the day he then turned to play rugby league - and got paid for doing it! He continued to play golf, and reputedly bought his first set of clubs with the £50 fee he received when he signed for Widnes. And later reached a high level at his 'second favourite sport', playing off a handicap of just four!

In 1970 Frank was thirty-one years old and one of the most experienced players on the tour. He was another one of those eleven who had experienced playing in the southern hemisphere, having been on the 1966 tour. He was a great skipper and always confident of his and his team's ability.

'There's plenty of pace and skill in our team. I think we're going to surprise the Aussies. If you go out there to do or die, you're not going to be far out in the end. That is what we intend to do. We have the best possible team and given time to acclimatize and freedom from injury we must have a great chance of returning with the Ashes. There are slight differences in rule interpretation in Australia but I think my boys will soon learn to cope with them,' said Frank on the eve of our departure. Frank always sounded confident and on this occasion I remember feeling almost as confident as Frank sounded. The squad did look stronger and a better team in depth than the 1966 and 1968 ones and I was sure we had the ability to win the Ashes.

Frank may have been one of the senior players on the tour but I recall it was the young forwards in the squad that many suggested would be just as important in deciding whether Britain would be successful or not. Following previous British shortcomings, especially in the forwards, it was predicted lads like Malcolm Reilly from Castleford, described then as 'a twenty-two year-old coal board fitter', and Rovers' Phil Lowe could have a crucial bearing on Britain's success...

Everybody was hoping for a successful tour and was determined to enjoy every minute of it - except one player, perhaps? Bob Irving, was probably hoping more than most that the eleven week long trip would pass quickly. He was due to marry his girlfriend, Valerie, as soon as he got back to Britain! As well as Phil Lowe I also had another teammate from Rovers with me, Peter Flanagan. 'Flash' had also toured in 1966. He was a real 'life and soul of the party' character, well known as a bit of a joker and someone who was just good fun to have around. But the one thing that most of the lads remembered about him on the '70 tour was his 'extensive luggage range'.

Travelling half way around the world meant at least a couple of well stocked suitcases for most players - but not 'Flash'. He used to carry everything he had on tour with him - in one carrier-bag! That was because of his very limited 'wardrobe'. He only had one pair of underpants for example. He used to wash them out every evening and then put them on the bedside lamp to dry, ready for the next morning. Each night he'd start them off by drying the underpants with the lamp on. Then when he wanted to go to sleep he'd turn the lamp off and leave them on the lampshade for the rest of the night and they'd always be completely dry the following morning. Needless to say on one particular evening this procedure ended in disaster - as many of us feared it would.

'Flash' was so tired one night that he fell asleep with the lamp still on. And was aroused from his slumber an hour or so later by the smell of a pair of very dry underpants going up in flames.

The next day I remember 'Flash' was up unusually early. He rushed off to the nearest clothes shop to replenish his dwindling wardrobe. And returned with - one new pair of underpants...

The tour started with a match against Northern Territory at Darwin on Friday May 22 - less than forty-eight hours after the British team had flown in. Malcolm Reilly's brilliant performance under the Darwin floodlights, even had the locals singing his praises. Watched by a crowd of 4,000 appreciative fans, he continuously broke the Aussies' defence to set up a series of scoring chances. The Lions had to overcome a 17-2 penalty count against them but still ran out convincing winners 35-12. After the match, referee Ray Pittey explained he'd awarded most of the scrum penalties against Bradford's hooker, Tony Fisher, for lying on the ground.

Another British hero that night was fullback, Terry Price, who kicked seven goals from eight attempts, including one from halfway and three from the touchlines. Our tries were scored by Hesketh 2, Myler 2, Sullivan, Hardisty and Hepworth. I was one of four substitutes used and went on for Alan Hardisty.

But I soon realised I'd have a difficult job to get into the side for the first test. Apart from 'Chuck', Mick Shoebottom put himself in the frame for the stand-off spot two days later, when he produced a sparkling performance and scored a hat-trick of tries in our second match against Queensland.

The Lions though allowed a healthy lead to slip with the Australians running in late tries in the final quarter. The 23-20 victory was criticised by the Aussie press who said the British side's high tackles and rough tactics may have disrupted their early opponents but would not trouble the more experienced Australian teams that we'd come up against later in the tour. And unless the British improved in these departments we should expect 'savage retaliation' and Australia should win the Test matches.

After Britain's win against Queensland, the Australian Team Manager, Norman Robinson declared, 'Britain may be able to get away with rough tactics against inexperienced sides but the stronger teams they'll meet in the coming weeks certainly will not put up with it.'

A more immediate problem we had to solve was the number of penalties we were giving away. We had already conceded thirty-eight in the opening two games but had been awarded only eleven. The British Tour Manager, Jack Harding didn't appear overly concerned, however.

'We certainly can't afford to keep giving away penalties like that. I believe it's only a matter of rule interpretation and we should be able to work it out this week,' he said. But it was obvious that if the problem wasn't solved quickly it would probably lead to serious repercussions in the following weeks. Jack went some way to help remedy the situation when he invited referee Henry Albert, who was due to officiate our match against Queensland at Brisbane, to discuss the 'rules interpretation' problems with the British squad...

Following my performance in our convincing 32-7 win against Queensland, my chances of being selected for the team to face Australia in the first test in Brisbane improved dramatically. I was widely tipped to be chosen ahead of my two main rivals Mick Shoebottom and Alan Hardisty. Unfortunately the selectors didn't agree with the media men and 'Chuck' was chosen at off-half with Heppy at scrum-half and 'Shoey' in the centre. But although we went into the clash as favourites, the match turned out to be little short of a complete disaster for Great Britain when we received a very rude awakening. There was a theory that some of those warm-up games were not challenging enough and we would have benefited far more if we had played more competitive games. But that was the way all the tours started, you started in the north, at the top of the country, and worked your way down. I think that's how it had always been, so we just got on with it...

We'd been unbeaten in our first five tour matches but never looked likely to win the sixth, the first test match, after going eleven points down after the first twenty minutes. Doug Laughton, Cliff Watson and Peter Flanagan, all forwards, scored our three tries and fullback Terry Price kicked three goals. It was the only game we lost on the tour. But on the day we were simply steamrollered 37-15 by a tremendous Australian pack, led by a certain Artie

Beetson. We'd gone into the game as firm favourites but finished up being well beaten. Their points came from fullback, Graeme Langlands who landed nine goals from eleven attempts to set a new Anglo-Australia Test record. The Aussie captain beat the previous record of 62 points set by Britain's Jim Sullivan with his first two kicks of the match in the opening six minutes. Their tries were scored by Jim Morgan 2, Johnny King 2, and centre John McDonald, with Phil Hawthorne landing two drop goals. The attendance was 42,757.

We moved down to Sydney the week before the second test and played New South Wales. Although we only managed a 17-17 draw, we got an idea of the likely support there would be for the test match when over 31,500 turned up for the game.

There was a certain amount of deja-vu as far as the run-up to the second test was concerned. Once again I played well in the tour games against Toowoomba, Brisbane and New South Wales. I was the man of the match in the first game, kicked four goals in the drawn game against New South Wales - and thought I had a good chance of forcing my way into the test team. Fortunately this time the selectors agreed and I was named at halfback alongside Keith Hepworth...

Following our inauspicious start in the first test, people were already writing us off. But on that Saturday when we were due to play the second, the whole place was absolutely electric.

The second test proved to be the culmination of one of my dreams. The dreams I had when I'd started out playing sport as a kid. Now I was there, living that dream in reality! To play professional rugby league. To appear in a Cup Final at Wembley. To go on tour. And to win the Ashes. These had all been boyhood dreams. And there I was, in the middle of one of those dreams - but one-nil down in the series and with everyone already writing us off. And amazingly the dream came true - we went out and took the Aussies apart! We won 28-7 in front of 60,962 fans.

The transformation from the first test defeat was unbelievable. We dominated the Aussies even more than they had dominated us in the first encounter - and for me everything went like a dream. I scored our opening try after only three minutes and finished with six goals, a second try and a drop goal for a personal tally of twenty points.

The Aussies badly missed their first test kicking hero, Graeme Langlands who was out injured. They used three different kickers that day but only John McDonald was successful, whereas I finished with a 100% record.

The twenty points I scored equalled Lewis Jones' record of points scored in a match against Australia, when he kicked ten goals in the second test at Brisbane on July 3, 1954. Lewis and I still top the list today. And I'm very proud of that record - it's been going now for thirty-five years!

Our victory in the second test was even more remarkable because we played the final twenty-four minutes of the game with only twelve men. Referee, Don Lancashire had sent off Syd Hynes following a clash with Artie Beetson. But the decision appeared particularly harsh especially as it was later reported the Leeds' centre had lost two teeth in the incident. And not surprisingly after the match the Australian Rugby League judiciary committee decided that a severe caution was a sufficient enough penalty.

Two weeks later, everything was then set up for the big one - the deciding third test! The thrilling climax to the series. It began with my sleepless night overlooking the Sydney Cricket Ground...

A huge crowd of 61,258 had gathered to witness the final showdown.

But although we outclassed the Aussies and scored five tries to one amazingly Australia still had a chance to win the match only four minutes from time. Referee, Don Lancashire again penalised Britain heavily 15-8 and fullback Allan McKean took full advantage, kicking seven penalties from nine attempts to keep the Aussies in the game.

We deserved to win the match far more easily after outclassing the green and golds from the opening minute. But amazingly we only led by a single point four minutes from the end after their hooker, McCarthy had scored their only try of the game. Had McLean managed to convert the Aussies would have led 19-18 and could possibly have held out to win. But had they done so, it would have been the greatest travesty in rugby league test history according to reporter Jack Reardon.

The victory was put into perspective by England soccer star, Bobby Charlton who said: 'The scoreline looks ridiculous - there was only one side in it as far as football was concerned and that was Britain. What a great match. What a great win. But what a fright they gave us.'

The Kangaroos had to play the final 19 minutes of the match with only twelve players after Artie Beetson had been dismissed for punching Cliff Watson. But the decision seemed to have little bearing on the outcome.

I completed the scoring in the dying seconds. As soon as I received the pass from Doug Laughton, who was voted the man of the match, I knew I'd score. I raced forty yards for our final try and beat four opponents on the way to the line. It was the perfect end to a perfect day.

The game ended 21-17 - I'd lived my dream - we'd won the Ashes.

Little did we realise at the time that to this day, a British rugby league team would never enjoy such an achievement again...

The twenty-six players who toured were: Peter Flanagan, Phil Lowe and I from Rovers. Derek Edwards, Alan Hardisty, Keith Hepworth, Dennis Hartley and Malcolm Reilly, all from Castleford. Terry Price and Tony Fisher from Bradford Northern. Ray Dutton from Widnes. Alan Smith, Syd Hynes, John Atkinson, Mike Shoebottom and Barry Seabourne, all from Leeds. Clive Sullivan from Hull. Frank Myler, the tour captain and Cliff Watson from St Helens. Dave Chisnall from Leigh. Chris Hesketh and Johnny Ward from Salford. Jimmy Thompson from Featherstone Rovers. Doug Laughton and Dave Robinson from Wigan. And Bob Irving from Oldham.

I remember one night of the tour we were all sitting down for dinner when the phone rang. I went to answer it - the call was for Ray Dutton. Ray for some reason wasn't about at that particular moment, so the caller left an obscure message. After I'd written it down, because I'd never have remembered it, the woman's voice at the other end simply said, 'Please give

Ray that message,' and then rang off. I recall it sounded like the sort of message they used in the war. A sentence that would be meaningless if intercepted by the enemy. But it meant a great deal to Ray. When I told him it turned out to be a coded message that his wife had given birth, so he was naturally over the moon...

Training under Johnny Whiteley was never easy. He did that much for the tour - in every way possible - it was amazing. He was coach, he was bagman, he was trainer, he was everything! And the hard work he put in was simply unbelievable. His attitude was infectious. It went right through the team. If you talk to the lads who went on the 1970 tour they'd talk about Pork Chop Hill. It's at the back of the Sydney Cricket Ground, a big hill that we used in training. Up and down, up and down we went and you'd see people like Dennis Hartley get to about the thirtieth time and he'd be nearly in tears because he'd got to go up it again. But they did it, they went through it because the team spirit was fantastic - that's what made the tour so special. And the things that happened on the tour cemented it even more. The competition for places was also brilliant - and the team had everything. It was the sort of team that you could say to the opposition, play it as you want. We can either play football or if you want a scrap - we'll have a scrap. The day after the third test we were scheduled to play at Woolongong. It was the only time in my life I ever heard of playing another game just a day after such an important match. But that's what they did to us - made us play again the following day. We'd had a good celebration of course the night before and had a good bit to drink having won the Ashes. But the first thing the next morning, Johnny was knocking at everyone's door to get us up, to take part in this final game.

Amazingly, more or less everyone wanted to play - including nearly everybody who'd played in the test team the previous day. I played along with the complete test front-row of Cliff Watson, Dennis Hartley and Tony Fisher.

And it certainly wasn't half-hearted, last day of the tour stuff either! After about twenty minutes, the referee stopped the game and started giving their front-row a real bollocking and asked them what on earth they thought they were doing. There was one with a split nose, one with a bleeding mouth and one with a cut eye. They were all taking the game 'very seriously'.

It came to a head when their scrum-half kicked Malcolm Reilly up the back-side. After that, Malcolm showed no mercy and just went round retaliating and hitting everybody he could. The referee took our skipper, Frank Myler to one side for a little, private chat. It was the first time I'd ever seen an official suggest to a captain he substituted one of his team, to avoid him having to send the player off. It turned into a very eventful game...

The strength in depth and the spirit of the squad on that tour was exceptional. It's not often appreciated that every one of the twenty-six tourists played test football on that tour, which was very unusual. I think the last one to play was Barry Seabourne. He didn't play until the third test against the Kiwis in Auckland. When you looked down the team and saw who was in - and then looked again at whom there was to replace them -

it must have been very difficult for John and Jack to pick the team. But a very nice problem to have...

At the time, winning the 1970 Ashes was my finest moment of my career so far. That was the pinnacle up until then, but things change as a footballer. To be on the Sydney Cricket Ground with 60,000 Aussies cheering and you've just beaten the Australians and won the Ashes, is a hell of a feeling! It was marvellous running around with the cup, an unforgettable day but then from there my game developed and the 'footballing' really started...

I think that test football brings the best out of you. It probably all goes back to when you first formulate your ambitions of what you want to achieve in your chosen sport. As a boy, I had my dreams of what I'd like to achieve. But it wasn't until I was well into my teenage years before I set definite goals. And I think it all goes back to then. When we won the Ashes - the first pinnacle had been reached...

Every time I pulled a Great Britain or England shirt on, I was so proud. Because that's how I'd been brought up. I was proud of my country and proud to represent my country. I was also proud to represent Hull K.R. of course but playing club football was very different. It was another level. Because every time you play rugby league you play at a level. Whether it's playing for the kids team, the under 17s, the A team, the first team, the Yorkshire team, then Internationals against France and finally the pinnacle is against Australia. When I played against the Australians it was undoubtedly one of the pinnacles of my career. Playing International football against the best team in the world - there's nowhere higher to go than that! And of course you didn't get to play that many games against Australia, whereas I was playing for Hull K.R. every week. I always looked forward to playing against the Aussies because that's where I was always tested the most.

I would say that I was selfish in a way, because all I wanted was to be picked for the next match. My attitude was that I always wanted to be the best. Because if you were the best then they couldn't leave you out!

I wanted to be in the team for every match and I didn't want anyone else taking my place. So every time at that level I went out and made sure nobody could take my place off me. That attitude then filtered down to club football - that to get picked I had to be play very well week after week.

I was fortunate to enjoy a long test career for Great Britain - twelve years from 1966 to 1978 - and ended up with 29 caps. But I always regretted it wasn't more. The reason for that was simple. For some competitions, such as the 1975 World Championship, they split the Great Britain side up and we competed separately as England and Wales. I got seventeen England caps during my career and I always thought if they had counted as appearances for Great Britain I'd have finished with over forty Great Britain caps. The legendary Mick Sullivan for example finished his career with forty-six...

CHAPTER TEN
FATE TAKES
A HAND
SEASON 1970-71

When a sportsman's career lasts for sixteen years I think it would be foolishly optimistic for him to imagine he'd constantly be able to stay at the top for every second of that time. And especially if he plays a team sport, there are bound to be some peaks and troughs to negotiate. After all, even that roller coaster doesn't stay at the top all the time! It gets its' momentum from the dips it encounters along the way.

The early 1970s were definitely one of those periods as far as Rovers was concerned. It's pointless to dwell on the problems too long. But a quick look at our achievements - or perhaps I should say the lack of them during those testing seasons - proves exactly what I mean...

I've always said you can be the best coach in the world but if you don't have the tools to work with, it just isn't going to happen for you. So when Johnny Whiteley was appointed as the club's new coach on Saturday August 8 1970 with Colin Hutton, club coach since 1957 becoming General Manager, I knew there were possibly very interesting times ahead. But I also feared it could well turn out to be a period when a fantastic opportunity could be missed...

Rovers' squad of players certainly wasn't what it had been when I'd joined them four years earlier. Nonetheless, they still possessed some pretty useful performers. And the Rovers' directors clearly thought that if any coach could bring the best out of them it was Johnny.

Johnny and Colin were two of the best, if not the best two coaches I've played under. Johnny had just been in charge of us in Australia and his methods were brilliant and the team spirit he'd built up in that squad of players was fantastic - it was all down to him. But then he came back and took on a job where he just didn't have the tools to work with. Rovers were in a transitional period at the time and I was very sad when he left because his presence at Craven Park could undoubtedly have signalled the start of something very special at the club.

Johnny and Colin were two individuals whose knowledge of the game of rugby league was unbelievable. And if they couldn't make things work then

I think that showed Rovers had more than a few problems to solve. And so it proved - the season following the Ashes win in Australia was a bit of an anti-climax for me. But then again, I imagine just about anything would have been after that tour. I only made a dozen appearances for Rovers in the 1970-71 season, scoring five tries and three goals, due to a series of injuries, including a broken ankle...

There had never been any mention on the Ashes tour about the possibility of Johnny returning to Britain and going straight to Craven Park. The appointment was regarded as one of the biggest bombshells to hit Humberside Rugby League for many years. John had been with Hull FC for over twenty years as a player and then coach. But he'd told Hull earlier in the week that he wouldn't be returning to the Boulevard.

Colin was happy with the changes and commented,

'I am pleased that Johnny Whiteley is coming to Craven Park. I have a tremendous respect for him. We have been friends from our Boulevard days and I am sure that the partnership can prove very successful. Both John and I live for this game and I am sure that we can make things tick at Craven Park.'

The pairing of John and Colin provided Rovers with arguably the strongest behind the scene's partnership in the game.

'I look on the post as a challenge and I am always open to a challenge.' said John. It may be difficult after so many years with Hull, but I am sure the players will accept me and I hope the supporters will too. Rovers came along with this opportunity... it was all a bit sudden though, and it will take time to assess the situation at the club. With the new fixture system this is going to be a hard season. Almost every game will be like a cup-tie, but Rovers are a good side with plenty of potential.'

His comments proved a chillingly accurate prophecy of his days ahead at Craven Park.

On the same day Rovers announced the signing of Castleford's goal-kicking centre, Ron Willett. However that news was offset by the announcement only days later that Geoff Wriglesworth, one of the most popular players at the club during the previous season, had been reluctantly allowed to go to York because of his work commitments on his farm.

Amidst all these happenings at the club, I threw another spanner in the works. The following week I put in a transfer request! The papers thought it was because I wanted to return to play in Australia. It wasn't!

It was a conscious decision that I'd made after a great deal of soul-searching. I had a good job with good prospects, away from rugby league to think about. Johnny's arrival had been an unexpected boost for the club and I can't deny it was a factor when I weighed up the pros and cons of whether or not to ask for a move.

But even the potential that his presence brought to Craven Park couldn't alter my decision. The travelling to Hull and back, two or three times a week had been getting me down and I could only see it getting worse.

I also knew I was going to have further problems making the journey for training as I'd started doing shift work. And I found that I was spending less and less time at home, which I didn't think was fair to Carol. She already had her hands full and was also expecting our first baby, Kay, the following December.

It wasn't a surprise that the board flatly refused my request. But I insisted I would be applying for a move again. I knew there would inevitably be problems in the future concerning my ability to get time off to train with Rovers because of my shifts. And you were no good to any rugby league side if you didn't train.

The following Friday night I played for Rovers against Salford in the first league match of the season at Craven Park. We were without Phil Lowe, 'Flash' and Terry Clawson but produced a brilliant tackling performance to beat a star-studded Salford side, including Chris Hesketh, Maurice Richards, David Watkins and Mike Coulman, by 13 points to 11. Johnny Whiteley was delighted with the team's display and I was voted the man of the match. But I put in a second transfer request immediately after the game. I had no complaints with Rovers, but the 120 mile round trip for training was getting me down. The Coal Board had been very good to me regarding giving me time off but there was a rule that you could only have three shifts off in a month. Training twice a week and a mid-week match would account for that in one week, when I was on afternoon shifts...

Once again the request was turned down!

Rovers held their annual meeting at the Spencer Arms Hotel on Wednesday August 26 when Chairman, Wilf Spaven diplomatically announced the clubs view of my situation.

'There have been no offers for Roger Millward and if there had been they would have been given the same reply as Millward himself - that we are not going to sell players of his calibre because we just cannot find replacements.' he said. 'There is no way you can force a player to play for you but I'm sure Millward will continue to play for Rovers, and let me wish him every success.'

With the problem set to drag on, fate took a hand and provided a solution. And for me it was a very painful one! On Friday September 4, after twenty-two minutes of the home league match against Warrington, I broke my ankle!

I was out of the side until after Christmas. I had my leg screwed together and was on the sidelines for four months, from September to January. My first game back was the Challenge Cup-tie against Keighley. But the injury had changed me in more ways than one...

I used the time wisely, studying for my examinations - which I was taking at Whitwood Technical College - and thinking about my life in rugby league. The result was that within a fortnight I'd changed my mind about wanting to leave Rovers and withdrew my transfer application. The travelling was still a problem but I decided it was something I'd just have to cope with - plenty of other players did! All I wanted to do was to get back to full fitness and get back out on the pitch again, playing for Rovers. I went through to Hull with Peter Small and told a delighted Colin Hutton of my decision. However the injury still meant I not only missed the first half of

Rovers' season but also the World Cup that took place in England during the Autumn. Needless to say after the euphoria of our Ashes win in Australia a few weeks earlier, it was a competition I'd have loved to play in...

The BBC hadn't shown much of the historic 1970 Ashes tour, limiting their coverage of the tests to a few minutes of highlights. Yorkshire TV however broadcast a Sunday afternoon programme that year, showing the Australian 'match of the day' which gave a good insight into the state of Aussie club football at that time. The coverage showed that apart from being at the top of the International tree, our club sides were still also regarded as better than their Australian counterparts. Nearly all of the British players who were playing down under were doing well. Yorkshire viewers saw players like ex-Saints star Len Killeen enjoying a new lease of life and scoring some spectacular tries and goals for Balmain.

Another comparison that is worth making is the number of matches the top players played in during a season thirty-five years ago, compared with those of today. Castleford's Dennis Hartley for instance returned from the 1970 Ashes Tour ready to start a new season in England. Since the beginning of the previous season he'd played in fifty-eight matches for his club and country. And what a successful year it had been for him. He'd won a second Challenge Cup winner's medal, been on his first tour down under, made his test debut against Australia, and had probably become the best number 8 in the world. Not a bad year for a man of thirty-four who hadn't started playing rugby until he was twenty-one.

A few miles down the road at Leeds, winger John Atkinson had played in an amazing 66 games during the same period, scoring 53 tries. He'd played in seventeen matches on tour including all six Tests and also played in all four home Internationals before the trip, the only player to appear in all ten games.

We may have returned from Australia in 1970 as the top team in the world, but it was a title that wasn't to last for long. The Australians arrived in Britain for the World Cup in October determined to exact revenge...

When the British World Cup Squad was announced on Thursday September 24 I was the only player who had played in the Ashes final who was absent. Because of my injury I hadn't been considered. Barry Seabourne was also unfit and the selectors also omitted Leigh's Alex Murphy, and named Keith Hepworth as the only recognised scrum-half.

The only notable absentee from the Aussies' Squad was their captain, Graeme Langlands, who was ruled out with a broken hand.

When the side was chosen for the first test against the Aussies on Saturday October 24 the only change from the side that had played in the final Ashes test in Australia was Ray Dutton of Widnes. He was drafted in at fullback with Mick Shoebottom moving up to stand-off to take my place.

'The side virtually picked itself after the remarkably high standard of rugby played in Australia. It was the finest Rugby League side I have ever seen.' said team manager, Jack Harding. '

But the team failed to reproduce the form that had conquered the Aussies only four months earlier and lost on home soil with a disastrous performance in the World Cup Final...

My broken leg meant I wasn't able to do much during the build-up to the World Cup. But I did manage to get to the British training sessions and help out as much as I could. What I'd have given to have been able to pull a jersey on and play in the matches as well, especially our first one!

Our opening game of the tournament was against the holders, Australia at Headingley. The Aussies had already trounced New Zealand in the first match of the series 47-11 and led at half-time against us, 4-2. But Syd Hynes emerged as Britain's hero after the break, scoring the game's only try and a drop goal, which gave us an 11-4 win. After the victory we were installed as firm favourites to go on and lift the World Cup. New Zealand then beat France 16-15 in a nailbiting game at the Boulevard. And in the fourth game Britain beat the French again 6-0 at Wheldon Road. The game was ruined though by torrential rain - and the only points of the night came from three penalties by Ray Dutton. We then beat the Kiwis 27-17 in our last qualifying game to secure our place in the final. And waited for the Aussies to beat France in their last match and join us.

The Australians did eventually face us in the final but only after the Odsal Stadium had staged the shock of the series. The scoreline of Australia 15 France 17 was one that nobody had anticipated. But unfortunately for the French their narrow defeat against New Zealand the week before at Hull had proved costly. And Australia went through to the final, thanks only to their superior point's difference. It was a game that few of the 20,000 crowd would forget in a hurry...

The match was a bad-tempered clash that continuously threatened to erupt from the first minute to the last. Syd Hynes and Australia's scrum-half, Billy Smith were sent-off following one of numerous second half flare-ups. And even after the final whistle, both sets of forwards continued to exchange punches in the centre of the pitch. The Aussies retained the World Cup winning 12-7. But the tabloids understandably had much more to say about the violence than the limited amount of rugby that was played!

'CRUNCH', 'BRAWL' and 'BATTLE OF SHAME' were some of the Sunday morning headlines. And one reporter later described the match as 'a tribal massacre with a gory finish.'

The final certainly did nothing to promote the game of rugby league. Rather than a contact sport played by athletes it was portrayed on national television more as 'an ugly bout of fisticuffs'. And another newspaper suggested 'that Rugby League is not mature enough to merit a national show on T.V.' Some of the comments were perhaps a little over the top. Punch-ups like the one seen at Leeds were after all not exactly unknown. If we're honest, they'd occurred throughout the history of the game. And after the questions of how we could ensure such scenes never happened again had faded from the fans' thoughts, there was another one that lingered on much longer. How could a team which had gone unbeaten for 240 minutes in the qualifying matches, lose the world title to a side who had only won one game during the same period?

I remember Johnny Whiteley coming over just after Christmas to talk to me about when I planned to start playing again. My broken ankle had been a bad injury - and I'd been out of the game for a long time. But the last thing I wanted to do was come back too soon and cause further problems. And again it was a time when my size was a positive help to me. I'd had my ankle screwed together and the leg was put in plaster. After two months the plaster and the pins were removed and another plaster was put on. That stayed on for another month, at which point I could start some light training. Everything went to plan and my size helped because I was so small and light. I remember Colin saying that once the second plaster came off I'd be able to regain fitness pretty quickly, and certainly a lot quicker than a bigger man would have done.

Those four months on the sidelines gave me a lot of time for thinking. And I spent many hours lying on the settee, contemplating exactly what stage my life and career had reached. What my ambitions were and what I wanted to achieve during the years that were to follow. You can get very philosophical when you've got a lot of time on your hands that you're not used to.

The lay-off also coincided with one of the proudest moments of my life, when my only child, Kay, was born on November 27. She was a full term baby but only weighed 3lb 4oz when she was born. We finally got her home on Christmas Eve, one month later, the best present Carol and I have ever had. Kay I'm proud to say, went on to have a far more successful education than I did and left school with eight 'O' levels and an 'A' level in Maths. Straight from school she went into Insurance, working for the 'Guardian Royal' for a number of years until she had a child of her own. When my grandson, Charlie was small and growing up Kay didn't work but recently returned to College. She's already passed all her exams and is now embarking on a new career as a beautician. And I'm obviously proud to say, she's done very well for herself. Her husband John is a joiner by trade but he has also successfully 'climbed the ladder' and is currently a site foreman for a construction company. Charlie will be six this October and I think it is safe to say that he is likely to remain my only grandchild. As far as I know Kay and John are definitely not planning any further additions to the family...

As well as my enforced absence from the team, Rovers had also been without Phil Lowe for the first two months of the season. He'd sustained a shoulder injury in an innocuous tackle during the Eva Hardaker Cup game on August 14. I'd kicked three goals and Phil crossed for a crucial try in a hard fought 12-12 draw. The injuries meant that Phil, like me, had missed out when the selectors chose the Great Britain squad to play in the World Cup. But he was back in action soon after when he made a try-scoring return in Rovers' 19-8 home win against Whitehaven in mid October, whereas I didn't return to the side until well into the New Year!

I'd been training at Castleford after the plaster came off. There were of course the usual rumours being banded about that Castleford had made an offer for me. But there was never an offer. And even if there had been -

Rovers would have thrown it out.

Off the field the New Year celebrations came and went - and on it our hit and miss season continued. We beat Wakefield 12-10 at a snow covered Craven Park on January 2 but lost a week later 12-8 at Whitehaven.

In between on the Monday night, the draw was made for the Challenge Cup First Round and we were drawn away against Keighley. I returned to training at Craven Park the following night...

After I returned following such a lengthy lay-off, I looked on it as a new challenge - the start of another era in my career. From then on things changed quite a lot as far as my football was concerned. I'd always been a player with good pace but that injury had slowed me down a yard or so. I had to change my way of playing a bit and luckily I had the brain and the hands to be able to do it. I reinvented myself slightly - I started working with other people - and I became more of a playmaker.

It never bothered me whether I played scrum-half or stand-off. But predominantly - I'd say for more than 90% of the matches I ever played - I was stand-off. In the later part of my career I played scrum-half on many occasions, but I never made a definite switch to that position. And I can't understand why a lot of people seem to think I did!

On January 12 we signed Joe Brown from York for £3,000. But another agonising defeat followed four days later at Swinton. David Wainwright scored a late try for us and had Terry Clawson been able to convert we'd have sealed a famous victory. For once however Terry was off target, his kick sailed wide, and we lost 11-10. The cup-tie followed eight days later...

The first round of the cup at Keighley was my first game back - it ended as a 9-9 draw. I scored our only try of the match in the 71st minute. And although Terry Clawson again couldn't add the conversion, the try looked as if it would take us into the next round. But the Keighley substitute, Green scored immediately and if Brian Jefferson could have tacked on the conversion, we'd have been out of the cup at the first hurdle. He also missed however and we faced a replay at the Craven Park, the following Wednesday night - but there was no way I could have played. I'd just got back after all that time out and if the truth was known, hadn't really been fit enough to play in the first match, let alone the replay. I'd done hardly any training whatsoever. And after my first game back, I was sidelined again - this time with a badly bruised right ankle - the opposite one to the one I'd broken. I'd only agreed to play in the away game to help out. It was a time when Rovers had a few problems and were going 'backwards' a little bit. A point which was unfortunately highlighted again when Keighley came to Craven Park for the replay and beat us fairly easily, 18-11. Johnny Moore was brought in at stand-off. But the game proved to be another disastrous one for us. Joe Brown was sent off two minutes from time for striking Evans and Jefferson kicked six goals in a fairly comfortable win.

Two days later though we went to Widnes and won 17-0 with a superb performance led by man of the match, Paul Daley. That match again summed up our topsy-turvy campaign. Paul had joined Rovers from Bradford Northern in November 1970 and proved to be a marvellous signing for us.

He also became another in my long line of travelling partners, although with Paul things were slightly different because he did the driving!

In my early days playing for Rovers, long before the M62 was built, we used to travel to Hull down the 'old road' - the A63 - and it could take us up to two hours to get to Gilberdyke. In fact I've known it take us that long just to get to Goole!

I used to finish my shift at the pit at 1.15 p.m. - go home for something to eat, get changed, then jump in the car and off we'd go.

We used to stop at the Mayphill Café at Goole for a cup of tea and a slice of toast, and then we still had another twenty-odd miles to go to Hull. I always thought it seemed a lot shorter going home though.

Over the years I've made that journey more times than I care to remember. And if you listed all the players who've accompanied me since the mid-sixties you'd be able to put two or three decent teams together.

Players like Paul Longstaff, Terry Clawson and Paul spring to mind. When I look back, we had some great times and a lot of laughs. But at the time I suppose it perhaps didn't always seem that way.

I'd been up at five o'clock in the morning, done a full shift down the pit, crawled about the face, 220 yards long, with a toolbox round my neck. Then I'd to get out, get changed, go home, get a quick bite, pick my gear up and then walk the best part of a mile to the meeting point - before I even started the trip to Hull!

I'd then do an hour or an hour and a half's training and invariably it would be about midnight when I got home. And then I was up at five again the next morning! It wasn't always easy to maintain 100% enthusiasm and do that two or three times, week after week, no matter how keen you were.

Not long ago I heard Paul on the radio reminiscing about his time at Rovers. Paul was a great little player. He gave one hundred per cent for eighty minutes in every game he played - and for a small man he was as hard as nails. He spent a very enjoyable part of his career in the early seventies at Craven Park.

But I wasn't surprised when one of the first things he recalled was the travelling we had to do just to get there for both training and matches.

'In the sixties there were some great players. I thought the rugby league was absolutely unbelievable in that era. I signed professional forms for Halifax in 1961 and during my career I think I played with some of the greatest players that this country has ever known,' said Paul.

'I think Roger Millward was about the best I've ever played with - and against - because he could do everything, could Roger. He'd score his thirty tries, he'd kick his hundred goals - and he could tackle as well. For a small man of that size he was unbelievable!

He was a natural - the type of player that only comes around about every ten years. To go over and beat the Australians in Australia was fantastic. Nobody has seen that happen again in the last thirty years! But Roger won it - and 'the Hill' gave him a standing ovation.

For a 'pommie' to go over there and receive a standing ovation, he must have been a great player.

Going to Hull K.R. was a great move for me. I remember Colin Hutton coming for me and Johnny Whiteley was the coach at Rovers then. And I had three great years there. I played forty-four games on the trot in the first team, that was great for me. When I played at Hull Kingston I had a white Volkswagen. And I used to pick Roger up at his home on a Friday night - we always played our home games on a Friday night when I was at Hull K.R. He'd have been working all day at the pit, he was an electrician. And he usually had a nap in the back of my Volkswagen until I got to Boothferry. Everybody used to stop at Boothferry Bridge. There was a café there and I used to wake him up and say, come on let's go and have a coffee and a round of toast, Roger. And he'd sit at the side of me - and I'd tell him how brilliant he was. I'd say, don't you do any tackling Roger - I'll do your tackling for you - you just score the tries.

Roger was a tremendous player and must have been Rovers' best buy ever,'concluded Paul.

As the season came to a close I got my International career back on the rails. I was picked to play for Great Britain against France at St Helens on March 17. It was a satisfying return for me - I scored two tries in a convincing 24-2 win. Rovers only finished in thirteenth place in the league that year. But in May, as the club looked ahead to better times, Johnny Whiteley said he was 'hopeful' for the following campaign.

However by the middle of February 1972 - less than nine months later - the Rovers' board had sacked him...

IN SUPPORT
Backing-up Great Britain's Cliff Watson...

HULL KINGSTON ROVERS 1969-70
The team which beat Wakefield Trinity 17-7 on February 28
Back row: Phil Coupland, Brian Mennell, Terry Clawson, Gordon Young, Steve Wiley,
Cliff Wallis. Front row: Ian Markham, Peter Small, Mike Stephenson, Roger Millward,
Peter Flanagan, Colin Cooper, Johnny Moore.

YORKSHIRE CUP WINNERS 1971-72
The team which won the Yorkshire Cup 11-7 against Castleford. Back row: Ian Markham,
Phil Coupland, Eric Palmer, John Millington, George Kirkpatrick, Paul Rose.
Front row: Terry Clawson, Joe Brown, Colin Cooper, Roger Millward, Peter Flanagan,
Paul Longstaff, Johnny Whiteley (Coach) Kneeling: Paul Daley and Mike Stephenson.

CHAPTER ELEVEN
TRANSFERS, TOURS & DIVISION TWO

After my previous season, which was marred by injury, I returned to some sort of normality and achieved a welcome treble in the 1971-72 season.

I captained Rovers to a Yorkshire Cup Final win - and then played for both Great Britain and Yorkshire. The season's new signings included two players who would feature later in Rovers' 'glory years', Roy Holdstock and Ged Dunn. But before those halcyon days, there were still plenty of problems to cope with...

The campaign started well. On Saturday August 21 we lifted another Yorkshire Cup, beating Castleford 11-7 at Wakefield. Ian Markham won the 'White Rose' man of the match and I kicked four goals. It was our third win in six years. John Millington deputised for Terry Clawson, who missed the match after being involved in a car crash the previous Sunday. With Terry out of the side, Johnny Whiteley asked me if I'd take the goal kicks in the final. I hadn't taken a goal kick in a match for nearly a year.

Johnny suggested I should try a few kicks at goal, as I might be a bit rusty. So I went out, put the ball down, kicked the goal and said, that would do. And I went into the Cup Final with only that one kick as practice. But it proved sufficient I'm glad to say. I kicked four goals to add to Paul Longstaff's try, which gave us victory. But I remember being scared stiff when I was taking one of the kicks - it was in their 'twenty-five' with the scores level at 7-7.

We left Belle Vue that afternoon with our fifth Yorkshire Cup whereas Castleford had still never won the trophy. They also missed out on a £40 a man bonus, which they'd have received if they'd managed a victory. And although we returned home with £50 I was so happy to be back playing rugby the bonus meant nothing to me!

Our Cup Final star, Ian Markham illustrated the problems of getting to far off grounds like Workington, especially for night matches, with a cross-country 'dash' only forty-eight hours after the final. We played the Cumbrians in a league fixture on the Monday evening but due to work commitments Ian couldn't travel with the rest of the team on the coach, which left Hull on the Monday morning at 9am. He set off by car three and a half hours later. He managed to get to the game in time and take his place at fullback - but to no avail. Workington, as so often in the past, dominated the match for long periods thanks to their heavier pack and ran out 12-4 winners. We never seemed to win in Cumbria.

And apart from that Yorkshire Cup Final win we weren't able to progress very far in any of the other competitions as the comparative decline at the club continued. I say comparative because when you look back at the results from the start of that season, we actually won 18 of our first 25 games, a very creditable performance by anyone's standards.

We beat the New Zealand tourists 12-10 at Craven Park on Wednesday, September 8. I hobbled off after only eight minutes with a thigh injury and I think it would be fair to say at that point few of the 5,663 crowd thought we had much chance of beating the Kiwis. But inspired by Cliff Wallis, and try-scorers Paul Rose and 'Flash' Flanagan, we produced a tremendous performance and played some brilliant attacking football to defeat them. What was particularly pleasing was that despite missing six shots at goal, suffering my early withdrawal and being without a number of regular first teamers including Phil Lowe, Terry Clawson, Paul Longstaff and Joe Brown, we still had enough strength in depth to beat a touring side. It was great to think that competition for places in the team would be a lot more intense than the previous year.

A few weeks later an 'A' team line-up was described by our second team coach, Arthur Bunting as 'the strongest he'd seen in his days at Craven Park'. It included Johnny Moore, Ged Dunn, Steve Hartley and Paul Daley in the backs, and Gordon Young, Cliff Wallis, Colin Cooper, Neil Dawson, Eric Palmer and 'Flash' in the pack. That list would not have disgraced the club in a first team match and coupled with our victory against the Kiwis, again highlighted the number of quality players we were accumulating at the club. A reception was held for the Kiwis after the game in the Stadium Club.

I received another bonus on the same day when I was named as stand-off ahead of Alan Hardisty for the first test against the Kiwis at Salford on September 25. I was originally named as vice-captain but following an injury to Doug Laughton, I actually captained the team, although with not the success I'd hoped for.

The first two tests again proved to be complete disasters for Britain. We started as hot favourites to win the series. But after leading 13-12 at half-time in the first test, we were beaten by the unfancied amateurs 13-18, when substitute Robin Orchard scored a late try for the tourists.

On October 16 we also lost the second test at Castleford, 14-17 and hence the series, in what was described in the press as the biggest rugby league sensation for years! Alex Murphy, then at Warrington, had been recalled to the test team after a five year absence. Again we led at the interval but again the Kiwis produced another second half comeback.

With two defeats I was set to become the first Great Britain captain to lose all three tests in a series. And I'd also have undoubtedly got some of the blame for the league's lackadaisical approach to selection, coaching and preparation for the games. Happily that didn't happen! On November 6, I led Britain to a 12-3 third test win at Headingley.

On the same afternoon Rovers beat Workington at Craven Park but only 2,121 watched the match - the lowest attendance since a match in December 1960 against Keighley. The International match, which was televised live by the BBC, it was said, spelled the end for Saturday rugby at Craven Park. Rovers' 13-9 win was the first Saturday afternoon game since the previous March. Although many fans also asked, 'Why was it played in direct opposition to the International at all?' it undoubtedly showed there was little appetite for Saturday rugby. And the problem wasn't just confined to Craven Park. A total of less than 15,000 fans had attended seven league matches on the same afternoon as the televised test...

Sandwiched between the test matches I also made two appearances as captain of Yorkshire. On September 29 I played against Lancashire at Leigh and kicked four goals and scored a try in our 42-22 victory. Then on October 20 we beat Cumberland 17-12 at Wakefield. That was a particularly poignant match for me. It was my old mate, Frank Foster's last game of rugby league. After the match the thirty-year-old Barrow forward announced his retirement.

On the same day, Rovers continued their team-building with the signing of Featherstone's twenty-year-old scrum-half, Terry Hudson for £7,500. But the season continued to be a 'see-saw' one of enjoyable highs followed by depressing lows.

In the newly introduced John Player Trophy, our first opponents were Salford. We beat them 17-14 but then on Saturday November 27 Wigan's Bill Ashurst kicked us out of the competition at the second round stage. He scored all of his side's points in an 18-11 win - it was our first home defeat of the season.

The following month was a traumatic one at Craven Park. And by the end of the year there was a great deal of unrest at the club. Terry Clawson was transferred to Leeds at the beginning of December and by the end of it we'd also lost Cliff Wallis, transferred to Castleford and looked set to lose Colin Cooper, who had announced his retirement. Joe Brown wasn't training and Peter Flanagan had been put on the transfer list. Ian Markham and Phil Lowe had also asked for transfers - but they'd both been refused. Christmas 1971 was definitely an anxious time for everyone at Craven Park! And equally worrying for the Rovers' board of directors was that the club didn't appear to be able to attract any new players.

In the same week as Cliff Wallis' 'whirlwind, overnight transfer' to Wheldon Road, Dennis Hartley turned down a move to Rovers from Castleford. And early in the New Year, Huddersfield's goal-kicking prop forward, Frank Davies also rejected the chance of a move to Craven Park because of the anticipated travelling problems from his West Riding home. Rovers' recruitment problems were clearly not money orientated but geographical - something of course I could readily identify with.

But the club's main problem centred on the lack of power in our pack. A number of experienced forwards had left the club in the previous two or three years and hadn't been replaced by players of an equal calibre. Basically, the backs including me, wanted more pack power. But they were unable to get it from a set of forwards that were regarded as simply not good enough. And the forwards wanted a few new faces to replace their departed colleagues. It all added up to a squad of very disgruntled players. New signings were needed desperately!

Another problem that I had to deal with at the time was just as hard to solve. I'd been sidelined since the start of December with a recurrent knee injury. And I was still absent when a 'lethargic' Rovers team lost 20-3 at the Boulevard on December 27. Steve Hartley deputised and once again the pack that day, which was described as 'one of the poorest packs to play in a Humberside derby' took most of the blame for the defeat.

Just after Christmas I was invited to 'clear the air' talks with the board. But the move backfired and instead of helping the situation, the meeting ended with me asking for a move as well...

Chairman, Wilf Spaven explained Rovers were searching for new players and that no more would be allowed to leave the club. But on New Years Eve the Daily Mirror carried the headline:

'MILLWARD TELLS ROVERS, I QUIT'

As the current Great Britain skipper it wasn't perhaps surprising that it was my name that was chosen to highlight the crisis at the club. In the last ten days of 1971 Phil, Ian and myself put in transfer requests - but Rovers response was the same as ever, 'We will not part with good young players'. But when the news broke that my request for a move had been rejected. And the reason for me wanting to leave was wrongly publicised as 'to play for a team nearer my home', once again people put two and two together and got five!

Wilf Spaven again insisted, 'If he wants to play rugby league it will be for Hull Kingston Rovers.' But to be quite honest I never wanted to leave Rovers. I was undoubtedly unhappy about the number of players that had left the club. And about the quality of the squad we had left and what we were expected to achieve with them. And I may have got a bit 'down' at times but I never actually wanted to go anywhere else.

At that stage though and with the leg injury, nobody believed me. They thought I was trying to pull the wool over their eyes.

But the injury was genuine enough - and very painful. I could play a match and everything would be perfectly OK. Then I'd play another and after ten minutes something just went! I'd gone! I couldn't continue a second longer! It went on and on and on. The injury plagued me for over a year. And although Rovers finally sent me to a specialist in Hull, he couldn't find anything wrong. That of course made things even worse and merely fuelled the speculation with some supporters that I wanted to leave - which just wasn't true. It was one of the most frustrating situations that I was ever faced with...

I remember one match at York shortly after the problem started. I was having a terrible match because every time I set off to run an excruciating pain would shoot down my leg. I was substituted almost immediately, and some of the Rovers' crowd actually cheered when I limped off. They thought I was swinging the lead and not trying. Well that hurt me - and I don't just mean my leg - because I've never gone on to a rugby field in my life and not tried. But nobody would believe me. People were suggesting that it was all because I wanted to get back to Castleford. But they couldn't have been wider of the mark. I'd never even dreamed about doing anything like that. The injury was very worrying - it recurred over and over again. And at times I thought if it continued it could even threaten my career.

In the end I had to take drastic steps. Nobody would believe there was a problem with my leg - so I actually paid for a second opinion!

I went to see a top specialist at Pontefract Hospital - he was regarded as a 'top-notcher' - and fortunately for me he turned out to be exactly that! I hadn't been on the table thirty seconds when he said,

'What have you come to see me for?' I explained the problem I'd been having and he just put his hand on the back of my knee and then said immediately, 'You've pulled your hamstring.'

It may sound stupid but his diagnosis was music to my ears. At last someone had finally found out what was wrong with my leg. But being me it wasn't any ordinary pulled hamstring of course. He explained that I'd injured the hamstring on the 'insertion' at the back of my knee. Not as most people do at the back of the thigh. And that was why the injury might have gone undetected. Then he just said,

'Five weeks rest and you'll be all right.' And I was!

I reported the diagnosis to Rovers and that was it. As soon as the five weeks were up I started playing again. The leg felt as good as new and I didn't have a single problem with it for the rest of my career.

But although things turned out OK in the end, it was an incident that upset me - and still does today. I found the fact that people actually thought I wanted to get away from Rovers and was feigning an injury to help my case in some way, very hurtful. Even the board of directors thought I'd been 'tapped-up'. But the injury was certainly real enough. And the lay-offs were costly in more ways than one. When the Great Britain side to meet France on February 6 in Toulouse was named, I'd lost my place to new cap, St Helens' Ken Kelly. Leeds' centre, Syd Hynes was named as captain and Phil Lowe was in the second row alongside Bill Ashurst of Wigan. Britain won the match 10-9 thanks to tries by Clive Sullivan and Billy Benyon and two goals from John Holmes.

But worse followed for me!

Whilst I was out of action I was also omitted from the World Cup Squad. And ultimately missed out on the summer's World Cup tournament in France. I don't have to tell you no player in the world would ever allow an imaginary pain in the leg to cause that!

But I never wanted to leave Rovers. It never once entered my head! I've been down on more than one occasion, even when I was coach. And there were times when I drove across to Hull day after day after day. And many times when I had a mental block after training. When I just couldn't get in the car and drive home. Many a time we'd go for a drink after training and

I'd end up at the Zetland Arms asking Colin if I could stay the night. I realise it may sound crazy but it's a terrible feeling to think you just can't make that journey again! I was travelling over five or six times every week along that motorway. There was a stage when I could tell you exactly how far I was away from home. The exact mileage! I knew exactly when the road surface was going to change - and that when I went off the concrete road and onto the tarmac one - I was exactly 29.4 miles away from Kippax. Now I know that admission sounds very sad but that's how it used to get to me! The New Year at Craven Park started with the club in continued turmoil. On the field we opened with a comfortable 24-4 home victory on January 2 against Doncaster. But I didn't resume training until nine days later following my two-week dispute with the club.

I returned to play for Rovers against Dewsbury at Craven Park on Sunday January 16 and kicked four goals in our 17-8 win. And Rovers clearly thought their 'get tough' policy with the other 'wantaways' and I had worked. The following week, on Wednesday January 19 Jim Neale was signed from York but his arrival was seen as only a small part of the much bigger solution. Two days later I played at Salford but we lost 22-11. And worse followed when we lost again on February 3 in the first round of the Challenge Cup at the Boulevard. It was a narrow but shattering defeat. Hull won 7-5 but I missed a late penalty chance that would have forced a replay. The cup defeat was sadly the final nail in Johnny Whiteley's coffin and he was 'relieved of his duties' a fortnight later. Arthur Bunting was appointed as Rovers' new coach and Paul Daley took over from Arthur as 'A' team coach until the end of the season when the situation was to be reviewed. It was of course less than 18 months since Johnny had arrived at the club, regarded as the best coach in the world, following Great Britain's Ashes win in Australia. But ever a realist and a gentleman, Johnny left Craven Park with a simple explanation for his departure:

'They've fired me. The board decided that results have not been good enough in view of the club's outlay on new players.'

It was an interesting statement. There were very few other people at Craven Park who thought Johnny was to blame for the club's problems. Most fans and the local press thought it was more down to 'the club's policy' and the board's 'small-time approach.'

I agreed. None of the players who had left the club or those of us who had asked for transfers had any criticism of Johnny. But as always with a struggling club the coach is usually the obvious scapegoat. And the first in line for the axe! Johnny hadn't been given either the time or the freedom to bring in the players he wanted to strengthen the side. Above all he wasn't even in a position to choose the side he would have liked to take the field each week! And he'd done much better than many fans had expected by keeping an understrength side in the top half of the league table...

But we had to complete the season without him. And it was a depressing ending for me in particular. Following my 'time-out' resting my hamstring, I spent the end of March again on the sidelines, after receiving an eye injury in a match against Castleford and recovering for a couple of days in

Pinderfields Hospital, Wakefield.

As the season drew to a close, I couldn't help but cast an envious eye at the Challenge Cup Final. My old pal and travelling partner, Terry Clawson, fulfilled his ambition of playing in a Wembley final when Leeds met St Helens on May 13. Despite kicking five goals Terry ended up on the losing side when Saints won a close game 16-13. But I was so delighted he'd achieved his ambition - there was hope for me yet...

My 'mysterious' hamstring injury meant I missed the 1972 World Cup in France and also ultimately missed out on a winner's medal.

Great Britain went through the competition unbeaten defeating Australia 27-21, France 13-4 and New Zealand 53-19. They finished at the top of the table and then faced the second placed Aussies in the play-off final.

The two teams drew 10-10 after extra time in the final but Britain were declared the winners because they'd scored more points in the qualifying rounds. My cousin Brian Lockwood and my Rovers' teammate, Phil Lowe were in the second-row. Terry Clawson kicked two vital goals. And skipper Clive Sullivan scored that amazing try in the final in Lyon. Clive's length of the field effort remains to this day the most famous touchdown in World Cup history. Whilst Clive, who also scored in Britain's other three matches, lives on in everyone's hearts - the last British captain to lift the World Cup.

During the 1972-73 season I scored 31 points in the league match against Hunslet with eleven goals and a hat-trick of tries. We won the game 58-5. The previous night Hunslet had played a home fixture against Halifax and sunk to a record home defeat 8-76. Bruce Burton, the Halifax stand-off had also scored 31 points against Hunslet with 14 goals and a try. So in less than twenty-four hours the Leeds' side had conceded 134 points, including 28 tries, with 62 of those points coming from the two opposition off-halves. This must have been some sort of record, albeit an unwanted one!

Phil Lowe set a new Rovers' record of 26 tries by a forward in a season, beating W. Sandham's record, which had stood since 1912/13. The club finished in a respectable tenth position, four places higher than the previous year. We also reached the John Player Semi-Final but lost 15-13 to Salford. And the four tackle rule was extended to six tackles. I made only one representative appearance playing for Yorkshire against Cumberland, due to injury and ended the season with 86 goals and 18 tries. And Ged Dunn finished at the top of the list with 27.

The first half of the seventies were fairly uninspiring years at Craven Park. And although the 1973-74 season was another successful one for me personally, it turned out to be catastrophic for Rovers. The league had again been split into two and we struggled in the new Division One set-up. We only finished 14th out of 16 and were relegated to Division Two!

We lost 25-9 to the Australian tourists. I played for Great Britain against Australia in the deciding test at Warrington on December 1. We'd won the first test 21-12 at Wembley but then lost the second at Headingley 6-14. Wakefield's David Topliss had been stand-off for both matches. I scored a try and a goal in the decider but we lost 5-15

Clive Sullivan was signed from Hull for £3,250. And Bernard Watson joined the club from Bradford for £4,000. But Phil Lowe was transferred to Manly for £15,000 and Paul Longstaff left for Castleford.

I was Rovers' top scorer with 63 goals and 14 tries. And Paul Rose and I were selected for the Australian tour at the end of the 1973-74 season. But some of the gloss was obviously taken off my selection because of Rovers impending relegation.

I remember we played against Workington late in the season at Craven Park. They had a young halfback called Arnie Walker who had expected to be picked for the trip down under. But I was selected instead. And I think all he wanted to do all afternoon was to knock my head off! It was a funny day that. But it had been a funny season! I recall we played Salford at the Willows and three other players who were widely tipped to go on tour with me that year were in the Reds team, Chris Hesketh, Kenny Gill and David Watkins. Kenny Gill had been picked at stand-off for the games against France that season. The only reason for that, or so I like to think was that I'd been out for a lot of the season, injured. But I remember playing at Salford and knowing I needed to put on a good display against Kenny as the selectors were due to pick the touring team the very next day.

I finished up scoring a hat-trick and I must have looked OK because the following day I was chosen for the tour. Mind you Kenny, Chris and David also made the trip, along with teammates Colin Dixon and Paul Charlton as Salford supplied no fewer than five tourists that year. That later became six when Maurice Richards was called up to replace the injured John Atkinson on tour.

I played for Great Britain three times during the 1974 tour, once as substitute. We lost the first test on June 15 by 12 points to 6 at Brisbane. But won the second on July 6 when we beat the Aussies 16-11 in Sydney. And I recall there was then a very bizarre situation that occurred before the third test, that any Aussie or Great Britain fan would probably have found difficult to believe if they'd seen it.

Whilst we were in Sydney, Jimmy Thompson and I went up to visit Phil Lowe and his wife, Avril at their house in Manly. Phil hadn't been picked for the tour. And was playing club football in Australia at the time.

I'd been injured in the second test when we'd levelled the series - the third was scheduled for a fortnight later. I was still struggling with the injured leg when we went to see Phil on the Tuesday, only four days before the deciding game. When we arrived, Bobby Fulton, the Australian captain and his wife were already there. Bobby and Phil were teammates at Manly. The afternoon ended with Bobby's wife, Anne, helping my recuperation by gently putting frozen peas and ice on my ankle. And I said that if anyone could have seen her, they'd have thought there was something very strange going on! Just imagine, the wife of the Aussie skipper getting one of his main opponents fit to play against her husband on the following Saturday! I suppose something like that could only have happened in rugby league...

Anne's treatment did the trick. I recovered in time and was substitute for the final test in Sydney on July 20. But Bobby had the last laugh. His team ran out 22-18 winners to again claim the Ashes.

Whilst I was on tour in 1974, I shared a room with Jimmy Thompson. I nearly always seemed to room with a 'flat-capper'. If Jimmy wasn't in the party it would be Steve Nash or Mick Morgan. Jimmy, Steve and Mick were all 'flat-cappers' - and I was from Castleford, only a stones-throw down the road, so I suppose that was the affiliation. The only exception to that arrangement that I can remember was on my first tour when I shared with Tommy Bishop.

After we'd been in Australia a few days, I wrote to Carol and asked her what she would like for a present when I returned home. She wrote back and said she'd love some perfume, called 'Sea Witch'. The next morning I said to Jimmy come on, let's go down to the shops, I know what Carol wants for a present. And off we went to one of the main shopping centres in the middle of Sydney. When we arrived at the first store, I went up to the counter and said to the assistant, excuse me, do you sell 'Sea Witch' perfume?

'Yes' she replied, 'I think you'll find some on that stand over there,' and pointed to a huge display rack containing hundreds of different perfumes in the corner. Jimmy and I went over to the rack and looked and looked but there wasn't any in the store anywhere. We spent two days looking in every shop possible to try and find some 'Sea Witch' perfume. And on the third day we were just about to set off for another search when Jimmy said,

'Just a minute, give me that letter from Carol to look at!'

The penny had finally dropped for Jimmy at least, but unfortunately not for me! He went into the toilet to read the letter. All of a sudden he burst back into the room, waved the offending piece of paper in my face and shouted, 'You stupid little pillock! It says here, 'Yes I would love some perfume, see which you like and get me that!'

I think you could say Jimmy wasn't very pleased. We'd been looking for a non-existent perfume for over two days! I admit I saw the funny side of it later on. But Jimmy never did. It was one of the very few times when the usually placid and laid back Jimmy lost his cool. But Jimmy was the best bloke you could ever wish for to room with, I couldn't fault him, even after the 'Sea Witch' episode. Every morning he'd bring a cup of tea up to the room and put it on the bedside table. He was as good as having your own private butler. Then he'd say,

'Come on get up, it's time for training.' And you'd enjoy the same every night, another cup of tea, delivered to the room.

We used to have some very eventful evenings in the hotel. There was an old chap there - the night porter in the hotel in 'Coogie Bay' - he seemed to be on duty every single night. We'd ring down about half past nine and order another cup of tea and some sandwiches. The old chap would bring them to the room without delay and he'd often sit down and stay and have a chat with us. He'd stay for as long as he could, or until he was wanted downstairs - but he'd always leave at five to twelve when he'd say,

'I'll have to go now lads because those two will be in.'

Now 'those two' we soon discovered were Steve 'Knocker' Norton and Les

Dyl. And they used to create havoc nearly every night. The hotel had a big staircase that turned at ninety degrees and then continued up again to the next floor. Where it turned there was a little landing and some big drape curtains. What 'Knocker' and Les did was annoy the old chap so he would chase them to the top of the stairs and into their room. But what he didn't know was that only one of them would return to their room. The other one would hide behind the curtains and when the old fella had gone past would quickly come down the stairs again and raid the kitchen. Steve or Les would help themselves to anything they could get from the fridge and then make sure they avoided the old chap, who by that time would be on his way down again, by returning to their hiding place behind the curtains. Once the coast was clear they could continue up the stairs to their room to enjoy a 'well-earned' midnight feast.

Why the old chap used to fall for the same trick over and over again, or whether he actually knew about the raids on the fridge, I never found out. But they used to play the trick on him nearly every night and it used to drive him crazy. Jimmy and I were never involved in pranks like that of course, in fact the only trouble we encountered was when we were checking out of the hotel. We'd given our key in and were walking out to board the coach, when the receptionist shouted after us,

'Mr Millward, Mr Thompson would you mind settling your bill, please?'

So I went back and insisted we hadn't got a bill or at least we shouldn't have! We've paid for everything as we've gone along, I said.

'No, no, you owe us some money,' she said with a smile. What for? I asked.

'For sandwiches on a night,' she replied. No we paid for them at the time I insisted again, we always do.

'No, I'm afraid it's quite clear you owe us $40,' she said with another smile.

By this time Reg Parker, the tour manager had appeared and was standing behind us, waiting to hand his key in. He'd obviously heard what was going on.

'You'll have to pay lads, if you've had it, you'll have to pay,' he said.

'But Reg we've paid for everything as we've gone along,' pleaded Jimmy.

'No, No,' Reg said calmly, 'you can't have done - you'll have to pay it now!'

Come on Jimmy we'll have to pay it, I said. So we settled the bill even though we knew we didn't owe anything.

Reg handed his key in next and started to walk off. But as he turned to leave, the receptionist called after him,

'Oh Mr Parker, can you sort your bill out as well now please?'

'But I haven't had anything!' he said in a surprised voice.

Come on Reg, let's have a look, I said. How much is it?

'$600!' he cried out, staring at the bill in total disbelief!

You'll have to pay it, I said, We had to...

And he did have to pay it. But we all knew what had happened. It was people like Terry Clawson, Colin Dixon and big Jim Mills, who had caused the problems. When they came in after a night out they'd order lobsters and all sorts of things to eat - and simply put them on other people's room bills. But it was so funny the way Reg made us pay our bill and then seconds later he had to pay fifteen times as much - there was just no way he could get out of it! It's memories like those that make tours so special, and you just enjoy them, at least afterwards...

Back in England, another new experience awaited me, one I wasn't too eager to face! In the 1974-75 campaign Rovers played in the Second Division. Neil Fox had been signed from Wakefield on May 25 and along with Clive Sullivan and Bernard Watson made his debut at Doncaster on August 25. It was the first game of a record-breaking season!

We were lucky in many ways that players of Clive and Neil's calibre were available at that time. We mixed them in with what we already had at the club and came up with a very competitive side. And under the shrewd guidance of Arthur Bunting, I know we didn't lose many games that year!

Neil beat Cyril Kellett's club record with 146 goals including one drop. He also crossed for fourteen tries - giving him a new club record of 333 points, beating Cyril's best of 290 points. Ged Dunn was an ever present and scored forty-two tries, another club record, beating Gilbert Austin's 1924-25 tally of thirty-seven. Ged scored six tries against Hunslet, a post-war record for the club and we finished the season having scored an amazing 1001 points, another club record.

We won the Yorkshire Cup for the sixth time, beating Wakefield at Headingley 16-13. The crowd was 5,824 and I won the 'White Rose' man of the match trophy. I think that victory in particular showed just how good a side we were becoming, and how near to a First Division team we were.

During the year, quality players continued to arrive at the club from different sources. We paid a record club transfer £8,000 for forward John Cunningham and Mike Smith was signed from the Colts. John arrived at Craven Park from Barrow with a tremendous reputation. At first he used to drive over from Cumbria which must have been a hell of a journey. And Mike of course went on to write his name in the Rovers' record books.

Nobody from anywhere in rugby league ever had a bad word to say about Mike. He was and still is just a superb guy. He always conducted himself impeccably, whether it was training, playing and even at after match events. Whatever aspect of the game you looked at, you just couldn't fault him. Today, Mike still holds the 'most appearances for the club' record, having played 481 games plus 8 as a substitute for Rovers in a magnificent career from 1974 to 1991. And with players playing far less matches these days, it's one record that's likely to last forever!

One of the main things Arthur tried to do that season was to make sure that the players knew what playing in the lower division was all about. It's not easy to get out of the second division and he knew some of the lads were going to play at places they'd never been before. We won most of our matches very easily. And we might at times have got a bit above our station, instead of remembering where we were and why we were there! It was of course all down to what had happened the year before. And it was Arthur's job to remind the players of that fact. The effort hadn't been good enough the year before. He had to make sure it was in the one which followed! Nobody likes relegation of course and at the time everybody was totally disappointed that we were down there. But that's where we belonged - due to the previous season's failings - you couldn't get away from the fact.

But we enjoyed a marvellous season, reaching the semi-finals of the BBC2 TV Floodlit Trophy and the John Player Trophy - tremendous achievements for a second division side. And it must be said better than we'd done as a first division one the year before. Thankfully we also achieved our main goal of the campaign - winning promotion back to the top flight! That had been our main priority, ensuring we returned to the first division at the first attempt. But that was something which never really worried me. I was always confident that we'd be promoted, we had a very experienced and talented squad. It was my International status that I was more concerned about...

I was a Great Britain regular at the time but couldn't help wondering whether playing for a second division side would affect my chances of staying in the team. Would people think that because I was playing at a lower level that I might not be able to still do it at International level?

Little things like that ran through my mind! But I needn't have worried. A year in the second division didn't affect my International career at all. Although I only kicked 16 goals, as Neil Fox had taken over as our regular first choice kicker, I scored 28 tries that season. I was chosen to play for Yorkshire against Lancashire. And I was named as captain for England's matches against France and Wales in the European Championship. In the first game against France, John Millington made his England debut and we won 11-9 in Perpignan. John only played one more match for his country in 1981. But finished with a 100% record when England beat Wales in Cardiff 20-15. In the second game of the European Championsip against Wales we won again 12-8 at Salford. And at the end of the season I was selected for my fourth tour. And along with Ged Dunn for England and Clive Sullivan and Glyn Turner for Wales I enjoyed another fantastic trip to Australia. You'd have to say that proved the gap between the divisions was not as big as it is now. Players could come from the second division and go on tour!

Seven years after my meeting with Alan Price and Georgie Fame, I actually made a record of my own. Well at least the rest of the England 1975 World Championship Squad and I did - with the aptly titled 'Up and Under'. Surprisingly enough it didn't make the charts or even the 'Guinness Book of Hit Singles' but we all had a great time making it. But what I could never understand however was why Dave Chisnall, probably the least photogenic of the English Squad, was featured on the cover?

In 1975 they split the World Cup into two sections. Half of the matches were staged in the southern hemisphere - in Australia and New Zealand - and then the other half of the competition was played in Britain. They also split Great Britain into two teams and we competed as England and Wales, with I have to say disastrous consequences.

The two things that stand out in my mind about the competition were first of all the match against Wales. For obvious reasons it became known as 'the battle of Lang Park'. And the Aussies must have killed themselves laughing, as us two sets of silly buggers, England and Wales, knocked 'seven bells' out of each other. The build up to the game was equally volatile with Alex Murphy and Les Pearce, the Welsh coach hyping the clash, and ultimately the whole thing got really nasty. Glyn Turner who was a teammate of mine and Ged Dunn at Rovers was there as a member of the Welsh squad. I remember we were in Brisbane one day and Glyn was walking down the other side of the street to Ged and I. We just waved and said 'Glyn, you all right?' and he just ignored us - that's how bad it got! But things like that were nothing compared to the actual match! It was totally crazy - fighting from start to finish! What was worse was we lost, 7-12. The other thing that still stands out about that tour was we then drew 10-10 against Australia on the Sydney Cricket Ground and then also drew with New Zealand.

In the games played back in England we beat Australia but they were declared the Champions even though they hadn't beaten England in either game. And it was that 'silly' match against Wales that had cost us the title...

The 1975 tour was my first as captain. Bill Oxley was the Tour Manager and Alex Murphy was the coach. Without any hesitation I'd say Alex was definitely the best scrum half I ever played against. Unfortunately, or perhaps fortunately for me, that wasn't too often - because he was playing towards the end of his career when I was just starting out on mine. So there weren't too many times when we faced each other. But as the coach on the 1975 tour, I recall that Alex's motivational skills certainly left a lot to be desired. They seemed to consist mainly of giving you a 'bollocking' before you went out to play the game, another 'bollocking' at half-time and a third one when you came back in. When he returned from the tour he became coach at Salford.

Steve Nash, another great scrum-half and a good friend of mine was playing at The Willows at the time and the next time I saw him, I just couldn't help but inquire how he was getting on with Alex in charge.

'Oh, Alex is all right,' replied 'Nashy', 'We get a 'bollocking' before we go out to play the game, another 'bollocking' at half-time and a third one when we come back in'... That was Alex!

As a boy I used to watch him and be amazed at some of the things he did. When we went out to play our own game of rugby the following day it would usually be Alex who I wanted to copy...

Alex was something else, when he was at his peak he was simply brilliant to watch. He had everything, there are no two ways about that - his only problem was that he occasionally opened his mouth a little too wide for his own good, that's all. But that's what made him Alex! And we wouldn't have wanted him any different!

I remember the first night in Australia. Bill and I were quietly chatting in the hotel in Perth when Alex came rushing in, shouting:

'They're all going home, we've got to send them all home!' I asked Alex what he was going on about? He told me that six of the lads, and don't forget we'd been flying all day for over 24 hours, had gone out for a few beers. A couple of them had enjoyed a few too many - and caused a few problems! Alex insisted,

'They're going home - every one of them - they're going on Thursday.' But

Alex I said as diplomatically as I could. We've only brought eighteen players, if you send six of them home we won't even have a team!

Luckily things were soon sorted out and apart from the Wales match, it wasn't a bad trip actually after that...

A little later, Bill Oxley told me about an old team-mate of mine, Frank Foster, who was the coach at Barrow where Bill was on the board. I always thought Frank was great. He was one of my first 'minders' at Rovers. He was a great friend and a great forward. One of the toughest I've ever played with. He was also well known as a bit of a 'hit-man' throughout a very stormy career. And by all accounts Frank hadn't lost any of his 'tough-guy' image. Barrow at the time were a bit of an 'up and down' club. And Frank had been under a bit of pressure from various quarters. I asked Bill if the Barrow directors had ever thought of sacking Frank?

'Oh many times,' Bill replied, 'But nobody dare tell him!'

Rovers were back in the First Division for the 1975/76 season, where we finished a creditable eighth out of sixteen teams. But the achievement was marred by the death of Wilf Spaven on Tuesday March 23 1976.

Even before I signed for Rovers, Wilf always seemed to take a big interest in me, like he did with all the Great Britain players. Our friendship started when I was drafted in as substitute against New Zealand. I was still at Castleford and he was the Great Britain Team Manager. Like Colin, Wilf became another father figure. He was someone you could always rely on - he always seemed to be there to 'look after you'.

It may have been one of the things that tipped the scales when Rovers came in for me. He was a wonderful man. I remember going to see him in hospital just before he died, he was a huge loss to the club. Wilf was another Craven Park fixture. His career there spanned three different decades. He became Rovers' Chairman for the first time from 1950 to 1952. It was the start of over twenty-five years of dedicated service to both Rovers and the sport of rugby league. He then served as Vice-Chairman from 1953 to 1958 and was instrumental in taking Colin Hutton to Craven Park from the Boulevard. Wilf was re-elected to Chairman again in 1958 and remained in the position until his death eighteen years later!

On the field, we reached the Yorkshire Cup Final for the second successive year but lost 15-11 to Leeds at Headingley. Neil Fox won the "White Rose' Man of the Match Award.

During the season I scored 64 goals and 15 tries for Rovers, enabling me to beat Gilbert Austin's club record of 160 tries in a career. I also played for England in the World Championship against Wales, France, New Zealand and Australia. And for Yorkshire against Cumbria.

The season witnessed the arrival of another of Rovers' all-time greats when Len Casey was signed from Hull FC for £6,000. However as one arrived another left the club, when Peter Flanagan along with Mike Stephenson, crossed the city in the other direction to join the Airlie Birds.

Off the field, we saw the departure of another coach when Arthur Bunting resigned and Harry Poole took the reins...

CHAPTER TWELVE
A BIT OF BANTER WITH THE REF'

It's funny how certain names crop up over and over again during your life, isn't it? And one that returned to haunt me throughout my career at least, was undoubtedly Fred Lindop! Fred wasn't a bad referee, in fact he was a very good one. But it just seemed that as far as I was concerned, most of the games where controversial things happened, he tended to be involved.

From my first Test series against Australia in 1967 - which we lost - to my last ever game at Wembley when I ended up with a broken jaw - Fred was there!

In between, I was sent off for the only time in my entire career in 1975, playing for England against the Australians. No points for guessing who the referee was...

The game was played after the World Cup matches, just after the Aussies had been crowned World Champions. We'd beaten them on the Saturday 16-13 at Wigan but they decided to issue a special challenge for another match on the Wednesday night at Headingley. I know why the Rugby League took them up on it - money! They knew they would fill Headingley. Some of the English players weren't so keen however and cried off. And Alex Murphy, England's coach, asked the Rugby League to be 'released' from the fixture in order to concentrate on his struggling club side, Warrington. Needless to say, we ended up going into the match under-prepared.

I'd been up at five o'clock in the morning to go to work. I'd worked the morning shift at the pit and when I'd finished went straight to the hotel in Garforth to meet up with the team. And from there we all went on to Headingley for the game.

There was a good crowd in Headingley as expected. I was playing scrum-half that night as I'd done at Wigan. But Australia brought in Tommy Raudonikis to face me instead of John Mayes.

At the very first scrum the ball came out and I dropped on it. The next thing I knew I'd been kicked straight in the head and I thought, this is going to be a good game!

Only a few minutes later at another scrum I again got the ball out. I was running off when Raudonikis whacked me. And I made a feeble attempt at whacking him back! He immediately started throwing punches and the next thing I was on the floor, laid out, with my jersey over my head, the lot!

The blow count was about ten-nil to Raudonikis. Fred Lindop blew his whistle and as I was recovering, I saw Tommy was already on his way to the dressing room having been sent off. Fred then turned to me and just said one word, 'OFF!'

So that was the first time ever - and still the only time in my life that I was sent off - and it really upset me. I was only on the field for eight minutes!

In hindsight of course I should perhaps thank Fred for his decision. The match was meaningless and he may well have saved me from a lot more punishment that night. But the decision did nothing for the depleted England side - Australia beat us 25-0.

INTERNATIONAL DUTY
Top: March 2 1968 Alan Burwell, left, watches as I score against France in Great Britain's 19-8 win at Bradford.

Middle and bottom: WORLD CHAMPIONSHIP September 20 1975 In action for England during our 22-16 win against Wales at Warrington.

Billy Thompson was another great referee. He stood no nonsense from anybody. And especially when he was officiating in the explosive atmosphere of a Hull and Rovers derby. The best way I can sum up a derby match - and Billy, who had refereed a few of them in his time, is with a story he once told me. We were discussing Boxing Day and some of the games we'd been involved in around the Christmas period.

'Boxing Day, I'll tell you what Boxing day was to me,' he said. 'Boxing Day was Hull versus Hull KR at the Boulevard - with an 11 o'clock kick-off! Two minutes past 11 there were twenty-four players fighting and I was blowing my whistle trying to sort it out. Three minutes past eleven I'd got everything calmed down. I got everybody in the middle and said, 'Hull fullback, Rovers' fullback - off!'

'But Billy we've done nowt' the fullbacks both said to me as one.

'Exactly' I proclaimed. 'Cowardice - now get off!'

The story may sound a little far fetched - and a little glamourised - but it was true, well almost!

The two fullbacks Billy dismissed were Hull's Gary Kemble and Rovers' John Lydiat. But it wasn't on Boxing Day - and it wasn't after only two minutes of the match! The incident actually happened well into the second half and the game was in April!

I remember one day I was playing scrum-half for Rovers at Wigan. Ronnie Jackson was the referee and I was trying to get the ball in the scrum. It was the time when you had to fight to get the ball from the scrum, not the rubbish we've got these days. Ronnie said to me, 'You're having some trouble there Roger, aren't you?' It was a time when you could have a bit of banter with the ref. Yes Ronnie I replied, I can't get it in for that 'Wigan lad', he's got his feet across the scrum.

'I've seen him,' said Ronnie. 'Put the ball in. I'll take care of things.' So I put the ball in and he immediately penalised me for feeding. I thought, thanks very much Ronnie!

So we stood back after Wigan had taken the kick to touch and waited for them to take the tap penalty. I was standing next to Ronnie. I could hardly believe it when he nudged me and said, 'Number eleven gets the ball here.' How do you know that Ron? I asked.

'I was here a couple of weeks ago and they worked this move, number eleven gets the ball and he'll come through just about where you are.' he explained.

Fair enough, I said. Anyway, number eleven did get the ball - exactly like Ronnie said he would - and I ran in, tackled him and stopped the move before it started. And as I was getting up Ronnie just ran by and said,

'There you are - I told you.' Ronnie was certainly one of the more unusual referees but he wasn't on his own by any means. The laughs you had with them! Bizarre little incidents like that went on all the time...

Dickie Thomas used to come into the dressing room before the game and say, 'I want to see the scrum half and the hooker.' When they'd gone over to

SIZE DOESN'T
MATTER

Left: Evading Aussie
skipper Artie Beetson
in 1975

Below left: Enjoying a
drink with Wales'
'Big' Jim Mills

Below right: Jeff
Grayshon and I
playing for Engand

him, he'd say in his broad accent, 'I want to see the ball there, your feet there, and if they aren't there then you're in there!'

There were a number of referees that all the players respected. People like Mick Naughton, Ronnie Campbell and Billy Thompson. And I'd better not forget John Holdsworth because he comes from Kippax. I know they have all dropped clangers in their time but that's life. But who'd be a referee to start with? I certainly wouldn't. In training I purposely used to give bad decisions to see how players would react. I'd make them react so I could have a go at them. But I wouldn't have been a referee for a gold pig - it's a hell of a hard job to do!

But I also think at times they let themselves down by not being strong enough, not positive enough and not consistent with their decisions. If they were I don't think anyone would complain. They're always going to miss some things, we miss things even now. I know when we watch games on television someone goes over for a try and there are people looking at me asking, 'What is it? Is it a try?' I just look back and say you've seen exactly the same as I have. But they seem to think because you've played rugby league you can always tell them what's happened. But you can't always. Exactly like a referee can't always get it right.

One of the funniest moments with Mick Naughton was at Craven Park. We were playing against Widnes but we weren't getting much of the ball. For some reason 'Watkie' seemed to be having a bit of trouble... All of a sudden at a scrum their hooker flew straight out of the pack, his hands clutching his face. Mick pulled all of our back three out. Rosey, Lowey and Casey. He got them all together then said to me, because I was the captain,

'Roger, come here.' I said what's up Mick?

He said, 'Phil, I know it wasn't you, but you other two bastards, I'm telling you now, that if it happens again, one of you will be going off!'

Casey recently revealed that was only one of the many occasions they'd run into trouble with Mick.

'In the third round of the 1980 Challenge Cup against Warrington at home we were in the dressing room before the game getting ready. Naturally everybody was very tense. The referee Mick Naughton and the linesmen came in and started to check everybody's boots and then our fingers for rings and things like that. He checked me and then Roy Holdsock. But when he got to John Millington, Mick let out a big yell as he jumped in the air with surprise. John had a huge false toe stuck to the outside of his boot, it looked just like the toe was sticking out through the leather! It just broke all the tension and everybody just roared with laughter at Mick's reaction - everybody except Mick that is,' said Len.

'And the joke worked. We went out and won the match 23-11 - and we were in the semi-final. But I remember equally as well, Mick's words of warning when we ran out of the tunnel before the game.

'No more messing about today you lot, else you'll be straight off,' he said.'

CHAPTER THIRTEEN
MORE IMPORTANT THINGS THAN RUGBY
CRONULLA 1976

Hopefully there aren't many places in the world that you've dreamed of visiting, only to eventually arrive there in floods of tears. And fewer places still that you've then had to leave, only a few months later, equally as distraught. But for Carol and Kay, Cronulla was one of them.

Because that's exactly what happened when our dream trip to Australia in 1976 initially turned into more of a nightmare! In the end I'm pleased to say our journey down under did provide all the fantastic memories that we'd anticipated it would. But when we arrived there - after a long and tiring flight from the U.K. - the experience proved a little overwhelming for an exhausted mum and her five-year-old daughter. And before we could experience any of the 'highs' of our new home, we certainly had our share of the 'lows' to overcome first.

It was an unforgettable experience in every sense...

When the plane touched down at Sydney Airport at 6.40am on Wednesday April 21 it heralded the start of another unique chapter in my life. I was wearing a big yellow jacket and black trousers. Jim Geraghty of 'Straight Talk Tyres', the company which had sponsored my season with Cronulla, had asked me to put a badge on the jacket. I had done - and looked a very impressive and noticeable 'advert' for the company.

As we were flying into Sydney I'd turned to Carol and Kay and said, just try and take it all in your stride now, whatever happens. Because I knew what was going to happen. And that there was no way we could avoid it.

I knew we had a few very hectic hours ahead of us. I knew there would be television cameras. There'd be radio reporters, journalists and all sorts, all over the place. And I was right, when we got off that plane they just hit us with everything!

I'd been before and I knew what to expect - what it was all about. But Carol and Kay, they just stood there with their mouths wide open. I know that got to them. And the travelling to Cronulla to our new flat did as well.

Phil Lowe had arranged to meet us at the airport and take us to Cronulla. He was playing for Manly at the time and it was great for us all to see a friendly face amongst the hundreds of strangers.

Cronulla is only about twenty miles south of Sydney, it's where Captain Cook landed at Botany Bay. But by the time we reached our destination Carol and Kay were both hot and exhausted.

A little later, as we tried our best to settle in, Cliff Watson came round to see us. But the moment he appeared, Carol and Kay just burst out crying - and I thought, oh my God, here we go!

Their tears had nothing to do with Cliff's arrival I hasten to add. I imagine any 'Brit' they recognised would have reminded them of home and produced the same effect. The crying was just a culmination of everything that had happened I suppose. Being tired from the long journey. The pressure from the media at the airport. An afternoon press conference at Cronulla's ground. And then arriving at a new home! Not surprisingly it had all proved too much for them...

Cliff told us he was thinking of having one final season with Cronulla. At the time he was with the south coast club, Helensburg, after spending a short spell with Wollongong, but he wasn't playing. Cliff had starred alongside Tommy Bishop in the 1973 Grand Final season with the Sharks. And my arrival at the club had influenced his decision to have a 'final fling' at the club. That was great to hear, Cliff was the type of player you always preferred to have on your side.

As soon as we let our feelings be known that our flat wasn't what we'd expected, Jim Geraghty immediately moved us. We were given another apartment, with the appealing name of 'Trade Winds' that overlooked the ocean - and for a while everything was marvellous. But nothing could have prepared us for the trauma that followed...

We'd only been in Australia for a couple of weeks, when Carol found a lump in her breast. Her mum Madge, had died from breast cancer three years earlier at the age of forty-eight, so Carol was in the habit of checking herself regularly.

Being in the position we were, she immediately went to see Dr Peter Malouf, the club doctor. And in only a few days she was operated on. In the meantime, Jim Geraghty from 'Straight Talk' asked me to contact my mum and Carol's dad and he arranged and paid for them to fly over to Sydney to be with us. So within the space of a couple of weeks everything was done. Carol was in and out of hospital and was recovering back at our flat in Cronulla. The people were all marvellous with her. The specialist, the doctors - the entire medical staff were all fantastic. They couldn't have done any more. We were so well looked after. And when we thought about it later, we both realised in a way we'd been lucky. That may sound like a strange thing to say. But if it had to happen, there was no two ways about it, Australia was the best place to be at that time.

It was the biggest crisis Carol and I ever had to deal with. Carol was only twenty-eight. I'd taken her half way around the world for a 'trip of a lifetime'. I couldn't help but think the whole thing seemed very unfair!

At times Carol was naturally terrified by the whole experience. But she also showed amazing courage and seeing how she responded and fought, I just couldn't help but do the same. The only thing that upset me at the time was that although we tried to keep it out of the papers, in the end because of who I was, that proved to be impossible. I kept on playing throughout Carol's illness, she insisted on that. I remember that on the actual day of her operation, I unfortunately had to play a match. Kay and I went to visit Carol straight after the game - thankfully everything had gone well. I can't begin to explain how I felt when I heard that news. Experiences like that put everything into perspective. For only the second time in my life - the only previous occasion was when Dennis Norton had been killed - passing and kicking a ball about didn't seem quite that important anymore. And at that moment I realised that there were more important things in the world than rugby...

When we came away from the hospital after visiting Carol one night, to try and take her mind off things, I asked Kay what she would like to eat. Bearing in mind she was only five years old at the time, I was a little surprised when she replied, 'a chinese'. But I was more than happy with that and I took her to our favourite Chinese restaurant 'The Fountain' in Cronulla. There were quite a few people waiting to go in and we joined on the back of the queue. We'd only been there a few seconds when the owner ran out, took Kay by the hand and led us straight in and sat us down. I can't deny I felt more than a little embarrassed. But things like that were marvellous. Reactions like that one meant such a lot to me. And I still find it amazing when I look back now and realise how highly everyone must have thought of us. They were all so helpful. And when Carol's dad Charlie, and my mum Ivy, went out to visit her they looked after them just as well!

Once Carol's recuperation got underway things soon started to return to normal. And in the end, she couldn't escape the limelight either. She had newspaper articles written about her, was featured with Kay in the 'Sunday Mirror' and also appeared in television programmes describing some of her favourite recipes. These included my favourite dish, roast beef and Yorkshire pudding, and of course, bacon and eggs.

'He'd eat bacon and eggs all the time if I let him,' said Carol - and I probably would...

In 1999 Cronulla invited me back to attend their 'Grand Final' dinner for captains of the club. Although I only captained the side once or twice, Jim Geraghty arranged everything and paid all my expenses. The only thing he asked me to take was a 1974 Great Britain touring jumper for the after dinner auction. He obviously knew what he was doing - it raised a staggering $500.00!

CRONULLA

Top left:
Straight Talk's Jim
Bradfield (left) and
Jim Geraghty,
welcome me to
Cronulla

Middle right: Carol
and I with Sharks'
coach, Johnny Raper

Other pictures:
Training with the
Sharks

CHAPTER FOURTEEN
KING OF CRONULLA
THE 'SUMMER' OF '76

I'd flown to Australia straight after Rovers had completed their season. Their last game was on a Friday evening in April against Oldham - it was my thirty-eighth of the season. Rovers had agreed to let me go to Australia on a free transfer. I was twenty-eight years old. I was due to return to Rovers by the end of August ready for the start of my testimonial season, 1976-77. Numerous Australian clubs had chased me before but this was my first taste of club football down under. Four Sydney clubs had approached me during the 1970 Ashes' tour but only Cronulla had persisted. I hoped I could repay their confidence...

The set-up at Cronulla was very good, exactly what I'd expected from the well organised Sydney league and I was looking forward to the challenge. We had lots of friends in Sydney, the weather was always good and I was going to be well paid for playing the game I loved. I was due to play seventeen games during my stay at Cronulla. And the deal would earn me about four times what I'd received for the season of thirty-eight matches I'd just completed in England. What more could I have asked for - it was an offer I couldn't refuse - and literally the trip of a lifetime!

It was muted in the Australian press that I might have been in line to return for another season after my testimonial year with Rovers. The fact that Carol and Kay were with me seemed to fuel the speculation. Had they come along to see what Australia was like, to make it easier for us all to return there the following year? The answer to that particular question was a definite - No! Quite simply, the opportunity was there to take them with me and we all jumped at it. But the chances of me spending another year with the Sharks looked extremely remote. Having just completed a season back in the top flight with Rovers, after an eye-opening one in the second division, I was determined to make sure Rovers stayed there.

Two summer tours in 1974 and 1975, a second proposed season at Cronulla, followed by another at Rovers, would have meant I'd have played almost four years of non-stop football. And by the end of it I'd have been thirty years old. I must say that prospect didn't sound all that appealing. I also hoped that my following season at Rovers would be one of the greatest I'd experienced there. I'd be returning to exciting times at Craven Park. The club had been rebuilding slowly. I knew it wouldn't be long before they'd be challenging for honours and winning silverware. I wanted to be a part of that.

It would also be my Testimonial Year. I'd always regarded spending ten years at a club and then being awarded a benefit as a great honour. And I couldn't deny that the money would also be very welcome. A benefit season was something I just couldn't contemplate missing a single second of. It was a highlight that every English player dreamed of. And hopefully it would be one of the best years of my career. So right from the start, I made it perfectly clear to everyone at Cronulla that I'd be returning to England at the end of my season with them. But what would happen after that, I couldn't say for certain...

At that moment however, my return to Craven Park seemed a million miles away. All I could think about was playing my first game for the Sharks. I was looking forward to the hard pitches - they'd always suited my game. And to running on top of the ground instead of through it, like we had to during the cold, dismal winters back in England.

The Australian game was so much more physical than the British one. And although that style had obviously never been my forte, playing off the big Aussie forwards I knew would be. I couldn't wait for the kick-off - it was going to be a fantastic experience...

One of the most satisfying things about our season in Cronulla was that nobody had done it like we did it - as a family. It was unique as far as I know. The only other sportsman who went on a sponsorship deal similar to mine was the cricketer, Tony Greig. My signing by Cronulla had completed a unique sporting double for Sydney. For what was certainly the first time ever, the two sports of cricket and rugby league both had their current England captains, Tony Greig and myself, based with Sydney teams.

The trip had been sponsored by one of Cronulla's main backers, the 'Straight Talk Tyre People' - a company with twelve branches throughout the metropolitan area. Our return flights, accommodation and my 'wages' of $150 per week, were all paid by the company. The only cost to the Sharks was my match bonuses.

The sponsorship deal cost 'Straight Talk' a reputed $15,000. And Cronulla lost no time in getting me started in my new role. I'd hardly cleared customs before a number of enthusiastic officials told me I'd been included in the line-up to face Eastern Suburbs the following Sunday. And that the training session had been put back so I'd be able to have a run-out with my new teammates later in the day. I was so keen to get started that I showed up early, although a little bleary eyed, for the evening's session. Earlier I'd tried to catch up with an hour or two of sleep but constant requests for television and press interviews meant even forty winks had been impossible!

Jim Geraghty and Jim Bradfield were the two directors of 'Straight Talk' - and Jim Geraghty was also the chairman of the Sharks' 'ways and means' committee. He sponsored me to go and play for the Sharks. Cronulla didn't do it! And I said to Carol when we landed and got off the plane, there were two ways of looking at the situation - two ways that Jim could handle it. He could have literally just put us in our flat, having done his job and said to us, I'll see you at the end of your stay. Or he could look after us. Fortunately he took the second option - and he was brilliant at it!

Jim and his wife Carmel were lovely people with a lovely family - three older boys, Paul, John and Steve - and a younger boy and girl, Peter and Julie who were great playmates for Kay.

They took us under their wing and really looked after us. Jim rang us every day to say we're doing this or we're doing that, come over and join us if you want to, he was marvellous! We became part of Jim's family and it carried on after we returned to England. When Rovers got to Wembley in 1980 Jim was the first person I rang - to invite him across - and he went to Wembley with us. We still keep in touch to this day, nearly thirty years later.

I remember the first thing he said to me when we first met was,

'You don't know anything about tyres do you?'

Not a lot, I replied, except you put them on a car before you drive it.

'That's what I thought.' Jim exclaimed, 'So I don't want you working in the garage. I want you to go out to the schools around the district and just coach and talk to the kids - Ken Morgan will look after you.' And that's exactly what I did. Ken who worked for Jim was another marvellous man. And he and his wife Loma also became great friends...

A senior Cronulla official, Bob Abbott, had first suggested me when asked by 'Straight Talk' if there was a player who would be worth sponsoring.

'Acting with the full co-operation of my club, I had no hesitation in suggesting Millward, the English skipper,' said Bob. 'This means Roger will play for Cronulla until the end of the Sydney competition. Without the sponsorship of Straight Talk Tyres there is no way Cronulla could have afforded to entice Millward out here,' added Abbott.

As well as playing for the Sharks, I also carried out promotional work for the company and gave coaching seminars throughout the area to schools and junior clubs.

'Straight Talk' was ironically in direct competition to another company that my new coach at Cronulla, Johnny Raper, did advertisements for. But the main reason for me being there was of course to try and help the Sharks survive in the most competitive league in the world. Cronulla weren't going through the best of times in 1976 - far from it. It was common knowledge that they had financial problems, including the rather worrying fact that they owed their players in excess of $50,000 in unpaid wages from the previous season. This had followed the suspension of football club grants by their Leagues club in 1975. But due to the fact that I was sponsored almost entirely by 'Straight Talk' I was happy it was something that wouldn't affect me in any way.

The Sharks' history was certainly an interesting one. Cronulla had only been formed in 1963 - and was one of the youngest clubs in the NRL. The club was originally named Cronulla Caringbah and played in the inter-district competition. The following year they changed their name to Sutherland-

Cronulla. And in 1967, as the NSWRL expanded the game in the rapidly growing Sydney suburbs, Cronulla and Penrith became the first new clubs to be admitted since Parramatta and Manly entered in 1947. They kicked-off their debut season by beating Eastern Suburbs but then managed only two more wins and finished the campaign at the foot of the table.

The formation of Cronulla co-incided with significant changes, both on and off the field in the game of rugby league. By the sixties the Australians had greatly improved the quality of their game on the field and were on a par with the traditionally dominant British. In fact the balance of power had arguably swung towards the Kangaroos. In 1963 the Ausies crushed Britain with a record-breaking 50 points in the second test match at Swinton.

Around the same time an off the field development helped the Australian game in an even more dramatic way. The restrictive betting laws were relaxed and Leagues Clubs in New South Wales were allowed to introduce poker and gambling machines. This immediately gave the clubs a tremendous financial shot in the arm through a new and unexpected revenue source. And it meant the leading Sydney clubs could virtually overnight, financially compete with their British counterparts. And not surprisingly, an ever-increasing number of British players, were soon enticed down under.

In 1963 Parramatta signed Derek Hallas from Leeds as the balance of power began to swing more and more in the green and gold's direction. Like Australia had seen in the past, it was now Britain's turn to watch helplessly as more and more of its' players were tempted to the southern hemisphere. In the sixties and early seventies we lost an entire test team to Sydney clubs. Dick Huddart went to St George, Dave Bolton to Balmain, Malcolm Reilly and Phil Lowe to Manly, Cliff Watson and Tommy Bishop to Cronulla and John Gray to North Sydney. Those names were just a fraction of the players who became rugby league stars on both sides of the world. In 1976 my name was added to the bottom of the list...

At the same time in England, Rugby League had scarcely broken out of its' northern heartland of Yorkshire, Lancashire and Cumberland. Attempts to introduce the professional game in places such as Cardiff and London were tried but only more recently with the relative success of the London Broncos, could it be said to have broken free of the restraints of the M62 corridor.

On the opposite side of the world however in Australia it was a very different story. There, rugby league was the national sport with an amazing number of players, all playing in highly competitive leagues and watched by fantastic crowds. And the importing of top British stars to further boost such a buoyant sport was a great way of making it even better.

It wasn't hard to see the attraction of playing in Australia for many of those leading British players. The thought of playing rugby league at the highest level in a climate totally alien to the frosty, wet and windy conditions of the British winter was an appealing one. And the challenge of testing their skills against the top players on the other side of the world at club level was understandably, a natural ambition for many of them. I was no different.

Two other players from Rovers, Alan Burwell and Phil Lowe, also took the opportunity to taste life down under at the same time as me, making the opposite trip to Artie Beetson who'd started the trend, at Rovers at least, by signing for them as early as 1968.

In the same year, the newly named 'Sharks' became the only club in Sydney to own their own ground when they moved from the Sutherland Oval to Endeavour Field. And the following year they joined the growing band of Aussie clubs who had started importing British Test players, by signing scrum-half, Tommy Bishop.

When Cronulla's coach Ken Kearney retired at the end of the 1969 season, Tommy took over as player-coach and transformed the club. His four years in charge saw the start of the Sharks' climb to become a force in the game.

The 1971 season was one to remember. The Sharks won ten matches and just missed out on a place in the play-offs. But Tommy suffered a serious achilles tendon injury that year otherwise the club could well have done even better. Tommy didn't play again until 1973. But once back in the side along with players such as Greg Pierce, Steve Rogers and John Maguire, Tommy made history by taking the Sharks to their first ever play-offs and ultimately their first Grand Final. There they faced defending Premiers, Manly. Cliff Watson led the Sharks' attempt to defeat the Sea Eagles against all the odds. But in what is regarded as the most brutal Final ever seen Bobby Fulton led Manly to a thrilling 10-7 victory.

Following the achievements of 1973, great things were expected of the Sharks in 1974. But a newly introduced $2,000 ceiling for player payments soon ended that! As a result of the new system, Tommy Bishop and Cliff Watson had little option but to leave the club. Tommy was snapped-up by Brisbane and Cliff went to become captain/coach in Wollongong. Noel Thornton was appointed as the Sharks' new coach, but the club managed only nine wins and finished third from bottom of the table.

Another change saw Johnny Raper installed as coach for the 1975 season. He'd played at St George for eleven seasons from 1959 and done everything in the game. Johnny was always a thrilling, running forward and combined the arts of playmaking and cover tackling. He was inspirational in 33 tests for the Aussies and his display in the second test in 1963 was recognised as one of the finest ever test performances. He continuously cut the Great Britain defence to shreds that day as the Kangaroos ran up a record 50-12 win. He spent his later years playing in Newcastle - a true rugby league immortal.

But even Johnny couldn't resurrect Cronulla's fortunes. The season was almost a carbon copy of the previous one. And the Sharks again missed out on the play-offs for another year. More importantly however, off the field events threatened the very existence of the Cronulla club...

The Sharks had started the construction of a multi-million dollar leagues club but before it was finished, funds had run out. Crippling interest rates then prevented the Sharks from taking out a $1 million loan to complete the building work. The project - and the Sharks - were fortunately saved following the help of the State government and a number of local investors.

Even the players joined in to collect donations at the local shopping centres for the fundraising efforts that included the famous 'Save the Sharks' campaign. And happily the Sharks Leagues club was finally opened in 1977- long after I'd left of course - and two years behind schedule.

I don't think I'd be exaggerating if I said Cronulla weren't having the best of times, compared with their immediate past, when I arrived in 1976. But I recall I didn't need asking twice when they'd invited me over.

Johnny was still coaching the Sharks in 1976. But only a handful of the 1973 Grand Final team remained, among them Steve Rogers and Greg Pierce. Both were still young - and destined to play major roles in the club's future revival. But the 1976 season was one of both consolidation - and change. It also proved to be Johnny's last campaign in charge. He quit the Sharks unceremoniously after another year of relative failure came to a close...

When I arrived at the club I was regarded as one of the game's greatest 'five eighths' as the Australians call a stand-off half. But I soon discovered it hadn't been decided whether I'd play at stand-off or scrum-half. What had been clarified however, was that I wouldn't captain the side. The current Sharks' captain, Greg Pierce would retain that responsibility. But opinions as usual, were split over the decision. Writing in his newspaper column about my imminent arrival, former Australian captain, Ian Walsh, said he thought I should be made the Sharks' skipper.

'The Sharks, despite all their troubles, might just be one of the surprise packets in this competition,' wrote Walsh. 'They are a pretty solid unit now and will improve dramatically when Roger Millward joins the fray. I think the captaincy should go to Millward, England's captain, when he arrives. Greg Pierce is a very fine footballer, but I don't believe he gives the Sharks quite the necessary drive as a captain. The Sharks should also move Pierce back to lock forward. That's his natural and best position,' concluded Walsh. But I hadn't gone to captain the side and it didn't bother me whether I did or not - I had enough on my plate.

It was suggested that I would have at least as much crowd-pulling power as Tommy Bishop had a few years earlier, when he coached the Sharks for three seasons starting in 1970. And my debut could, the Sharks' officials hoped, create a new ground record. The pressure, I suppose you would have to say, was already on. If Cronulla had got their calculations correct, my arrival would not only boost their attacking capabilities but would also greatly increase their attendances. I'm glad to say it did both.

Tommy and I had played together for Great Britain on many occasions and I knew I had a lot to live up to. Our paths had continuously crossed throughout our careers. When I played in my very first test series against Australia in 1967 Tommy partnered me at scrum-half. We hit it off well, both as a halfback combination on the field - and enjoying each others' company off it. We were both then picked to go to Australia in 1968. And although Tommy didn't play on the Ashes winning tour of 1970, I recall that he made a significant contribution to one particular game on that tour - for the opposition! Just after we'd won the second test, the Aussies quickly arranged a mid-week match and Britain played against what they called 'a Sydney Colts side'. They picked Tommy, who was playing at Cronulla at the time as captain of that Colts' side - and we played the game at Endeavour Field. You'd have thought Tommy was an Aussie that day because he went around 'cracking' everybody he could. It was unbelievable!

He went on to become captain-coach of Cronulla and also took them to the 1973 Grand Final before moving to Brisbane. And then of course I arrived to play for the club in 1976. So I think you could say we had followed each other around quite a bit. But although Tommy was a former Great Britain halfback, who'd played for the Sharks - that's where the similarity between the two of us began and ended. And even before I pulled a Cronulla jersey on, I made sure the fans knew that the two of us had little in common as far as our playing styles were concerned. I'm not another Tommy Bishop, I'll just be doing my best to play well and help Cronulla, I said.

It was fantastic to arrive at a place where so much was expected of me. I had the advantage of already being a favourite with the Australian fans following my successful tours with Great Britain. But I knew the Sharks would be hoping I could repeat Tommy's success. And I knew that despite my warning, the Sharks' fans would naturally be quick to compare me with him...

During the mid-seventies, the Sydney competition was taking on a very cosmopolitan appearance both on and off the field. A handful of top English players were due to join Australian clubs for the 1976 season to add to the list of outstanding players, including Phil Lowe, Brian Lockwood, Mick Stephenson and Bill Ashurst, who had already made their mark there.

As well as me, Gary Stephens and Steve Norton were joining Manly, Eric Hughes and Mick Adams were going to Canterbury, John Burke to Souths and David Topliss and Henry Oulton were due to join Penrith. When I arrived there were some very flattering headlines in the papers.

Phillip Jenkins wrote comments in 'Rugby League Week' such as:

'The Little Big Man - Here To Save The Sharks' and 'arguably the most popular Englishman of them all with Aussie crowds' - I had a lot to live up to! But two of my former International colleagues had mixed reservations about the season that lay ahead for me in Sydney.

Chris Hesketh, who'd toured Australia as Great Britain captain two years earlier, feared for my safety and predicted I'd be a marked man in Sydney. He suggested that the big Aussie forwards would be out to 'bury' me' but there was nothing new about that I thought!

'I have played with and against Roger for a long time and I am worried about what could happen to him in Sydney. I just hope he gets a fair deal out there, particularly from the referees, for I have no illusions how the Aussie forwards will try to stop him,' said Chris.

It was of course nice to think that people back home were concerned about my welfare. But I knew what to expect. I'd learned to look after myself, whether it was in a league game in England or a test match in Australia. And I was confident that I was experienced enough to be able to stay out of any serious trouble. I wasn't bothered about the possibility of being closely

SHARKS-1976
Back row: Warren Fisher, Fred Dennehy, Paul Khan, John McMartin, Glen Stolzenhein
Middle row: Steve Kneen, Steve Rogers, Greg Mullane, Dave Chamberlin
Front row: Greg Pierce, Steve Edmonds, Roger Millward, Peter Ryan
MY SHARKS' DEBUT
Below: Tackling Easts' Bruce Pickett in my debut for Cronulla

marked. I always thought if the opposition was paying more attention to me than they should, then it followed they were leaving someone else alone. Nor was I overly concerned that I'd be facing one of the leading sides, Eastern Suburbs, in my Sharks' debut game. I'd always thought that you knew what to expect when you faced the best sides. It was the poorer teams that tended to spring the 'surprises'. But I cannot deny it was a little unexpected when I arrived on the Wednesday and discovered I'd be playing against Easts at Endeavour Field on the following Sunday. I'd played my last match of the season at Craven Park on the previous Friday evening and wouldn't have been too disheartened had I been given a weekend's rest. But taking on the best sides that the Sydney league had to offer was after all what I was there for - and I couldn't wait to get started!

It was great to be back in Australia. I'd been looking forward to it for weeks. In fact the last few matches I played for Rovers reminded me of the times before, when I'd been preparing to go on tour. The games seemed to get harder and harder the nearer I got to the trip - and I was glad when they were over.

Another Great Britain teammate and friend, Malcolm Reilly, who'd guested for Manly with outstanding success in the early 1970s sounded slightly more confident about my chances when he gave his opinion about the impending ' English Invasion' of Australia for the 1976 season.

'I can't put any more raps on Roger than what have already been put on. He's been established in international football for a number of years and at the moment he's playing really well for Hull Kingston Rovers,' said Malcolm.

'I'm sure he'll be a real asset for Cronulla. He'll open up the three-quarter line for them - I think this is what they're expecting - and he's a real opportunist, as the Australian public has already seen. If there are any tries going begging, he'll have them. My first words of advice to any half-backs who hope to cope with this character is, get some spiked running shoes on because he's pretty fast. Millward comes through off the forwards very quickly and before you know it, he's in a wide-open space. And if he has anyone with him there's a try laid on because normally, when he breaks, there's only the full-back between him and the line. But even in signing Millward I don't think for a second that Cronulla has got the answer to everything. There's no one man in Sydney who can win a Premiership. It has to be, as Jack Gibson has proved, a team effort. You can have brilliant individuals, like Bobby Fulton and Phil Lowe, and still come unstuck. At the same time, I don't think there will be many half-backs in Sydney who will be able to keep Roger quiet for long. '

'I think he'll be looking forward to meeting Tommy Raudonikis again because the last time they played against each other they were involved in a bit of a tussle at Headingley in the last international between England and Australia. Roger ended up getting sent off and I must admit that I thought it was a bit unjust. I think he's still feeling a little upset about that and he'll be out to prove something to Raudonikis... But its Roger's pace which sets him apart and gives him the name he's got. When he goes through that gap he's really motoring,' concluded Malcolm.

I recall my biggest regret at the time was that I had to watch the Challenge Cup Final on television. Normally I would have made the annual trip to Wembley with a party from my 'local' in Kippax. But in May 1976 I had to watch the St Helens versus Widnes clash from my armchair, 12,000 miles away. Eric Hughes was allowed to play before going to Australia for a season with Canterbury - but Widnes still lost. In the end I enjoyed Saints' 20-5 victory but I have to admit it wasn't a patch on being there and watching it 'live'.

Thankfully my Aussie career got off to an excellent start against Premiers, Easts, during the Anzac Day weekend at Endeavour Field - but not a winning one. I didn't know whom I'd be facing at halfback virtually up to kick-off time. Two internationals, John Mayes and Kevin Junee had been bracketed to face me. Both however had missed the Easts' previous match because of injuries and their chances of recovering in time were unclear. The whole thing was shrouded in mystery but Mayes seemed to be my most likely opponent. Nursing a damaged shoulder he assessed himself as being 95% fit and appeared more optimistic than Junee who was nursing an injured shoulder. And so it proved when Junee finally dropped out of contention on the eve of the game. When my Sharks debut duly arrived on Sunday April 25, the gate was an incredible 15,380 - more than Cronulla's first two home attendances against Manly and Parramatta put together! Before the game I was introduced to the local State member Mr Ian Griffiths. But there was a far more familiar face in the Roosters' ranks opposing me when I ran out onto the pitch. We'd played alongside each other for Rovers in the late sixties, and against each other much more recently, as captains of our respective countries. I'd had more than a few interesting encounters with my old pal and adversary Artie Beetson, over the years.

The previous day Artie had given me a warm welcome to Sydney - thankfully only verbal - with just a hint of a warning thrown in. Easts may have been the current Premiers but Artie suggested they weren't having things all their own way in 1976.

'As if we didn't have enough troubles without the Sharks timing the arrival of that great little player Roger Millward, to coincide with their clash with the Roosters at Endeavour Field tomorrow', he said in a pre-match interview.

'We know from Millward's previous ventures here with British teams that he has no trouble adapting to Australian conditions. In fact, they seem to suit his will-o'-the-wisp running style. Roger and I were rival captains in last year's World Series and no one knows more than I do how many times he has stood between us and victory. So let me simply welcome him to our premiership scene and assure him he won't find his first match any picnic.' It was the sort of reception I expected from Artie...

We lost the game but it turned out to be a memorable one, especially for Artie. But afterwards, in the dressing room, he had to admit he didn't recall much about the opening forty minutes of the match at all. He was pole-axed in a first half tackle and spent some time in 'dreamland' for the first time in his career. He laid motionless on the turf for three or four minutes following a late, high tackle from a Sharks' forward. But he recovered enough to help Easts to a 20-5 lead before retiring at half-time. Although he was obviously groggy and at times played as if he was in a trance, his amazing and instinctive overhead pass set up a try for the Roosters' fullback, Eric Ferguson. Peter Fitzgerald grabbed another only seconds later as Easts scored two tries in as many minutes just before the break. That double blow virtually ended our chances of recording a famous, if unlikely win - the Roosters eventually running out as 22-11 victors against us. The main problem I had during the game wasn't as predicted the Easts' forwards, but the blistering heat! I was unlucky to make my first appearance on one of the hottest days of the year - and remember finishing the game looking a lot more like a beetroot than when I'd started it!

My 'crafty debut' - including a try-saving tackle on winger, Bruce Pickett - and our skipper, Greg Pierce's 'non-stop effort' were reported as the side's high spots. We certainly had the better of the second half and finished far stronger than the Roosters. And although the Sharks' record crowd had seen their side beaten, they'd obviously enjoyed my performance and I think they went home happy.

The good thing for me was that I knew I could play a lot better. I'd made my debut at scrum-half and had more than a few problems with referee, Jack Danzey's interpretation of scrum rules. For my next match, I was chosen in my regular position of stand-off. One other thing I was happy about was the way Artie had reacted to the well documented 'tackle' that had resulted in him missing the second half of the game. He insisted there would be no retribution, no 'get square' measures, when the Sharks and the Roosters met again. It was good to think we both thought the same about those type of incidents - there are plenty of players I could name who didn't. Artie knew very well who had hit him with a late tackle.

'I'm well aware who sent me on my way, although it's hard to believe he wasn't at the wheel of a truck at the time,' he joked. 'But anyone who thinks I'm the type who harbours a grudge for months on end just to settle old scores, is way off the mark. The tackle may have been a bit late, but that's part of this game I love so much, and like many other players who have been flattened before me, I just have to accept it.'

I remember thinking that I could have said those exact words on numerous occasions, following many misdemeanours I'd been subjected to during my career. And I would have meant them. I also couldn't help thinking however, that saying them in the cold light of day in his regular newspaper article was one thing. But sticking to that philosophy in the heat of a match, especially for somebody of Artie's nature, might be an entirely different proposition...

I was happy with my debut, I think I made an impressive start and all the comments following it were complimentary.

'Roger is something of a mixture of some of the outstanding attributes of Bishop and Saints' great 'war-horse' Billy Smith.

'I could be buying myself a big argument, but I regard Millward as a more talented player than Tommy Bishop, and that's about the biggest rap I could give any half-back.' enthused Artie.

'His timing was fantastic. He put so much thought into his game. I expect him to lift Cronulla out of their rut. I had my hands full trying to pin him down.' said Roosters' Ron Coote.

'He is an embarrassment to other players. He shows up their limitations. The NSWRL are fortunate to have such a glamour player here to further boost the record crowds.' wrote Frank Hyde.

'A great acquisition for Sydney football. He is so unpredictably brilliant that he not only caught Easts napping but also most of his own side! He'll be a constant headache to the opposition.' added Keith Barnes.

The final 'pat on the back' came from my old mate, Tommy Bishop.

'Cronulla hit the jackpot when they brought Roger Millward to Australia - but they won't reap the full benefit from him. It is almost pointless having Millward for only one season. Millward would send the Sharks to the top of the ladder in three years. But Cronulla will never be able to have him for any length of time. His club Hull Kingston Rovers would put a $40,000 transfer fee on his head and his wife would be too homesick. But while he's here he'll give Cronulla plenty of value. He will be a turnstile clicker if ever there was one,' he predicted.

During my second week at Cronulla, coach Johnny Raper informed me he was moving me to stand-off for my next match. He'd thought I'd be a lot less under the referee's gaze at 'five-eighth'

'Millward is outstanding value, whether he's in a winning or losing side. It is up to me to build a side around him - a side that can capitalise on his attacking genius. He is so fit. He has just played thirty-eight games with Hull Kingston Rovers. He could not have arrived at a better time,' commented Johnny. But I couldn't fail to smile at his following prediction. 'I'd like to make a long-range forecast. I think Roger will be back with the Sharks again next year even though he's on a one-year term.' he said.

My second game for the Sharks was significant for three main reasons. It provided me with my first win in a Cronulla jersey. It gave me my first and only try of my time with the Sharks. And it also highlighted that late tackles were something that not just Artie Beetson had to contend with.

The away match at Penrith couldn't have got off to a better start for me. In only the second minute I stabbed the ball through the Panthers' defence and regathered to give us a three-point lead. But we then had to wait until a minute from half-time before we got our second. As the interval approached, I carved out an opening for our full-back, Warren Fisher to score, and we led 12-7 at the break. And there was no doubting our superiority after the interval. The game swung our way two minutes after the restart when I combined with Greg Mullane who passed to Dave Chamberlin - and Warren Fisher raced over for his second try under the posts. Steve Rogers' conversion put us 17-7 ahead and virtually out of Penrith's reach. It was the start of a tremendous second-half performance We ran in four more tries and ended as 28-10 winners.

It was widely regarded that I had much the better of my opposite number, fellow 'Brit' David Topliss. But I didn't manage to finish the game, after having to leave the field twice in the second period, following late tackles. After the first one I spent four minutes on the sidelines but begged Johnny to let me go back on. Ten minutes later I supplied another pass to Fisher who put Steve Edmonds over for our fifth try. But I then received another late shot that meant I missed the closing minutes after being led off again. Although I was slightly concussed at the end, I was happy I'd got my first win and adamant I'd be playing the following week against Newtown. After the game Johnny appealed for greater protection for top players.

'The public want to see the best players on the field, and its up to linesmen and referees to make sure they can complete the match,' said Raper.

'I was disgusted at the treatment Penrith dished out to Millward. It was a disgrace to this great game. Millward was the victim of blatant late tackles. He won't last the season unless referees stamp out the thugs. Interest in rugby league is skyrocketing but it will soon wane if the players of the calibre of Roger Millward are continuously 'spotted'.' And he also warned Manly, Penrith's next opponents, to beware of their 'rough-house' tactics.

'I hope Manly have better luck with their costly imports, Gary Stephens and Steve Norton. Penrith have an unpredictable attitude towards English players. They don't mind recruiting them - but delight in trying to knock their heads off when opposed by them. Beware of the Panthers, Manly. With Phil Lowe, Norton and Stephens in your side you'll need lots of plasters,' he warned.

I'll admit my third game, away at Newtown, was a bit of an anti-climax. We lost 22-18. We didn't appear to be a team who could reproduce our home form away from Endeavour Field. The theory proved true throughout the season. After our rare away win against Penrith, we beat South Sydney 39-5, Balmain 17-14, Penrith 16-15, Canterbury 24-8, North Sydney 19-8, Newtown 28-11 and Wests 20-17, all at home.

I was voted player of the round against both South Sydney and Canterbury. I think my performance against Canterbury was undoubtedly my best for the Sharks. They were going very well in the competition - and I just couldn't believe the game I had that day. I just couldn't put a foot wrong. Everything just fell into place. I assisted in three tries, kicked seven goals from seven attempts and we beat Canterbury easily. They were near the top of the competition and we were only mid-table and nobody expected us to do anything with them. But those away victories always seemed to elude us. Of our nine wins only two were away from home. We also managed a draw at Canterbury but ended the season in eighth position and out of the play-offs.

Unfortunately a rib injury forced me to miss the last two games of the season, so we left Australia a fortnight earlier than planned. There was no point in staying any longer as I wouldn't have been able to play any more matches. So I got in touch with Rovers, and told them I'd be back for the start of our season, the start of my benefit season in fact.

During my short stay with the Sharks I scored 17 goals and a try - 37 points. But I like to think I also played an important part in helping Cronulla move forward a great deal, both on and off the field that summer.

During my season with the Sharks, the Endeavour Field attendances improved greatly. And as well as the rugby I played, I also personally met over 5,000 kids at thirty-five schools, which I visited to help their Rugby League training programmes.

I made a guest appearance for a Charity night for an injured Rugby Union player. I drew the winning raffle ticket at the Netball Association - and faced up to 800 girls! I presented trophies to the N.S.W. Police and Citizens Boys Club Soccer Week to 700 boys. And I presented the 'Straight Talk Tyre Trophy' at the Orange (N.S.W.) Jockey Club.

As well as numerous other promotional duties for Straight Talk I also made an appearance at Grace Brothers Stores and spoke at the Sydney Rotary.

I held 'clinics' and gave talks at local clubs and schools and Endeavour Field, giving instruction, hints about training, or just talked to the kids about my career in rugby league. I presented trophies on sports days, attended just about every sport's competition you could think of - and ploughed through countless dinners! Not a bad workload for a shy, little Englishman - and all in less than four months! By the end of my stay it was frightening to think what I'd packed in to such a short time. It had been non-stop - but I'd enjoyed every minute of it! And after their initial traumas, I know Carol and Kay did as well.

It was strange to look back over our visit. When we'd first arrived, they were both crying their eyes out and wanting to go home. But by the end of the trip they were crying because they had to go home! They loved it that much. After Carol's operation she finished up wanting to stay in Cronulla even longer than we'd planned.

So from the first days' problems - and with all that Carol went through - it may sound a stupid thing to say but our stay in Cronulla was probably one of the best few months of our lives. It was a brilliant time. We were looked after superbly. But we had to return to Britain. I had to start my testimonial season with Rovers. And more importantly, Carol had to commence her radiotherapy and chemo treatment. As soon as we got back to Yorkshire we went straight to the hospital with a note from the specialist in Australia, to arrange Carol's ongoing treatment in England.

Carol, Kay and I had arrived in Cronulla on April 21 - and left nearly four months later. Carol's dad and my mum, were still with us. We all flew out of Sydney on Monday August 16 at 3.30pm on flight QF 1.

But we'd return only three years later...

CHAPTER FIFTEEN
HARRY? HE COULD HAVE DONE ANYTHING

I returned from my summer with Cronulla to one of the most eventful and traumatic seasons I ever had. The events that had happened to me on the other side of the world in Australia had changed my life forever. Back in England, it was changed again although by very different circumstances.

My testimonial year was a great success - I received an estimated £10,000 - and Rovers finished fourth in the league after some very encouraging performances. But it was another season marred by tragedy! Where everything else paled into insignificance when compared to the shattering event which took place the week before our Challenge Cup Semi-Final against Widnes...

Harry Poole was one of the most popular players to ever wear a Hull Kingston Rovers' jersey. He played in a hundred and twenty three games for Rovers, scoring twenty-seven tries. He'd been a leading figure during Rovers' revival during the early sixties and led the side out for their first ever appearance at Wembley in May 1964. He was transferred to Leeds in 1965, the year before I arrived at Craven Park. And less than another year passed before he was named as the Captain of the 1966 Tour to Australia and New Zealand.

Harry's career was continuously hampered by injuries. And even down under, the injury bug robbed him of the honour of leading Great Britain in any of the three tests against Australia. He was fit enough however for the two tests against New Zealand in Auckland - Britain won them both.

After his playing career came to an end Harry coached at Hunslet and Castleford. He returned to Craven Park when Arthur Bunting resigned as Rovers' coach only days before we were due to face Leeds at Headingley in the 1975 Yorkshire Cup Final. But with only a few days in his new position before the game, he just failed to take Rovers to another Cup Final victory. Leeds beat us narrowly that day 15-11. It was the only County final I'd lost out of the five I'd played in. I'd won against Featherstone, Hull, Castleford and Wakefield, the latter only twelve months earlier when we'd been a second division club.

Once in control however, Harry showed that none of the enthusiasm and commitment that had been his trademarks as a player had left him. He was immediately given full powers of team selection, the first time a coach had had the responsibility since the days of Bryn Knowlden in the early fifties. Up until Harry's appointment, the board had picked the team. That was the old way but when I became coach it was something that I never agreed with because how could they know what the players had been like in training? Or what they were feeling like? Or tactically how they fitted into my plans? Harry's arrival changed all that. He took over from Arthur who had resigned. I'm not blaming Arthur because his hands had been tied, he had to do things in a certain way. He'd be on the training pitch with us and get a call half way through the session - and the 'selectors' would tell him which players they'd chosen for the next match. That was the system then. That's how it used to be. But I think that's one of the biggest problems Arthur had. He didn't have the responsibility of choosing the team and I'm sure that must have been very undermining. As a player you needed somebody to talk to. And to know that's where it began and ended. That's what Harry believed in too. Everybody respected him and those kids would have died for him...

The season that Harry arrived at Craven Park things started to change! It was our first season back in the First Division. Attitudes changed - he introduced a new regime - the transformation was nothing less than remarkable! Harry started a new movement off at Craven Park. Everything had been put in position for the future. His principles were in place. He'd done it all. He made such a great impact in such a short time. Harry did things his way and I know the fact that he could pick the players who he wanted to play for him helped him enormously. But the build-up to the 1977 Challenge Cup Semi-Final sadly saw all that disappear!

Only days before Rovers were due to play Widnes, Harry died from a heart attack at the age of just forty-one!

It was undoubtedly the saddest day in the history of Hull Kingston Rovers and cast a shadow over the rest of the season.

I'd always dreamed of becoming Rovers' coach, but I remember the day that I was appointed as Harry's successor, I felt absolutely nothing. The whole thing seemed of no importance. Once again fate had put the triumphs - and the trials and tribulations of the sport we all love - cruelly into perspective! Whether Harry would have guided Rovers to the success they achieved after his tragic loss will always be open to conjecture. What can be said with absolute certainty is that his players thought the world of him, as did the supporters. And Harry would have given it his best shot - it wasn't in his make-up to do otherwise...

I'd actually been with him on the night he died. Harry lived in Townville in Castleford and we'd arranged to meet and go to watch Castleford play Widnes at Wheldon Road. With Rovers due to face Widnes the following Saturday, it was obviously a great opportunity to take a last look at them before the cup-tie. We watched the game and then went in the clubhouse. After a couple of beers and a discussion about what we'd seen, we went home. It was the last time I saw him.

The next morning his brother rang me at 5 a.m. to tell me he'd died!

I just couldn't believe it! I'd been with him only six hours earlier. It was such a shock. And the loss to the club could never quite be put into perspective. He was doing such a fantastic job with Rovers and that was proved not only by what was going on out on the park every weekend but also by the people who were coming into the club.

The attitude from the players was tremendous, they all wanted to be there. Harry was steeped in rugby league and loved talking to people about it. Even the hardest people respected Harry and wouldn't mess him about. What might he achieved in the following years? I honestly think he could have done anything...

I was the only one that he would travel over to Hull with because I was the captain and a fixture in the team. Which was quite right, as far I was concerned. I know later when I was coach I would always drive across to Hull on my own. I didn't want anyone to think I had any favourites. If I picked anybody in the team it was on merit - not because he was a mate of mine. So I'd always travel on my own, even though there were usually about nine or ten other lads travelling across at the same time.

The journey might have been a little lonelier - but I decided that was how it had to be.

After Harry's death, I was appointed 'temporary coach' and although we lost 14-5 against Widnes in the Semi-Final at Headingley the following weekend, I had to continue what he'd started, things had to carry on...

Allan Agar and David Watkinson were signed during the 1976-77 season. Allan arrived from Hunslet for £3,000 and David from York amateur club, Heworth. What a pair of incredible 'bargains' they turned out to be!

They both became legends at Hull KR, there's no two ways about that! When you talk about Allan and Watkie you immediately link them with the best years that Rovers ever had. In each of the following seasons - the last three I played - Rovers won a major trophy! They were very hardworking, sensible and exemplary professionals. They were also both winners. They knew what they wanted from the game and exactly what had to be done to achieve their aims.

That was marvellous as far as I was concerned because when you've got two players in your side like that it rubs off. Most of that team I'd have to say was equally as professional. There was the 'odd joker in the pack', but that is usual in most dressing rooms. It was something I didn't have a problem with - in fact quite the opposite. Having someone who can relieve the tension at the right time can be an incredible benefit to a team. And the way that set of players started to mould themselves into a team, who wanted to become totally professional, to do everything in the right way and to become the best players they could be, was spot on. All I had to do was to find different ideas and training methods to help them move forward and achieve those goals. Allan and David were both totally dedicated players - and both great leaders. And although it's easy to say that now, when they've won everything and proved themselves over and over again throughout their tremendous careers, I knew it from the first day they arrived at the club. When I was 'out of the game' for a while at Wembley, Allan organised things and kept things together. It was great to have someone on your side who could just take over and get on with it.

'Watkie' was even easier to sum up - a true professional who simply hated losing! He later took over from Len as Rovers' captain, and his professionalism and leadership qualities were rightly recognised when he was also picked for Great Britain. It would have been an injustice had he achieved anything less!

Another of the season's signings, Colin Tyrer, who had joined us from Wigan, topped the club goal kickers with 52 and Ged Dunn, who was again an ever-present in the side, crossed for 26 tries ahead of Clive Sullivan with 21 and Steve Hartley with 17. But the season ended controversially when Rovers were 'booted out' of the Premiership Trophy after beating Warrington at Craven Park in the first round. The reason for our expulsion was that Phil Lowe had played for us when allegedly his return from his Australian club, Manly, hadn't been ratified.

In many ways that disappointing ending just about summed up the season. It was definitely one I couldn't have been blamed for wanting to forget. But looking back on it now it was one where I learned a lot about both myself and the people around me. We were gathering a good squad of players together at Craven Park. And I knew there was a lot of success just around the corner to look forward to...

Before my first full season as Rovers' coach however, I had another trip to Australia to enjoy. I hoped my fifth tour down under would hopefully see Great Britain return as World Champions. And but for one of the most notorious refereeing decisions in rugby league history, we would have!

My Craven Park colleague, Len Casey, was also selected. And I recall when we got the news of our selection, Len and I were on our way up to Workington with John Sexton, the Hull Daily Mail reporter. Two other players who played a significant part in my future were also in the touring party, Phil Hogan of Barrow and a young George Fairbairn from Wigan.

Reg Parker was again the Manager, David Watkins was the coach, Bill Francis was on the trip and best of all England and Wales were back together as Great Britain!

We won our first two matches of the tournament, 23-4 against France in Auckland and 30-12 against New Zealand in Christchurch. But we came unstuck in our final group match when the Australians beat us 19-5. I scored a try in all three of our games and George kicked a total of fourteen goals. And as the second placed team we then had to play the Australians again.

I was captain and Billy Thompson was the referee in the final. But we were beaten again by Australia when Billy 'ballsed' it up. Stuart Wright had broken away and was in the clear, he would definitely have scored. But Billy called him back for an infringement by the Aussies, when he should have played the advantage and waved play-on. He brought us back, put a scrum down and gave us head and feed!

'I blew for an Australian offence and before I realised what had happened, Wright was away,' said Billy after the match.

'I knew straight away that I had made a mistake and should have allowed play to continue.'

It was one of the few times I can remember a referee admitting he'd made a mistake. We all make mistakes from time to time and I admired his honesty. He was in my mind, a great referee - and later of course, a great after dinner speaker. The decision cost us the match - we lost 13-12 - and ultimately cost us the World Championship as well.

It was heartbreaking. They were a good set of lads, they were all playing well and but for that controversial decision we'd have finished as World Champions...

ANOTHER TOUR, ANOTHER BREAK...
Great Britain's Bill Francis, left, and David Ward, right, watch as I break through the
Australian defence in 1977

TESTIMONIAL YEAR
Receiving my testimonial cheque in 1977 from, left to right:
Frank Morton, Malcolm Willcox, John Sexton and Colin Hutton

FLOODLIT FINAL SUCCESS
Rovers won their first-ever
major trophy in 1977, the
BBC2 Floodlit Trophy,
following a 26-11 defeat of
St Helens in the final

Kay and I, with the
Floodlit Trophy

CHAPTER SIXTEEN
GLORY
DAYS

Rugby league became an even bigger part of my life in 1977. I finished at the pit where I'd worked for fourteen years, to become Rovers' full-time coach. I can't begin to describe how proud I felt. I was still only twenty-nine. I know a lot of people suggested I didn't have enough experience to be successful. But I like to think I proved a few of them wrong!

In my first full season as captain-coach we won the BBC2 Floodlit Cup - beating St Helens in the final - and for the second season in succession we finished fourth out of sixteen teams in the first division.

Saints, coincidentally had been the team I'd beaten with Castleford in my only previous floodlit final, in the competition's inaugural season, twelve years earlier. It was the first major trophy I'd won, the only one in fact I'd won at Castleford. They'd gone on to make themselves uncrowned 'floodlit kings' with four wins from the first dozen competitions, including a hat-trick of wins in the first three years.

The Floodlit Trophy had been introduced in the 1965-66 season and was in its' thirteenth season. And thirteen certainly proved lucky for Rovers!

When we beat St Helens 26-11 in the 1977 final on December 13 - it not only provided a fantastic night's entertainment for the success-starved Craven Park fans - but also the club's first-ever, major trophy.

I was fortunate to be part of a tremendous team performance that night - we produced some irresistible rugby - and with tries from Ged Dunn 2, Mike Smith, Steve Hartley and Paul Rose - and four goals from Dave Hall, the result was never in doubt.

It was the first time we'd beaten Lancashire opposition in a cup final since the League Championship of 1925.

There was a good crowd at Craven Park and we fully deserved our victory. The way we played that season, beating St Helens was a perfect way to say we'd 'arrived'. We're here now - this is where we start. And anything under that performance from then on wasn't good enough. We'd set a benchmark that night. We'd got there and achieved something. But we then had to move on to more success. It was like a carnival atmosphere on the field after the game - just brilliant. I think two girls finished up in the bath with the players afterwards...

With the signings that we brought in the club was obviously progressing. The directors wanted to go places, they might not have been breaking the bank with the players that they got, but to their credit, they got players who wanted to play for Rovers. That was one of the main things we insisted on. They might have been the best players in the world but if they didn't want to be there and they didn't like the travelling over to Craven Park then they were never going to be happy at the club. We only brought in players who wanted to be at the club - who wanted to play for Hull KR. Everybody we signed from then on had ambition. They all wanted to succeed in the game and were professional about their career...

My cousin, Brian Lockwood was signed from Wakefield Trinity and Steve Hubbard joined from Hull & East Riding RUFC. They'd become a famous 'double act' in the not too distant future.

I was very pleased the day Brian signed for Rovers, I'd played with him throughout my early career in the Castleford Under 17s, 'A' team and first team. But if anyone had told us on the day he arrived at Craven Park that in the near future we'd share a 'dream occasion' together that would be the climax of my career, I'd have taken the prediction with more than a pinch of salt. Brian had already experienced two wins in Wembley Cup Finals with Castleford. Incredibly he would go on and enjoy two more - and with two different clubs before his playing days came to a close.

On the International front, I captained England against both Wales and France. Colin Tyrer was again the club's top goal-kicker with 54, and the ever-improving Steve Hartley was the top try-scorer with 17.

My second season as coach was even more amazing. We finished at the top of the league for the first time in over 50 years. It was an incredible achievement!

The season opened with some frantic transfer dealings. Len Casey was sold for a world record fee of £25,000 to Bradford Northern, with Paul Harkin joining Rovers as part of the deal. And Rovers then broke the record again paying Barrow £35,000 for International forward, Phil Hogan. Geoff Clarkson also joined us from Wakefield for £4,000.

Geoff was the type of forward every Championship-winning side needs. The type of player perhaps we hadn't had enough of for a few seasons. He was a smashing bloke, very limited as regards playing rugby - and he would have been the first to tell you that - but could he tackle? He knew exactly why he was there, knew exactly what he had to do - and he just got on with it. But a player who recognised his limitations I always thought, was better and more useful than one who didn't.

Geoff was a big tough forward on the field but off it he was as nice as pie, a brilliant kid. He was so polite, so well mannered and well spoken. And he had a very good job. He was a civil engineer, but you'd never have guessed it when you watched him charging around a rugby pitch!

I remember one game in particular that epitomised what Geoff was all about. It was the match away at Leigh at the end of December. They were the sort of matches we had to win if we were to win the Championship - and thanks to Geoff, we did.

There was a lad called Billy Platt playing for Leigh at loose-forward that day and he was knocking everybody about - and scored two first-half tries. We weren't playing anything like we said we were going to play and at half-time I went bloody crazy!

There were cups of tea flying everywhere in that changing room as I demanded to know who had decided to change the game plan?

We need a good hit on that Platt - he's got to 'go' as soon as possible, I demanded. We'd been losing 10-3 at one stage and although we led by a point at the break, I don't really know how we'd managed it - we'd never really been in the game...

The very first tackle in the second half was a memorable one! Geoff hit this lad, Platt - completely legally - and he just went! He just stood there at first, looking round. But he then had to go off and we finished up winning 21-13. I'll always remember that tackle of Geoff's - it was definitely the turning point...

But it was only one of hundreds of memories from what turned into a groundbreaking season for the club and another sensational year for me. In October I scored two tries in our 19-14 win at Salford to become the only player to ever score 200 tries for Rovers. I crossed for the record-breaker in the opening minutes and added another in the second half. But I didn't even know I was near to setting a record. I'd never gone after records, I got a bigger thrill creating tries for other people. The win maintained our unbeaten start to the campaign and we leap-frogged St Helens to take over at the top of the table.

By November 11 we'd won our first eight league games of the season. And our sensational start just went on and on. We only lost two of our first twenty matches. That amazing run included an 18-10 victory at Workington in February - it was the first time we'd ever won there! And we achieved a record win at Craven Park when we beat Oldham 67-11 in the first round of the John Player Trophy.

Steve Hartley topped the Rugby League try-scorers list with thirty-five. Whilst Phil Lowe and Clive Sullivan also had fantastic seasons and finished with 24 and 21 respectively. Steve's tally was his best ever for the club and included five tries in a match when we beat Huddersfield 57-3 on Good Friday at Craven Park. Steve Hubbard, who shared the goalkicking duties with me that year, kicked twelve goals in the same game and ended the season, his first in senior football, with 123 points.

We finally clinched our first Championship in fifty-four years with away victories at Castleford and Featherstone. And although we actually lost our final three matches, all away from home, we finished at the top of the pile, two points ahead of our nearest rivals, Warrington.

It was a fantastic feeling to lift that trophy. We'd reached the next rung of the ladder, arrived at the next level, but what was even better was that I knew we were destined to go a lot higher!

An old friend of mine at Castleford, John Sheridan, once said Hull K.R.

would never win anything because they couldn't 'travel'. I suppose at the particular time he said it and with our record, he might have had a point, especially regarding the league. But I'm glad to say we proved that theory wrong! And more than that, we did it in devastating style!

When we won the Championship it was a big feather in our cap. I've always thought that winning the Championship is the greatest accolade a club can achieve. When you compare how much soccer clubs get for winning the title, I think it should be the same with rugby league because that's the result of a long, hard season's work.

You can win the Challenge Cup by winning only five matches. And with the luck of the draw, some years it can be relatively easy. But to win the title, it takes a whole season of hard work and commitment. That consistency and dedication, should in my opinion, be rewarded a lot more than it is.

Our victory I supposed proved just how difficult it is to win the Championship - it was the first time we'd finished at the top of the league since 1925! The achievement reflected the work of everyone at Craven Park, from the board of directors, the players and coaches, right through to the stewards and the people who worked in the bars and restaurants. And also every single fan who came to support us that season. They were all a part of it. Everything at the Club was organised superbly well at that time - it was totally professional from top to bottom...

On the International scene however, the season turned out very differently. When I'd made my Great Britain debut, I never imagined I'd be lucky enough to play International rugby for over twelve years. But I like to think I was still playing as well as when I'd started - although in a very different way - when I made my last test appearance in 1978.

During the autumn, I played in all three home tests against the Aussies but Great Britain unfortunately again lost the series in the deciding match. The Aussies won the first test at Wigan 15-9 on October 21 and we squared the series a fortnight later at Bradford 18-14. Again Britain stood only eighty minutes away from winning the Ashes but again we fell at the final hurdle when Australia stormed to an impressive 23-6 victory at Headingley.

But Rovers' achievements that season were reflected when the Great Britain party for the 1979 Australian Tour was named. I was selected for my sixth tour, along with four other Rovers' players, Phil Hogan, Brian Lockwood, Mike Smith and David Watkinson.

Brian had a great season with Rovers and also played for England against both Wales and France and for Great Britain against Australia.

Later, on the summer tour he was selected as substitute against New Zealand. But things didn't turn out as well for me. I was carried off with a torn cartilage in our 20-11 win against Northern Division in Tamworth. And after making only three appearances I returned to England. My sixth tour in eleven years turned out to be my last. I never played International football again...

CHAPTER SEVENTEEN
WE'RE THERE!
SEASON 1979-1980

Another amazing season with a very special climax followed...

Early in the season on December 18 - 8,000 fans saw us lose 13-3 in the last ever Floodlit Trophy final at the Boulevard. But we never even attended that night - we didn't 'turn up' for that game. It was a big disappointment! I was still out with a broken jaw - but it was matches like that one that worried me! We had the ability to get to the final but then produced a flat display like that when we should have been buzzing. It was impossible to explain! We never really competed and I started to think how we could change things to make sure it didn't become a habit. It was something that became an obsession with me. To find different ways of training and to introduce new methods that would keep the players focused...

Rovers went on to finish the season in seventh place out of sixteen in the league. Steve Hubbard beat Neil Fox's points in a season record with 366 (138 goals and 30 tries). He also received the Greenall Whitley-Sunday People award as rugby league's joint top try scorer. Len Casey rejoined the club from Bradford Northern for another world record fee of £38,000 and Mick Crane was signed from Leeds for £9,000. Paul Rose received £16,000 for his Testimonial Year. Roy Holdstock was voted R.L. Young Player of The Year. And Craven Park saw numerous changes including new floodlights, a new supporters' club and office block - and improvements to the dressing rooms.

But the only thing any Rovers' fan remembers about 1980 was May 3! I remember it as the unforgettable climax of the season and the highlight of my glittering career. It was the match that I'd waited sixteen years to play in, the Wembley Challenge Cup Final. It didn't arrive until my very last season - and my last ever game as a first team player...

The final against arch-rivals Hull is now of course part of Rovers' folklore. And although a club the '10-5 Club' was named after the historic scoreline - and people still remember the camaraderie and idiosyncrasies that made the day so special - no one can actually appreciate what the game meant to the players who took part. And especially for two of the Rovers' side in particular. Those two individuals were of course Clive Sullivan and I. We'd

141

both enjoyed fantastic careers and although we'd both achieved everything else the game had to offer - neither of us had ever appeared in a Wembley Cup Final. After the semi-final win it was just one hell of a feeling. The first person I ran over to after we'd beaten Halifax was Clive. I used to say every year - this is the year we're going to Wembley! And I'm sure Clive said it too. Year after year I said it. But year after year it just didn't happen. In 1980 however it was somehow different. All the lads kept saying, 'this is it - this is the year!'

I remember that on the day of the Cup Final, Clive and I were sat together on the bus going to Wembley. As we got nearer and nearer to the stadium, the scenes were absolutely incredible. And I'll never forget one couple we noticed. They were strolling along, arm in arm, one dressed from head to foot in black and white and one in red and white - it was marvellous - and just showed what the weekend was all about.

In the run-up to the final a number of people from around where I lived had said there was no way they would be going to the final. They expected there would be trouble with 'those two sets of fans' around. But I said to them - there's nothing wrong at all with Hull people - they're tremendous people. They'll go down to Wembley and all enjoy themselves. And that's exactly what they did!

95,000 watched the Wembley showpiece. And although nobody would ever describe the final as a classic, the occasion put the spotlight firmly on the city - and it's supporters did the whole occasion proud.

The barriers were still up around the Wembley pitch - but they weren't needed. There wasn't a hint of any trouble throughout the entire weekend as the fans of both clubs mixed together and enjoyed a truly unique occasion. I thought they were all marvellous!

The 1978-79 First Division Champions

CHAPTER EIGHTEEN
WEMBLEY –
THE ULTIMATE
DERBY
1980

'You're either a 'red and white' or a 'black and white' - there's nothing in between.'

I always took sayings like that one - and that Hull fans wouldn't eat bacon with their breakfast because it was red and white - and Rovers' fans would avoid zebra crossings because they were black and white, with a pinch of salt. But I hadn't been in Hull long before I discovered things like that were actually true. People who thought like that really existed...

We went down to London on the Wednesday and went straight to Windsor Rugby Union Club, where we'd arranged to train for the three days before the final.

We stayed at the Runnymede Hotel in Egham which Ron Turner and I had chosen a few weeks earlier. I was player-coach - so Johnny Moore and I received rooms of our own - but the players of course had to share. It was a lovely hotel and perfectly situated for our needs, only about ten or fifteen minutes from Windsor. At the back there was a huge conservatory which overlooked the River Thames. And at the front there was a little 'pitch and putt' golf course. The lads spent a fair bit of time there each morning before getting on the coach to go down to training.

It was all new to us. The whole experience was something we'd never done in our lives before. I remember when we arrived for our first training session at Windsor, I was quite nervous. Everything seemed very fresh and very strange to me. And I became a bit uptight and was 'having a go' at some of the players.

Allan Agar walked by and just simply and quietly said,

'Roger, calm it.'

That's the way we were then. We were a team - but we were friends as well - and we all helped each other through those tricky moments, whenever they arose. I took it straight on board. I knew everyone was in the same position as me. Only one or two had been in this situation before, facing a Wembley Cup Final. And they'd all be feeling exactly the same as I was. But there were some experienced guys around in that squad, like Allan, Brian and Clive, who probably helped me as much as I helped them. And after that little hiccup, it was a really good build-up to the final.

In fact, the try we eventually scored in the final, we worked out on the training field, later that day. And it wouldn't work at all. We never got it to work once in training! But the first time we put it on in a match was in the final - and it worked like a dream!

The night before the final we had dinner at the hotel and then it was up to the players what they did after that. They ran their own race from there. Some had an early night and some stayed up to watch TV. They knew where they were playing the next day. They knew they were playing the game of their lives in the biggest stadium and on the biggest occasion they were ever likely to play in. They didn't need me to tell them anything about how to conduct themselves.

The following morning a lot of the players were naturally very nervous. A lot of them got up early. I however had a habit especially on matchdays of lying-in. There were many times that Carol had to wake me up at eleven or even half past eleven to make the trip over from Kippax for a game at Craven Park. But that morning even I was up fairly early - it wasn't like me! It was about nine o'clock. I had a cup of tea and a slice of toast, which wasn't like me either because I never used to eat anything before a game. After that, and an hour or so on the 'pitch and putt' course, we just had to wait until it was time to leave the hotel for Wembley. But the time seemed to go so slowly. And we weren't due to set off until 12.30pm. Something was needed badly to break the tension - and it arrived in the shape of Bill Land. Bill was the Rovers' Chairman who would be leading us out at Wembley. A man who was going to be seen by millions of people that afternoon. He appeared about midday, ready to get on the coach, wearing a mid-blue suit. Unfortunately he was also wearing a pair of white shoes.

'Millo' took one look at him and said,

'For God sake Bill, you can't wear those shoes!' Never the fashion guru, Bill happily took 'Millo's advice and immediately went back to his room and changed them - for a brown pair!

Earlier, back in Hull, the exodus to the final had started from Paragon Station at 6am with ten special trains carrying 5,000 supporters to London. That was only the tip of the iceberg of course with an estimated 60,000 fans from the city attending the Wembley showpiece. Hull were averaging about 10,000 at the Boulevard that season. Thousands of cars and coaches also made the trip south. And thousands more fans were already in the capital having packed the normal trains in the three days running up to the final, many not planning to return until the Tuesday after a long weekend in London.

Up to 20,000 fans went by road to the capital, a journey of over 200 miles. But unfortunately the Humber Bridge still couldn't provide a route for them. It was several years behind schedule and only half-completed. And even when it was eventually finished many people expected it was set to become a white elephant.

Many fans went by taxi to the final, with fares reported to be around £60. For a party of four that seemed a fair price. The price of a standing ticket at Wembley was only about £3 and a match programme cost 60 pence...

I remember getting to Wembley at about half past one and the coach pulling in round the back. The journey only took about three-quarters of an hour despite the heavy traffic because we had a police out-rider with us. He was a smashing bloke, he'd actually been to see us the night before to finalise all the arrangements, so it wasn't too surprising I suppose that the whole thing went without a hitch.

We then got off the coach and went for a look at the dressing room. We had number one, the North Dressing Room, with Hull in number two, the South Dressing Room.

At about half past one we had a walk out onto the pitch. There were probably only about 30,000 of the 95,000 crowd in at that time but they all started cheering as we walked out and I'm not kidding the hairs on the back of my neck went straight up. It was just a brilliant feeling. The atmosphere was already amazing. And the rivalry between the two sets of fans as intense as ever. I knew it would be a bitter pill to swallow if we didn't win and a lot of the kids would be pretty upset. But it was the occasion that mattered most. And the main thing that I was hoping, was that everything went off OK and the supporters behaved themselves...

It had taken me all those years to get to Wembley and at times it was hard to believe I was actually there. And all I could think to myself was - come on, get a grip of yourself, you've got to go back into that dressing room and start talking to a team about winning a rugby match in half an hour...

All the players had worked very hard during the month since we'd got to the final and they were all in tip-top condition. They all knew what they had to do and were all ready to do. I knew I'd got a lot of good footballers there with me and I couldn't see anything going wrong. This is what I'd waited many years for and it was a hell of a feeling to finally be there and just walk around the pitch.

We'd been to Wembley the previous day but only for a walkabout. You weren't allowed to train on the pitch - at least that's what we'd been told. A certain member of the Hull side however later suggested that wasn't strictly true...

Hull had only one Hull born player in the side, Keith Tindall. But if any Hull player deserved to be at Wembley it was surely their hooker, Ronnie Wileman. He had scored the winning try in Hull's semi-final win against the cup-holders Widnes, that took the black and whites to Wembley for the first time since 1960. But by the end of the first ever all Hull Wembley final, I'd have cause to remember him for something very different however!

Hull had signed Wileman at the beginning of the 1979-80 season from York. It was a coincidence his opposing number nine in the final was Rovers' David Watkinson. He hailed from the same area and had joined us from the York amateur side, Heworth.

Hull had to make a late change to their line-up when their three-quarter,

Graham Evans, missed the game due to injury. He had been pencilled in to be on the Airlie Birds' bench but sustained a leg injury in training only forty-eight hours before the final - he tore a muscle at the back of his leg - playing soccer!

I don't suppose it was until we went back to the dressing room that things began to sink in. I got changed and put my brand-new tracksuit top on. We were all talking - all the time - we never shut up. We then sat down and went over our plans. We discussed what we were going to do. We picked their players out, one by one. We knew how they played and what they could do. But we'd played each other so many times we knew they'd be able to do exactly the same with us. That's what made it such a tight game. And it was always going to be something unexpected that would decide the outcome...

Melvyn Hayes and Windsor Davies from the popular television comedy, 'It Ain't Half Hot Mum,' led the community singing. And at 2. 45 p.m. we were called out and we lined up in the tunnel and waited to be led out onto the pitch. We were on the left and Hull on the right. We nodded at the opposition and asked them if they were OK, you had to be courteous - after all there were some lads from Castleford that I'd known for years in the Hull side.

Then Bill Land, the Rovers' Chairman, led us out of the tunnel to deafening applause. As the captain I was next in the line, then Dave Hall, Steve Hubbard, Mike Smith, Steve Hartley and Clive Sullivan followed. ...

As I looked down the line-up of players behind me, I couldn't help but appreciate what an amazing amount of talent we had at the club...

Mick Crane didn't play in the final but I couldn't leave him out of my autobiography. He was a real character, I can tell you that! You used to say to Mick lets have a warm up - and the next time you looked at him he'd lit up a Woodbine! But what a lad he was - and a hell of a player! He was so, how can I put it nicely? - I don't think I can! He was always 'miles away from you' if you know what I mean. And his concentration span was very short - but what a player! Off the cuff he was unbelievable. We bought him from Leeds and then sold him to Hull. He'd played in Leeds' Cup-winning side in 1978 when they beat St Helens 14-12.

In his two spells at Hull he played 324 matches. And although he only made 18 appearances and scored four tries for us, what an impression he left on everyone at Craven Park.

David Hall was at fullback - he was in brilliant form. He could read the game perfectly from there and communicate to the people in front of him. He was tremendous bringing the ball away because he had a hell of a side-step and he could join the line at any time.

Steve Hubbard always appeared to be a very awkward player. Every time he ran he looked like he was going to fall over. But he always seemed to get to where he wanted to be. And as far as kicking a ball, he was simply terrific. When Steve was at Rovers, he was part of a team that was at the top of the tree! The forwards set things up. The middle backs cleared the way. And Steve and Clive ran in the tries. Don't get me wrong they also had often to work hard to score some of those tries themselves. I saw him score one against Castleford at Craven Park where he must have busted six defenders out of the way and went the full length of the pitch. But when we were playing at our best, the forwards were opening things up on the outsides all the time. And these lads were just great at finishing those chances off. When we also had people like Steve Hartley and Mike Smith in the centre hitting holes, these kids were going to score tries. It was a very good team and when you look at it, a very balanced one.

Clive of course became a legend at both Hull and Rovers. He scored a total of 400 tries in a tremendous career and was the only player ever to score over 100 tries for both clubs. He also won a Challenge Cup Winner's medal with both us and the Airlie Birds. He played for his native Wales, toured with Great Britain and captained them to World Cup victory in France in 1972. But what few people realise is that a road accident had threatened all this! In 1963 Clive was nearly killed in a car crash. He received mutiple injuries including three broken ribs, two broken shoulders, a broken arm, a fractured shoulder blade, torn muscles in both legs and his left arm, a punctured lung - and internal bleeding. He was told it would take him two years to recover - but such was Clive's fighting spirit, he was back on the rugby field only three months later!

I recall one match though when even Clive 'put a foot wrong'. We were playing at the Boulevard and Clive raced over the try-line but as he was running around to touch down behind the posts he stepped over the dead ball line. That really proved to me that nobody's perfect!

Mike Smith and Steve Hartley were in the centres, they were a fantastic partnership. There was Mike at one side, who was strong and solid and with good pace. And Steve at the other side with electric pace who just took people on and just went! That era must have been the time when Rovers had more home grown players than ever, playing at the top level.

Then there was Allan Agar and I at halfback, making the link with the forwards. It was just a good combination and the players who were being signed at the time found it easy to slot into the side.

To give Allan a rest for instance we'd bring Paul Harkin in. He was only a 'baby' then but we gave him a few games and he got used to how the side worked. It was the same all the way through the team.

Then there were the kids coming in from the 'A' team who I knew would be OK because of the excellent job being done at both 'A' team and Colts level. We'd got a superb system that worked perfectly. From John Edson with the Colts, up to Ged Dunn with the 'A' team and then finally to Johnny Moore and I with the first team.

The front row was Roy Holdstock, David Watkinson and Brian Lockwood. I think you could safely say there was a bit of everything in that front row. Roy was a big strapping lad who only knew one way to go - forward! He'd always take the ball up for you. He was popular with the other players and the fans and it came as no surprise when just before the final he was named the 1980 Rovers' Player of the Year. 'Watkie' was a superb organiser. He could dictate the play or run off from acting halfback - and was always

OPPOSING CHAIRMEN
Rovers' Bill Land and Hull FC's Charles Watson lead out the teams
SHAKING HANDS WITH ROYALTY
I'm introduced to Her Majesty, Queen Elizabeth, The Queen Mother, watched by
David Hall and Steve Hubbard

capable of upsetting the opposition in more ways than one from that position. Brian was a pure footballer. He was a great thinker and a superb ball-handling forward. But he could also play it the hard way as well when necessary.

Behind those three were Phil Lowe and Paul Rose, possibly the best second-row combination Rovers ever had. Phil was an out and out runner - and hell could he score tries. 'Rosey' was perhaps underrated in many people's eyes, but he was undoubtedly one of the best second-rowers that I ever played with. You could have it anyway with him. He took no prisoners! I'd have to say they were the best partnership Rovers ever had. Two great players, two great professionals - two great lads. And they complimented each other perfectly... Paul liked nothing better than to get in where it was tough and run where there was traffic. He never held anything back, whether he had the ball or not. And a Cup Final appearance was a tremendous way for Paul to crown his testimonial year. Phil was a different type of player. He was marvellous to watch, especially when he hit the holes and got those long legs going. And the side-step he had. They were two exceptional players - the type that don't come along very often - and an era ended when the two of them left me.

If Lowe and Rose were the best second row, then I'd have to say adding 'Case' must have completed the best back three combination we ever had. Case had a beautiful pair of hands and when the time came to use them he always did! Len was known for his fiery, no-nonsense style but that often hid what an extremely skilful player he was.

I was lucky because when I finished playing, 'Case' became my first club captain before 'Watkie' took over. And I couldn't have wished for two better skippers. Every player around them respected them both!

All the good packs I've ever seen or ever played behind have all known that they had a job to do and exactly what their role was. And they've all had a bit of 'devilment' in them. If you take that away from them, I think you're taking the heart out of the pack. It's up to the bloke in black in the middle to sort that out and decide how far the players can go with that 'devilment'. All the best sides will go as 'close to the edge' as they're allowed to!

The Wembley substitutes were Phil Hogan and John Millington.

Well, what do you say about a player like 'Millo'? Put him in a dressing room and he'd keep anybody entertained whether we were at Wembley or wherever we were. But then he'd go out onto the field and do the job for you, whatever you'd asked him to do.

There are thousands of stories about 'Millo'. He's done some amazing things. But there aren't many of them that I could put into print. He was a very funny lad, one of life's comedians. I remember when we signed George Kirkpatrick, a Cumbrian centre, 'Millo' for obvious reasons immediately nick-named him 'Mr Pastry'. The name stuck and always got a laugh. But when he got on that field the joking usually stopped. And he never looked out of place with all those good players around him - he was one of them - and he used to love it!

I decided on Phil Hogan as the other substitute. He was a good player in his

MIND THE JAW
David Hall moves in as I tackle Hull's winger, Graham Bray
OPPOSING HALFBACKS
Allan Agar and I combine to stop Hull's stand-off, John Newlove

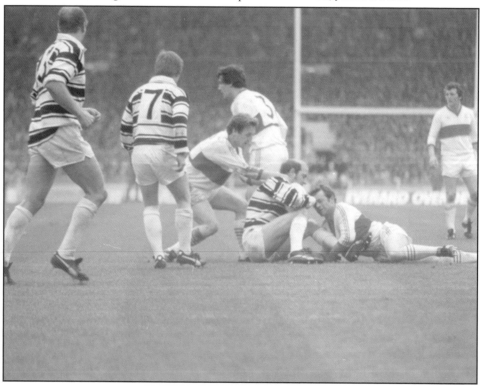

own right and when I had to pick a team to go out on that park, I decided Phil was the best man for the job. I could only pick fifteen - although I could probably have picked twenty on the day - but Phil offered me the best options. He could cover for our forwards or our backs. 'Millo' could cover us up front, if one of the back three got injured I would have simply brought 'Millo' on in the front row and dropped Brian back into the second-row, that's where he'd started his career. I had all sorts of options with those two, in fact there were times when I found it harder to pick the subs than to pick the team. Because I had to think of every eventuality when picking the subs. Sometimes I'd sit at home and quickly write the team down but when it came to the subs I thought yes but what happens if 'so and so' gets injured, how would I cover that? I could pick the team in five or six minutes and then take another hour deciding on the two subs. They were a vital part of the game...

Next to us, Charles Watson, the Hull Chairman, led the Hull side out. My old halfback partner Arthur Bunting, now the Hull coach followed immediately ahead of the team's captain, my old mate from Castleford, Steve Norton. As we emerged from the tunnel - the fans saw us - and the whole stadium erupted. It was then that the atmosphere really hit me - and it was a hell of a feeling! I don't mind telling you that I was very nervous. I remember I was trying to chew a piece of gum and take big gasps of air at the same time. But I couldn't afford to be nervous for long. Once that ball was kicked, the nerves had to stop!

On the television, even commentator Eddie Waring mentioned that I looked nervous. And then suggested Wembley had seen many great Cup Finals and said he reckoned it could be one to surpass every other. I'd have to say from a purist's point of view as regards free-flowing football and spectacular tries, that prediction was very wide of the mark. But for any partisan red and white, or black and white supporter, the game undoubtedly provided as many incidents and talking points - and as much excitement - to match any previous final!

When Eddie then asked summariser Alex Murphy who he thought would win, Alex evaded the question, merely answering by informing the viewers he thought Rovers looked very relaxed. The only thing I didn't like about Wembley was that they'd put that bloody fencing up. And there was no need for it!

We then walked to the middle of the pitch and lined up in front of the main stand. And Bill Land, wearing his brown shoes, presented the Rovers' players to the Queen Mother. She wore a blue hat and coat. I can remember everything as if it was last weekend, rather than twenty-five years ago.

We'd all been told to be careful shaking her hand because she shook so many hands, and they were frail and arthritic. So we had to remember not to grasp her hand too tightly. It had to be a very light handshake.

Next to be introduced was Fred Lindop, the referee, a man who had cropped up on many occasions throughout my career. And as kick-off time approached I chewed my gum and tried to take as much of the atmosphere in as I possibly could.

The National Anthem followed and then the teams were announced to the crowd, each player being individually introduced, Rovers first. And as our names were read out, we peeled away and ran to 'our' end of the ground. The main thing I wanted to do was to enjoy the whole occasion. I'd not played at Wembley before but everyone who I'd spoken to who had, told me to try and remember everything - and not to let anything pass me by. And I knew what they meant later on because I barely seemed to be on the field five minutes, and it was half-time!

Then we went back on the field and it didn't seem another five minutes had passed before 'Millo' came on. And the first thing he said was,

'Come on lads there's only eight minutes to go.' I couldn't believe it. The whole game had just flown by.

As Cup winners, Rovers won £12,555 and as runners-up, the Hull team received £6,000. It didn't seem a lot when you consider all the effort we'd put in. But I can honestly say I'd have happily played for a penny that day!

WEMBLEY BOUND
Introducing the 1980 Wembley Squad:
Back row: Jack Ounsworth (equipment) Johnny Moore (Assistant Coach) David Watkinson, Len Casey, Steve Hubbard, Roy Holdstock, Paul Rose, David Hall, John Millington, Mike Smith, Cliff Wallis (Physiotherapist) Mick Crane, Phil Lowe.
Front row: Ray Price, Clive Sullivan, Steve Hartley, Bernard Watson, Steve Leighton, Ian Robinson, Allan Agar, Paul Harkin, Phil Hogan.

CHAPTER NINETEEN
MY FINAL DREAM

What I've seen of the match since, and it's not a game that I sit and watch very often, I'd have to say Allan Agar went pretty close to winning the man of the match award. It was a fairly poor game when you analyse it, a bit dour! And the reason for that was - it was a game that nobody dared lose. That was the one thing that came across on the day, every player seemed terrified of losing the match! It was the same for the Hull side as us. I think there was probably more pressure on the two teams not to lose that day than there had been in any previous final...

The final was in complete contrast to when Rovers played against Widnes the following year. Or when Hull played the Chemics in the 1982 Final. There didn't seem to be the same amount of pressure on the two teams in either of those matches. But in the all-Hull final the pressure was intense, simply because of who the two teams were.
It was all about the cross-city, east versus west rivalry. It was all about two sets of fans with a traditionally intense passion for their teams. And it was all about what it would be like afterwards for the team that lost.
This was a unique match!
The first time that two professional clubs from the same city had ever faced each other at Wembley. It would never happen again. We'd never get another opportunity to win a Wembley Cup Final against Hull. And equally there wouldn't be a second chance to redeem ourselves if we returned home as losers. And that's why in the mind of every single player who was there at the time - the one thought that came up over and over again in the dressing room - was that we just dared not lose...
But you didn't even have to be involved to sense the 'fear'. It was the first thing author Les Hoole, highlighted in his account of the game in his 1998 book, 'The Rugby League Challenge Cup'.
'With their fiercely partisan groups of supporters behind them, both sets of players knew the game was as much about the championship of the city of Hull, as a major final at Wembley. From the kick-off, both sides seemed over-cautious, almost petrified of making a mistake,' wrote Hoole, an

observation I'd have to agree with.

But I just couldn't wait to start. I was still chewing my gum vigorously as the game kicked off - in great contrast to thirteen minutes later...

Our shirts had no collars, an innovation I'd introduced many years before, to stop opposing players grabbing them in a tackle. Hull did have shirt collars. But I noticed a number of their players, as if to emphasise my theory, had already tucked them in.

We lost the toss and my halfback partner, Allan Agar, kicked off. But we were awarded our first penalty in only the second minute. It was the first of many!

After eight minutes, the dream start that we'd hoped for materialised - albeit from a very surprising source. Steve Hubbard scored a tremendous try off Brian Lockwood's delayed, cut-out pass. It was Steve's 30th of the season and left him joint top of the try-scorers list. But if I'm honest the try was the result of a move that nobody had any confidence in.

We knew we had the ability to win the match. And we didn't concentrate very much on what Hull may or may not do. We knew their game well enough and in the days leading up to the final we focused more about what we were going to do for ourselves.

We'd discussed 'the move' after the training session at Windsor - most of the players said that it would never work. But I said let's keep it in mind and if we want it, we'll use it. I think it was more or less the first free kick we got in the right position and I told them, put it on! And it couldn't have worked better. You can't legislate for things like that, they either happen or they don't. The timing was superb on the actual day but if you'd seen it in training, you wouldn't have thought it would work in a million years.

Steve missed the difficult conversion from wide out on the left side of the pitch. But added a penalty from in front of the posts, the result of a foul by Hull's fullback Paul Woods, who was adjudged to have struck Steve as he touched down.

It gave us a 5-0 lead. But I can't help but smile whenever I think about that try. We'd practised it all the previous week in training - and it hadn't worked once!

After our try Hull seemed to lose their heads even more and Fred Lindop awarded a string of penalties against them for a series of head-high shots and other infringements.

Almost immediately Ronnie Wileman committed the most serious, flooring me with a high and late tackle. I copped that now infamous shot from Ronnie in the thirteenth minute but again there was no hint of a sending off. In fact amazingly Lindop did nothing except issue a brief warning to Wileman and award us another penalty.

Les Hoole appeared to agree, he described the incident as follows:

'Hull's bad tempered start began to worsen and in the 13th minute their hooker, Ron Wileman, caught Roger Millward far too high and late and left the little stand-off lying semi-conscious with his jawbone broken. Referee Fred Lindop showed remarkable tolerance when he allowed Wileman to stay on the field for what the majority of the crowd thought would be an instant sending-off... The incident did little to distract the Hull players from their chosen tactics and within minutes Hubbard kicked a penalty goal awarded when Stone had punched Holdstock.'

The 'stiff arm' had broken my jaw but I was determined to play on, even though I don't recall a great deal about the following ten minutes or so. But I've no problem with Ronnie Wileman. I've no axe to grind with him - in fact I've spoken to him many times since. Once you're out there you do what you think is right - and what Ronnie decided to do in the thirteenth minute was obviously what he thought was the right thing to do at that particular time. It doesn't bother me whatsoever. If he thought taking me out of the game would win them the Cup - then all I would say is thanks, Ronnie. At least he respected me and saw me as the main danger.

I've found out one thing about rugby league and that's it's no good holding grudges. Hell, the amount of grudges I could hold is endless! Starting right from when I was sixteen - every game I played in there'd be someone out there that I could hold a grudge against. I couldn't go through the rest of my career with that mentality...

I'd had two broken jaws already that season. But they were a lot more difficult to remember - I couldn't even recall which teams I was playing against until I looked them up. The first was against St Helens in the Floodlit Trophy on December 11. I took a calculated risk when I made my return in our 13-18 First Round Challenge Cup win at Wigan. It was an impressive victory where it was reported I 'benefited from the strength and cover' which I received from the recently re-signed Len Casey.

But my dream of appearing at Wembley was put in jeopardy when I broke my jaw again in the dying seconds of a game against Widnes. I went in to tackle Widnes' Mick George - but that's all I remember about the incident, except my jaw was very painful and swollen after the game.

The third one was at Wembley, when an old International colleague from Castleford, Steve Norton, unwittingly helped me get it back into place. But the broken jaw was just one of those things - I'd waited all those years to get to Wembley - then in the first thirteen minutes somebody clocked me one!

It took me about about twenty minutes to come round properly, but in that time I'd 'hit the corners' a few times and then just before half-time I landed a drop-goal, so I couldn't have been that bad. I'd certainly fully recovered by the time we went back into the dressing room and talked at half-time. Up to then it was a bit of a blur but fortunately we had Allan in the side who took over tremendously well and led the side brilliantly for the rest of the match in effect - so things were all right.

These days I'm sure Wileman would have been sent off - but back in 1980 that was never likely to happen, especially in a Wembley Cup Final - and especially with Fred in charge! The funny thing was I'd actually warned the players about Fred before the game.

I'd told them to be careful because it was Fred's first final for ten years. And ten years before, in 1970, he should also have sent someone off - but he didn't. Fred should have dismissed Keith Hepworth in the 1970 final after

CELEBRATION TIME!
No words are needed,
and none could describe
how I felt at this
moment...

he put Colin Tyrer out of the game with a late, off the ball tackle. Everyone agrees 'Heppy' should have gone - he should have been the first man ever sent off at Wembley! But it wasn't until the following year, that Leeds' Syd Hynes became the first player to be dismissed in a Wembley Challenge Cup Final, for allegedly head-butting Leigh's player-coach Alex Murphy. The referee that afternoon was Billy Thompson.

So watch yourself today, I told them, because Fred won't make the same mistake again. Well hindsight is a wonderful thing. And I was definitely proved wrong with that prediction, because unfortunately for me he did make exactly the same mistake again!

But Lindop's leniency did nothing to help the game. Another high shot by Charlie Stone on Roy Holdstock resulted in another Hubbard penalty success, which put us 7-0 ahead.

After the game, Hull's coach Arthur Bunting admitted:

'We lost the match in the first twenty minutes when we gave away so many silly penalties. I think the penalty count was about 9-2 at that stage.'

Hull also continued to squander field position when straight from the restart Charlie Birdsall went in high on Phil Lowe. And the only chance they got to open their account was when we were penalised for off-side but Sammy Lloyd pulled his shot at goal wide.

As the half-hour mark approached Hull managed to get back into contention when John Newlove raced away from a scrum and Tim Wilby crashed over for a try. I can't deny it was good to see Sammy Lloyd having to tee the ball up three times in the blustery wind, and then pull his kick to the right of the posts.

It was Sammy's first time at Wembley. Before the kick-off Sammy had appeared on Grandstand with Tony Gubba and described how he'd had a 'secret' practice session at Wembley the previous day.

'I was very privileged to be able to have a walk out on the hallowed ground. It was marvellous. I had my ordinary clothes on and had my boots in my pocket,' he explained. 'I had a pair of very, very tight cords on. I took two or three kicks but most of them were unsuccessful. I thought with the ground being completely enclosed that it would be quite still in there. But it surprised me - there was a nasty swirling wind. I just hope that I do better than I did yesterday - and that I've got those kicks out of my system.'

But fortunately for us Sammy faired little better in the final and his numerous missed kicks at goal undoubted aided our victory. Sammy showed his obvious frustration seconds later with yet another high shot, this time Paul Rose was the recipient.

My drop-goal followed just before half-time and was crucial because it opened up a five points gap. It may only have taken the score to 8-3 instead of 7-3 but that one point was important. Because without it, Hull only needed a converted try to win the match.

Fortunately by half-time I'd recovered quite a lot and I could get my words out. When Hull had scored their try, we'd said that if we didn't stop making mistakes we were going to get beaten. That was also the main topic of discussion in the dressing room. That it was our own errors that were

TREASURED MEMORIES
Top left: The moment I'd waited my whole career for - lifting the Challenge Cup at Wembley
Top right and bottom left: The fantastic 'homecoming' in Queen Victoria Square
Bottom right: Carol and I with the Cup at Craven Park

causing us our main problems - not how well or how poorly Hull were playing. We highlighted the mistakes and the pressure we'd put ourselves under. We'd never really got any rhythm going at all during the first half. But unfortunately it continued like that again in the second half, more or less. It was one of those stop-start games almost all the time. The Hull players constantly tried to 'spoil' it - and to be fair to them they made a good job of it. But they gave a lot of penalties away and I think we surprised them with just how good our defence was. We took everything they could fire at us.

But everything went so quickly. I suppose it was just the occasion that got to us. The adrenaline was pumping and before we knew it, the game was over. None of us could believe just how quickly the match had gone - especially as it wasn't even a particularly exciting encounter.

It was a fairly dour match, a typical derby in many ways. But it wasn't about being pretty. It wasn't about putting on a rugby spectacular. It was about winning! One team had to win the Challenge Cup that day - and we made sure it was us!

In the second half both teams had their chances to win the match convincingly. After forty-five minutes Sammy Lloyd missed a simple penalty. And at the opposite end Len Casey raced clear but was brought back for a forward pass. Then I sent Steve Hartley under the posts but he was also recalled for a forward pass. I'm sure both 'flat ball' passes would have resulted in tries today.

Next, Hull attacked down the right and Graham Bray raced over in the corner. But much to my relief, Fred Lindop pulled Sammy Lloyd up for obstructing David Hall in the build-up, and the try was disallowed. The decision was another debatable one as I'm certain if Sammy hadn't blocked David, Hull would have scored anyway. But it merely added to the series of missed opportunities and gave the fans even more to argue about in the pub later.

Keith Tindall touched-down after sixty-five minutes but again was recalled for another forward pass, but there was little doubt about that one!

We thought we'd sealed victory ten minutes from the end when Steve Hubbard slid over in the right corner but the 'score' was ruled out for a double movement. I've watched the video numerous times and still find it difficult to decide whether it should have stood or not. It was just one of many incidents that emphasised how difficult a referee's job was in those days. There was no big screen, 'square in the air' or help from 'wired-up' colleagues in the stand for referees to rely on twenty-five years ago! But it did appear Steve's momentum had carried him over. On another day the try might easily have been given. And even the BBC summariser Alex Murphy, never the greatest Hull K.R. fan, admitted he thought it looked a good try.

As the game went into its' final few minutes Sammy Lloyd missed another kick at goal and was then adjudged to have obstructed me deep in the Hull half. Steve Hubbard made no mistake with his twenty-eight yard penalty to complete the scoring.

But the tension still wasn't over!

Hull had to score twice to win the cup but one converted try would have forced a replay at Headingley. They didn't manage either - although there were a couple of incidents very near the end when they went desperately close!

With only two minutes left on the clock, Graham Bray broke down the right but Clive Sullivan's copybook tackle took him into touch. And even in the last minute, Len Casey gave them another chance! He did something 'daft' and Hull were awarded a penalty. And he knew he'd 'cocked-up' straight away because he was shouting and bawling at everyone.

Hull put the ball into the corner and then we had to face another two tackles virtually on our own line! I couldn't believe it. Only seconds earlier we'd had the ball - we'd been going away from our line with it - all we had to do was hang on to it and we'd won!

But now we were under pressure again! That just proved you had to keep thinking for every single second of the match until you heard that hooter - even at Wembley.

On the other flank, with time now seeming to stand still, Steve Hubbard was stretchered off after falling awkwardly and we brought 'Hogey' on. I remember twenty-odd thousand fans chanting:

'There's only one Stevie Hubbard'. And as Steve was wheeled away he shook his fist at his teammates as one last act of encouragement.

At first it was feared Steve may have broken his ankle and our physio Cliff Wallis strapped Steve's legs together as a precaution. But Steve's worries were soon eased when the doctor told him that he'd only sprained it and after a week in pot it would be as good as new!

Substitute, Phil Hogan, wasn't so happy. He later complained that it had been terrible just sitting on the bench, until the last few seconds, unable to help the rest of the lads.

'It was murder,' said Phil. 'I kept saying to Johnny Moore there'd be hell on if he didn't let me on the pitch. It would have been awful to have come to Wembley and not get on the field. I don't want to go through that again just sat on the bench. But now I can always say to my grandchildren that I've played at Wembley - even if it was only for a minute or two.'

Seconds later, the final hooter sounded. And the feeling at that moment was simply brilliant! I jumped on the nearest Rovers' player to celebrate. It was Dave Hall. And as the cheers from the Rovers' fans grew louder and louder, 'Sully' ran over to join us. I looked up at the scoreboard.

It read 10-5... the most famous result in Rovers' history.

After the hooter had sounded I went around congratulating every member of the team. I also remember shaking hands with the Hull players. The fourth hand I shook was Ronnie Wileman's. I was then congratulated by my old Castleford and Great Britain colleague, veteran scrum-half, Keith Hepworth. He hadn't played in the final but his smartly tailored suit told everybody that even at the age of thirty-eight he was very proud to still be a part of the Boulevard squad.

My next job was to receive the cup from Her Majesty Queen Elizabeth, The

Queen Mother. I started to climb the steps. Clive followed closely behind me.

'Millward and Sullivan - who knows when they will give up playing?' asked television commentator, Eddie Waring, as we approached the top step. We didn't know then, but his rhetorical question would soon have two very contrasting answers...

At the top, in front of the Royal Box and watched by a blur of Rugby League officials, including General Secretary - David Oxley, the Chairman - Mr S. Baxendale and the President - The Earl Of Derby, I shook hands for the second time that afternoon with Her Majesty. And collected the Challenge Cup!

I raised the trophy above my head. The roar from the Rovers' supporters was deafening. It was a moment I'd waited my whole career for and one that I'll remember for the rest of my life.

Steve Hubbard was the last to collect his winner's medal. He managed to negotiate the stairs despite his injury. But only after the Hull team and the officials had collected their mementos of a unique occasion. Back on the pitch, as we savoured our victory, Steve was helped around his lap of honour by Bernard Watson and Cliff Wallis. And Brian Lockwood had an extra trophy to carry, after he was awarded the Lance Todd Trophy for his man of the match performance.

I was hoisted onto Watkie's and then Phil Hogan's shoulders. Surrounding us, the national press photographers snapped away, each one hoping to get that perfect photo for the Sunday papers. And illuminated by what seemed like a thousand camera flashbulbs, I raised the Cup proudly above my head again...

In the excitement I remember somebody stuck a red and white 'cowboy' hat on my head - and every time I look at the photographs now, I cringe. I finished up with it on when we started the lap of honour. I know I didn't have it on when I went up the steps to collect the Cup, I'm glad to say. And I didn't have it when I got to the bottom of the steps either - so where it came from I don't know. But that didn't surprise me - I didn't take everything in - and I didn't see a lot of things that happened at the time. Apparently at one point Kay was standing only a few feet from me, waving from the stand - and I didn't even see her. My mum and dad were with her and she was shouting at me but I didn't notice any of them. She was only ten and if I'd seen her she would have got my medal straight away!

After we'd left the pitch, Grandstand's Frank Bough asked me about the injury to my jaw. And knowing I'd broken it for a third time, I said I thought I'd got the hat-trick up. I finished by suggesting I would probably get drunk later on to celebrate - even if I had to use a straw! I said I thought we'd deserved it. My interview with Frank was broadcast on national television. And a few days later I received a letter from a woman complaining about my 'drinking habits', which she obviously didn't approve of. But that wasn't the crux of her complaint. The main thing she objected to was that I'd also used the word 'Humberside' in my interview and not 'East Yorkshire'.

Frank also talked to our nine-point hero, Steve Hubbard.

'I thought at first the ankle was broken but it's starting to feel a lot easier and I just wanted to get up there with the lads. I knew it was going to be my day as soon as that move came off. It was fantastic...

The try came from a move which we worked on at the training ground at Windsor and everything just happened - a huge gap just appeared and I couldn't believe my luck. Hull had some fast lads and I thought they'd have got to me but they just seemed to lay off. And when I saw the line... all I wanted to do was get over it. It was Brian Lockwood who called it and it just went well on the day,' said Steve.

Although I was obviously very happy for all the lads, I was particularly pleased for Clive and Brian. Clive and I had waited all our careers to win at Wembley. But although Brian had done it twice before with Castleford this win he later admitted was a very special one for him as well.

'This final was the one that gave me the most satisfaction,' he said. 'When I'd signed with Rovers I said I'd like to regain my international spot and also play at Wembley with Rovers. I've done both now and I've also won the Lance Todd Trophy - and that's the greatest thing I've ever achieved. But I'd have given fifteen trophies out today because there were fifteen winners out there. I thought we won it in the first half. The start was great - we went out just to hold them for the first twenty minutes but it worked out just the opposite - they had to hold us,' said Brian.

I had to agree with Brian's assessment. We'd played very well for the first twenty minutes but then had gone off the boil a bit. In the second half I thought we dropped too many balls and we also had a lot of trouble getting the ball out of the scrum. That was the only time I got a bit worried. But the lads tackled very well. They'd all been marvellous throughout the build-up to the game. I couldn't fault any of them. They all built themselves up for the win and they all helped to make my job easy...

Carol had travelled down to London on the Friday with the other players' wives and girlfriends. They stayed at a fantastic hotel on the Friday night where they saw Tony Christie in cabaret.

Kay stayed with my mum and dad in a hotel at Richmond. Then on the Saturday after the game they all came over to Runnymede and stayed with us. On the evening everyone attended a celebration banquet and dance. It was a wonderful night.

All the players' wives, girlfriends, families and invited guests had joined us - but not many of them, I'm sure would remember what time they went to bed. It was just one of those marvellous nights that went on and on...

One particular guest and I had a lot of catching-up to do. Jim Geraghty my sponsor from Cronulla, and now a great friend, had flown half way around the world to watch me in the Cup Final. But the condition of my jaw meant our conversation was much more one-sided than usual that evening...

It was the first time any professional club from Hull had ever won at Wembley. And now that the new stadium is nearing completion that's a record that will live forever! Rovers were actually victorious at Wembley twice, they also won the Silk Cut Plate there in 1997 against Hunslet Hawks. The next morning we set off back to Hull for the civic reception. I remember coming back on the coach. We stopped at Leicester for a meal, and then arrived at Gilberdyke at exactly the same time as the Hull team did. We were changing there to get onto an open-topped coach for the parade through the city. Both teams went on tours of the city and the reception we both received was fantastic. But when I looked at the Hull players' faces - I just thought, I'm glad that's not us!

We were going to enjoy our day. And although the Hull players got a great reception at the Boulevard from their fans - and so they should have, they deserved it - I knew they'd feel totally different to how we felt.

The difference between winning and losing is a significant one! Some of the Hull players were in tears when they saw the welcome the fans gave them. I recall Arthur Bunting saying later they couldn't have had anything better had they won! But I had to disagree. They could have experienced what we did in a packed Queen Victoria Square.

To lift the cup again on that balcony and see and hear all those fans singing and chanting was simply marvellous. It's another sight from a weekend full of memories, which I'll never forget. I just looked out at the sea of red and white. The only thing I had to do was thank the fans. The players had won the cup - but the supporters had made the weekend what it was.

On behalf of all the lads I thanked everyone who'd made the trip to Wembley. I said how proud I was of the way they'd all behaved. For the fantastic support they'd given us at the stadium. And for being part of such a marvellous advert for the city!

David Oxley perhaps summed the whole occasion up better than I did when he said,

'It's been a fabulous weekend for the city and it couldn't have come at a better time. The industrial and employment scene is rather bleak but the two rugby league teams have brought sunshine and smiles to the faces of their fans. And what wonderful fans both sides have - there was 60,000 of them that made the trip to Wembley and there wasn't a single incident. They're a credit to the game, a credit to the city and to the two teams that mean so much to them.'

We stayed at Colin's on the Sunday night. On the Monday I of course had a date at the Hull Royal Infirmary, to have my broken jaw looked at. We then went back to the clubhouse at Craven Park before returning home to Kippax.

It was May Bank Holiday weekend. It had been quite an eventful one...

MY LAST MATCH
Above: Being led off against Batley 'A' at Craven Park after suffering my fourth broken jaw

Above left: A quiet word with Hull's Aussie coach, Brian Smith

Left: 'Enjoying' the game with Paul Lyman

Below: About to shake hands with Len Casey during his coaching days at the Boulevard

CHAPTER TWENTY
THE MOST FAMOUS PUNCH, EVER!

I only ever played in one other match after Wembley. It was on October 4 1980 at Craven Park.

We had a lot of young kids in the 'A' team at that time. I planned to have a month or so with them - to settle them in - and at the same time get my fitness back. But that never happened!

I had my jaw broken again in my 'comeback' game against Batley 'A'. That finally told me, that's it! I knew it was a 'bad one' on that day because as I was walking off, blood was pouring out of my mouth - all I remember after that is getting into an ambulance. At the Infirmary they put me in a bed. And a little later the specialist who had looked after me on the three previous occasions I'd broken my jaw appeared. I'll never forget the question that followed. He just stood at the bottom of the bed and asked, 'Is that it?'

I stared back at him and answered as best I could, That's it!

And then with an approving look he simply said, 'Right, we'll do it then.'

So the decision was made there and then. He'd asked the question.

'Is that it?' and I'd replied, That's it. Just five little words - but five words that meant my playing days were over...

Four broken jaws in ten months were enough - and I couldn't see how things were going to get any better. It's obviously not the way I would have liked my career to end, but it was finished!

I didn't quite think of myself as being at the 'pipe and slippers' stage but I knew it was time to call it a day.

In hindsight I should probably have hung my boots up after we'd won at Wembley. And nursing another broken jaw I asked myself many times why I hadn't! But as I've said before, hindsight's a wonderful thing.

It was a very nasty break. The jaw had gone down at both sides and caved in and it needed a fair amount of work to pull it out - and I was wired up for four or five weeks. There are certain times in your life when something comes along to tell you to stop doing something. For me that day had arrived...

My career had reached a major crossroads. I was no longer a professional rugby league player. The job I'd done for the past sixteen years was over. But they say when one door closes, another one opens. And fortunately another door was already wide open for me.

I'd been coaching the team for the previous three seasons - with a fair amount of success. There was no need to change that, just because I wouldn't be playing anymore. Rovers were a good side at the beginning of the eighties. I knew they were on the threshold of becoming a great one! More Cups and Championships were there to be won. More achievements were just around the corner. And I was adamant that I was going to be a part of it. I'd been a player and player/coach at Hull K.R. for fourteen years. I was now determined to give 100% effort - and win more silverware, as their coach!

Everything changes, and you just can't keep doing things in the same way forever. If you get the opportunity to change something that needs changing, you change it. I knew that time had arrived for me. And after winning at Wembley that was also the situation that Rovers were in...

One of the first changes saw Johnny Moore appointed as my assistant coach. It was a fantastic appointment as far as I was concerned. Everything John did was faultless - and I knew I couldn't have hoped for a more dedicated person to work with.

He'd enjoyed a tremendous career and played in 430 matches for Rovers. But in his first year at Craven Park he probably thought he might never play in even one! He'd been at Rovers since April 28 1962 but due to a knee injury didn't make a first team appearance until August 31st 1963 with a try-scoring debut against Castleford. But when I first arrived he was a regular fixture, playing in the centre. He was such a solid player and a more loyal club man you could never wish to meet. He was a professional in every sense of the word.

He used to 'second sight' you. I swear he often knew what I was going to say before I turned round and asked him the question! He was just a marvellous bloke to have at your side. And certainly helped Rovers in a big way, not only as a player for ten years but as a top class coach as well.

Off the field John was a hell of a guy and a true gentleman but that didn't mean opponents could mess him about. He was a very hard man and I've seen him throw a few 'short arms' when he needed to. On the field he did his job - professionally and effectively - if something had to be done, he got on and did it.

But there was one thing about Johnny that not many people knew about. It was one of his after-match rituals - and I admit it used to worry me a little... I'd estimate it used to take him about forty-five minutes to get dried after his shower. I've never seen a bloke get as dry as he did in my life. He would literally have the towel between every toe. The other players would sit there and watch him, they couldn't believe it!

The 1980-81 season was another successful campaign. We finished third out of sixteen teams in the Slalom Lager sponsored Division One

Championship. Phil Lowe and David Hall shared a testimonial. And jerseys bearing a sponsor's name 'Rank Xerox' were worn for the first time in the club's history at the home match against St Helens on January 11 1981. I remember the game very well. We were in the dressing room when the shirts were brought in with the 'Rank Xerox' logo on them. And the players were going to refuse to go out and play in them because they hadn't had a cut of the sponsor money. It was a problem - I had to go upstairs and get the Chairman to talk to them. I'm sure we finished up going out and playing in the shirts - and I'm also sure that not long afterwards there was a payment of some kind made to the players.

We signed a number of new players including Colin Dixon from Salford and Chris Burton from Huddersfield. But it was also a time when a number of players who had been at the club for a while, were for one reason or another, ready to move on. And we saw the departure of Allan Agar to Wakefield, Clive Sullivan and Brian Lockwood to Oldham and Mick Crane to Hull. But that's the way things had to be. It was pointless trying to keep a side together indefinitely, just because it had won a cup final. Changes had to be made, we just couldn't stand still, we had to keep moving forward. But what we also had to ensure was that the people who were coming in, were as good or better as the people we were letting go. And that's what we always tried to do at Rovers. When we signed players from Australia and New Zealand, they had to be better than the lads that we had at the club already, otherwise there was no point in bringing them.

Once they were here they had to prove that they deserved to be - and with one or two exceptions they all did. I always made it clear that I wasn't there to stand their corner. They had to stand their own corner! But that was the great thing about the players that we brought over, they all wanted to come and prove what they could do and get into the team on their own ability.

That was proved in the following years when despite the fact that I'd retired, players such as Brian and Clive had moved on and all those great players had gone, the club still continued to move forward.

I was sorry that Brian had left us. But there's a time and a place for everybody they say, and Brian had done his job for us at Rovers. And I had some good young forwards coming through, like Steve Crooks. He was only a young lad but he needed to be in there and he needed to be playing. If Brian had stayed Steve wouldn't have got his chance so early and it was a conscious decision that I went for Steve instead of Brian.

Steve took his place in the front-row at Wembley in his first season. The changes were significant and had already started by the time we made our second consecutive Wembley appearance in 1981. When you compare the team that faced Widnes to the one that had won the cup against Hull just twelve months earlier for example, there were six new faces in the line-up - nearly half the side...

That 1981 final taught me something else about changing things, when I received a harsh lesson about team selection. I suppose you could say the lesson was the old adage - 'don't mend something if it's not broken'...

But I'd be the first to admit I tried to! And I made a major mistake when I took David Hall out of the pack and moved him to fullback. We all make mistakes and I'd be a liar if I said I hadn't made any. I've made plenty. And probably that was the biggest one. I should have left Paul Proctor at fullback and played David at loose-forward.

I think we'd have caused Widnes a lot more damage doing it like that. David was playing some of the best football of his career and created so much at that time. But I decided not to take a chance on young Proctor. But I should have - because a fortnight later I did - and he played out of his skin when we beat Hull in the Championship Final at Headingley. So I think I've got to hold my hand up there and say the game was probably lost at the selection stage. And the decision I think undoubtedly contributed to our downfall...

My first Challenge Cup Final as a coach was also the end of an era for Eddie Waring, 'the most famous voice in rugby league'. It was the last final he commentated on before retiring. Eddie had started commentating over thirty years earlier. In 1952 he was the voice on the first Challenge Cup Final to be broadcast on nationwide BBC Television. Workington Town, brilliantly led by their 41-year-old captain and coach, Gus Risman, beat Featherstone Rovers 18-10. Risman's success was an amazing feat, coming fourteen years after his initial Challenge Cup Final success. In 1938, he'd enjoyed his first win when Salford beat Barrow, 7-4. The only try of the game in the dying seconds was one of the few highlights of a final, described as 'the worst ever seen at Wembley.'

Our match against Widnes was far better I'm glad to say. We reached Wembley for the second successive year by beating Barrow at home, 18-13, York at home, 23-7, Salford at home, 19-8 and St Helens at Headingley in the Semi-Final, 22-5. Unfortunately the Chemics, with Brian Lockwood in their ranks, following another move from Oldham proved too strong for us. They ran out 18-9 winners, but I was excited with how the club was progressing. We had mature players who were playing well and some very good youngsters who were coming through. Kids who'd been there a couple of years started improving and it was just a great time to be at the club - we always seemed to be involved in one cup competition or another.

Earlier in the season we'd lost the Yorkshire Cup Final, 8-7 against Leeds at Huddersfield. We also lost 12-20 against the New Zealand tourists. But after those two disappointments there was plenty for the Craven Park fans to enjoy. No fewer than eight of our players made representative appearances that season: Roy Holdstock, Len Casey, Colin Dixon, Mike Smith, Steve Hartley and David Watkinson all played international football. Paul Harkin appeared for Great Britain U24s and Zook Ema played for the Great Britain Colts. Our Wembley hero from 1980, Steve Hubbard, finished as our top points scorer with 108 goals and 25 tries, whilst Steve Hartley scored 23. Our average home attendance was a healthy 8,904. And I was honoured to receive a special 'Greenall Whitley-Sunday People' award for services to Rugby League.

The City of Hull was certainly a brilliant place to be at the beginning of the eighties. Rovers and Hull were two of the top teams in rugby league. Every side in the league struggled against both of us. We finished third in the league in 1981 and Hull were seventh. And following the all-Hull Wembley final, it seemed inevitable that we'd meet in another major final, sooner rather than later. The fans didn't have to wait long...

We clashed with Hull again when the two sides reached the 1981 Premiership Final, another first for both clubs. And the rugby-crazy Hull public filled Headingley to almost bursting point on May 16 when 29,448 - a record attendance at the time - watched their second major 'derby' final in only twelve months.

With any Rovers versus Hull game, you could forget all about the form-book! Those matches could always go either way. I recall the fantastic atmosphere as the two teams walked out on to the pitch. You can imagine that Headingley with nearly 30,000 fans packed in, was a hell of a place to be! Len Casey won the Harry Sunderland Trophy and we won another tension-packed final against our arch-rivals, 11-7. I remember Steve Hartley's match-winning try. A pass from Phil Lowe put him free and he sprinted more than half the length of the pitch, leaving Hull's fullback Paul Woods in his wake. It was a superb moment and a fantastic way to win any cup final...

During the following season, 1981-82, the team continued to progress. Winning at a place like St Helens said everything. All of a sudden we'd come of age and here we were winning at Knowsley Road, a ground we hadn't won at for half a century. That tells you the way we were going - it must have showed we were doing something right.

But even before a ball had been kicked that season we'd already made the headlines. In the summer of 1981 Rovers broke the world transfer record when we signed George Fairbairn from Wigan for £72,500.

It was probably the best bit of business I ever did when I signed George. He's another Rovers' legend. He was a hell of a good fullback - a true, dedicated professional who always knew what he was doing. He used to get upset with himself if things didn't go right. I know he cost the club a fair bit of money but I also know he repaid every penny, many times over. And he has to rank amongst the very best of my signings, simply because of the way he played the game. There was never any shirking with George, he always put 100% effort in. Plus, when his playing days were over, he still had so much to offer. He's a great bloke to discuss things with - his knowledge and enthusiasm for the game is tremendous. And of course he followed in my footsteps when I left in 1991 and he became Rovers' coach.

The year also saw the re-appointment of Colin Hutton as the Great Britain Team Manager and also Chairman of The International Selectors. He was also selected as part of a special fitness committee that included me, which would be responsible for preparing the Great Britain squad to meet the Aussies in 1982-83.

We played in another major final on January 23. Hull again were our opponents for the John Player Trophy Final as another huge crowd of 25,245 packed into Headingley. But on this occasion we were beaten 12-4.

Bank Holiday Monday - May 3 - was a very strange day. It provided me with a sight I'd never seen before, or since, on a rugby field. The match in question was our first round tie of the Premiership Play-Offs against Bradford Northern at Craven Park. It soon turned into a very bad-tempered game. Bradford were constantly being penalised for a combination of blatant fouls and stupid little indiscretions. And as the match progressed, they got madder and madder and in the end, just lost it! The referee, Robin Whitfield, was in the middle and he had to decide how to deal with it. And the way he chose to deal with it was to send off no fewer than six players. Bradford's Gary Van Bellen and Rovers' John Millington were the first to be dismissed, followed by Northern's Dean Carroll and Rovers' Steve Hartley. It was a rare event for Steve and co-incided with the culmination of an otherwise successful campaign for him. He was just completing his joint testimonial season - shared with John Millington - which realised £25,000. And he also topped the club's try-scorers list that year with twenty-two.

Bradford's Ian Ellis was next to be sent off - but when Jeff Grayshon became the visitor's fourth player to be ordered from the field, something very strange happened!

I don't know how Bradford would have coped with only nine players, but we never had the chance to find out. Because when Jeff, their captain was dismissed, he simply walked off and the rest of his players - what was left of them - followed him. It was one of the most bizarre things I've ever seen on a rugby pitch!

When the Bradford team had disappeared down the tunnel, I remember telling my players to stay on the field. There was no way that they were to leave the pitch until the referee told them otherwise. Then there'd be no way that the situation could escalate, or be blamed on us. I kept thinking it hasn't anything to do with us - it wasn't our problem!

Phil Hogan, Bernard Watson and Ian Robinson had scored our tries and George Fairbairn had kicked four goals. And when Robin Whitfield abandoned the game after 56 minutes we were leading 17-8. We were later awarded the tie but went out in the following round 16-15 at Widnes. Northern were banned from three competitions for the following season, a decision that was later suspended for three years. And Jeff was suspended until the end of September...

We finished fourth in the league that year with our average home attendance rising slightly to 9,039. John Moore celebrated twenty years at the club. And in his first season at Craven Park, George Fairbairn beat Neil Fox's goal-kicking record with 166. George was also voted the Daily Express-Hepworth Tailoring 'Player Of The Year' and completed a memorable season by playing in both of Great Britain's Internationals against France and also for England against Wales...

Before the 1982-83 season commenced, Director Colin Hutton was elected as Rovers' new Chairman following Bill Land's decision to stand down. As a result Colin resigned from the International Selection Committee.

The club obviously wanted to continue its' momentum and tried desperately to strengthen its' squad still further for the start of the season.

We were constantly on the look-out for good players but at the time the choice was very limited. The natural thing was to then 'widen the net' and look abroad - and we found two absolute gems in Gary Prohm and Gordon Smith. And if you're talking about value for money, well I used to feel sorry for Gordon because it seemed like nearly every time he went out onto a field he used to come off and have stitches. The value for money you got from that lad was unbelievable - and he was an exceptional footballer too. 'Prohmy' of course was something else - he became a try-scoring machine. The first time I sent him out onto the park, I played him at loose-forward. Then all of a sudden he went back to his normal position at centre and he became one of the best players to play for Rovers in that position. He was an incredible player.

When Andy Kelly arrived at the club, a lot of people had already labelled him as 'the new Phil Lowe'. I think it was a bit strong to say Andy was going to be like Phil, frankly I don't think that was ever going to happen. He came with a big reputation, but didn't quite fulfil every thing that he thought he would at Hull K.R. But having said that his contribution was always first class, the other lads got on with him and the fans liked him. But to put him in the same category as 'Lowey' I don't think was fair.

As one new player arrived another 'old favourite' departed. Paul Rose had made his mind up to leave - in fact he was adamant about going. He'd been upset about a few things and probably I hadn't helped with my team selection. He thought it was the right time to go. I wasn't going to stand in his way - and off he went to the Boulevard for a record 'outgoing' fee of £30,000. It was sad to see him go because he'd been a good friend of mine all through my playing days. And I knew that I was part of the reason for his departure. It didn't feel right. But he went and I think he enjoyed himself when he got there.

Like every coach, I was constantly faced with the difficult choice of selecting a team. But when it all boiled down I had a job to do. It wasn't easy, I often had to talk to people and tell them I was leaving them out of the side that week. Or worse still, that they were not in my plans for the club and if they wished to leave I wouldn't stand in their way. There's no easy way to say things like that especially when I'd been a friend and teammate with someone, sometimes for many years. It's not nice - but that was the job. I knew there would be problems like those to deal with when I took the job on - so I'd just got to get on with it...

On October 10 we lost 30-10 against Australia at Craven Park in the first game of their tour. The Aussies were a very formidable side that year. They were most years. Their squad of players included such names as: Wally Lewis, Eric Grothe, Brett Kenny, Mal Meninga, Gene Miles, Wayne Pearce, Steve Rogers and Peter Sterling.

We hung onto them for a long time. But I have to say some of their tactics were not to be found in any of the coaching manuals I'd read. They certainly did nothing to endear themselves to the 10,000 plus Craven Park crowd and were slated in the press afterwards. Rod Reddy was sent off for punching Steve Crooks, Les Boyd for using foul language and our own

David Watkinson for a flare up with his opposing number nine, Ray Price. Referee, Fred Lindop, in an unsavoury first half dismissed all three. Tries by Steve Hartley and Gary Prohm had given us an 8-5 lead at half-time. But trailing to any side was a situation the Kangaroos didn't find themselves in very often during the rest of the tour.

They beat Wigan, Barrow, St Helens, Leeds, and Wales before returning to Hull on October 30 for the first test at Boothferry Park. I think that year was the time where the standards between the two countries got as wide apart as ever! Certainly at International level, as far as technical ability was concerned, we were at our lowest ebb!

That was cruelly confirmed when the Australians won a totally one-sided encounter 4-40. They went on to record equally impressive victories in the rest of their matches and left unbeaten. They won the second test at Wigan 6-27 and the third test at Headingley 8-32, were dubbed 'The Invincibles' and hailed as the best rugby side of either code, ever to visit Britain.

They also showed us in no uncertain terms, just how much of a gulf there was between the two sides. I think it was then that the alarm bells really started ringing. And it's taken us over twenty three years to get into a situation where we may be getting close enough to be able to compete with them again...

At the start of 1983 the sin-bin was introduced into domestic football and I have to say it was an innovation that up to a point pleased me. But on the other side of the coin it was also suggested in some quarters, that it was a rule that referees could hide behind. It gave them the opportunity to cop-out and to not make a decision. Rather like today, I don't like this 'crossed-arm job' and the option of putting people on report. I mean if the referee's seen an offence - and often it's obvious that they have - they should do something about it there and then! At times, it's just another way out for them, as far as I can see. It says the referee doesn't want to make the decision, they want to leave thirteen players on each side and make it a game. And I don't always agree with that! I think the sin-bin should be used up to a point, because then you can hit players for an offence when it happens. And I think it's a rule that would do soccer the world of good as well. Where they would be penalised for what happens on the day and not three or four weeks later. Often it's the team who a side plays two or three weeks after who benefit from a player being put on report and subsequently banned - not the team he's actually committed the offence against. Where's the logic or the fairness in that? If a player has obviously committed a foul and it's been seen, they should be dealt with there and then! But if we are going to use the sin-bin, let's use it correctly - and not have referees hiding behind it.

The sin-bin was introduced in England on January 1 1983. And I remember the first player to fall foul of the new law, only twenty-four hours later, was one of the finest ever to play for Rovers, Gary Prohm. The referee who showed the first yellow card was Ronnie Moore. That was about right for Ronnie - somebody had to be first and he'd have probably wanted to get his name in the record books somehow!

There was a bit of a surprise for me as well at the beginning of 1983 when I was honoured with the MBE. It came completely out of the blue but made it a very special new year for my family and I.

I learned in the November that I was going to get the award but I had to 'keep quiet about it', at least until the New Year when they are announced. I think I told my mum and dad in the week running up to Christmas but not many other people knew. We had a fantastic time at Buckingham Palace and it was a marvellous honour not only for my family and I but also for the club and the people of Hull. I always liked to share things and they after all had been the main support and the reason I'd been awarded it.

Dave Borrill, who had the Jaguar franchise in Hull and was a Rovers' director, organised a chauffeur-driven Rolls Royce to take us down to London and bring us back. He also arranged for us to stay at a superb hotel in London. We went down and stayed overnight, then the next morning it was off to Buckingham Palace, wearing my top hat and tails, and into the historic Palace grounds.

Then came the nerve-racking bit as far as I was concerned. I had to go in front of the Queen receive my medal, bow, and then off I went again. I shouldn't have worried - the whole thing only took a couple of minutes!

I was surrounded by sports stars, pop stars, politicians, film stars, just about everyone I could think of in fact. But it was very much like Wembley had been, very surreal. It seemed like you were there but you weren't there! They were all just faces! But the occasion and just being at Buckingham Palace was just something very different!

I came home after the medal ceremony - and by the time I walked through the front door in Kippax - it was like I'd never been to The Palace at all!

The season was another successful one. The club's top try-scorers were our new-signing, Gary Prohm and Garry Clark with 17. And George Fairbairn topped the goal-kickers list with 83 and 5 drop-goals. A slight surprise was that our average home gate fell to 7,400 - that was difficult to explain because we were playing some very good football then. We finished second in the league behind Hull. Our goal for the following season was to go one better and win the Championship! And twelve months later - following a magnificent season we did exactly that...

We clinched our second Championship in five years with a 44-16 win at Leigh on April 15. There were over twenty-five coach loads of Rovers' fans at Hilton Park to see us lift the trophy - it was another sensational experience. The club picked up £12,000 in prize money. But winning the Championship wasn't about money. We'd lost only one of our last twenty-two league matches - I think that made us worthy Champions.

A month later we achieved a unique 'double' when we defeated Castleford 18-10 at Headingley in the Slalom Lager Premiership Final. It was the first time any club had won both the Championship and Premiership in the same season. And John Dorahy achieved another first when he became the first overseas player to win the Harry Sutherland Trophy as the man of the match.

On October 16 1983, we played the Australian State champions, Queensland in their opening match of a mini-tour of Britain. The match produced probably the most famous instance of 'foul play' by a Rovers' player in the club's history. And even though I was the coach of the side that night it's an incident I'm happy to include here. And one that I won't deny, I recall with fond memories - and more than a little smile...

We'd played the full Australian side in the first game of their tour 12 months earlier, and just like that game the clash against Queensland proved to be another bitterly contested one.

It was our first sighting of a player who was already regarded as the best player in the world, and went on to become one of the game's 'greats', Wally Lewis. He captained Queensland on that eventful night, whilst the side was coached by a man well known to the older fans in the Craven Park crowd, Artie Beetson. We knew any side coached by Artie would provide formidable opposition but none of us were prepared for the torrid encounter that followed.

The crowd of over 6,000 had come to be entertained by the Australians renowned skills - after all the Aussies were the current World Champions and supposedly 'years ahead' of the British. But all that the fans saw that evening, was a team which produced a sickening collection of fouls, aggression and violence. And unfortunately referee, Robin Whitfield, did little to stop it!

I remember in the first half-an-hour, both Roy Holdstock and David Watkinson were carried off and Steve Hartley had to leave the field with a broken arm! It was lucky that we'd arranged for there to be four substitutes allowed that night instead of the usual two, otherwise we'd have been in a terrible situation.

The only time Queensland showed any of their footballing ability was when Lewis raced over for a try after thirteen minutes. Added to an early Lewis' penalty that gave them a 6-0 lead.

George Fairbairn kicked two penalties for us, as the visitors continued with their violence-based gameplan, and the teams turned round with Queensland 6-4 ahead at half-time.

The defining moment of the match had happened four minutes before the break however. It was a moment that everyone who saw it will remember for the rest of his or her life. And one that transformed that ill-tempered game from the second it occurred!

Mark Broadhurst was a New Zealand international prop forward, who was playing in our front row that evening. He'd been a boxer in his earlier sporting days. And had what you'd call an uncompromising approach to rugby league.

He may have been an extremely mild and friendly bloke off the field, but he was as hard as granite on it! But Mark always played the game as it should be played. And I'd never seen anything that made him lose his temper - until that night!

The Queensland hooker, Shane Bernardin, had repeatedly niggled Mark throughout the opening half. But the referee continuously refused to help the situation. And the running confrontation continued to simmer until the 36th minute. Then, as the two clashed again at the play-the-ball, Mark finally lost his cool. He could take the provocation no longer and without warning, hit the Aussie with the most powerful left hook you could imagine. Bernardin was jolted upwards by the force of the punch then slumped slowly to the ground. The crowd roared their approval. Even Mr Whitfield had to turn to one side for a discreet smile. He could have sent Mark straight off, but seemed happy to simply award Queensland a penalty. The way the match was going, I thought what 'Broady' did was something that just had to happen! If he hadn't done it, I'm certain someone would have been badly hurt.

I remember before the match I was in the office and Robin walked in. He asked, 'Is there anything you'd like today Roger?' I replied that I'd like him to remember he was an Englishman. I also remember he didn't seem to appreciate my reply very much. Although I wouldn't normally condone retaliation in any form, I did on that occasion. Mark's action undoubtedly saved us from further unsavoury incidents that evening. I dread to think how the match may have developed without it. After it, lacking their physical and intimidating dominance, which had been shattered by Mark's punch, Queensland were never quite the same. Mike Smith scored a try for us when he touched down a kick by Gordon Smith. It proved to be the only score of the second half and we beat them 8-6. And even Wally Lewis' nerve let him down when he missed a relatively simple penalty that would have given Queensland a draw.

The teams were: Rovers: George Fairbairn, Garry Clark, Mike Smith, John Dorahy, Gary Prohm; Steve Hartley, Gordon Smith; Roy Holdstock, David Watkinson, Mark Broadhurst, Phil Hogan, Chris Burton, David Hall.

Subs: - David Laws, Paul Harkin (not used) Andy Kelly, Tracy Lazenby, Tries: Mike Smith. Goals: George Fairbairn 2

Queensland: Colin Scott; Steve Stacey, Gene Miles, Brett French, Mitch Brennan; Wally Lewis (c), Mark Murray; Paul Kahn, Shane Bernardin, Brad Tessman, Bryan Niebling, Chris Phelan, Wally Fullerton-Smith

Subs: - Jones, Patterson, Lindenburg, Kilroy. Tries: Wally Lewis.

Goals: Wally Lewis. Attendance: 6,383

Those games were all right but they could cause a lot of problems afterwards. I lost Steve Hartley for a few weeks following the game. And it could have been far worse after Mr Whitfield's lenient handling of a number of the early incidents had 'Broady' not took charge in his own unforgettable way...

After us, Queensland played Leeds and then St Helens and defeated both of them easily. The next thing I knew, they wanted to play us again! They might have come over as World Champions but beating them once was more than enough for me! And I said to Colin, 'no bloody chance!'

We were the only British club to beat them, but few people remember that fact. Everyone though, still recalls the moment that led to the famous victory. It's now part of Hull KR folklore. When a placid Kiwi in a Rovers' shirt, produced the most famous punch ever seen at Craven Park...

We were crowned Champions again the following season!

We had to win our last away game of the season at Barrow to clinch the 1984-85 Championship. Barrow were relegated that season but they weren't a bad side at the time, especially at home. But we came back as Champions after winning 30-14.

We had a particularly hectic run-in to the campaign that year, finishing with eight matches in only three weeks. But I was delighted that we won seven of them to clinch our second successive title.

We stayed overnight at Grange Over Sands at a large country house. I recall it proved to be an eventful stop. The driver was parking the coach when a huge branch of a fir tree crashed straight through the window. The other funny thing about that weekend was that we met Ron Hill, the former Castleford player who now commentates for Radio Leeds. Ron had chosen the same hotel to take his wife to for 'a quiet weekend away'. You can imagine when we all walked in, his wife's face was a proverbial picture. And needless to say Ron got the biggest rollicking of his life because she was convinced he must have known we were going to be there. But it didn't stop him staying up until two o'clock in the morning with us.

We lost our final game of the season at home against Widnes but still finished three points ahead of St Helens. And Gary Prohm's two tries in that match aagainst the Chemics set a new club try-scoring record, beating Ged Dunn's 42 tries in a season which had stood for a decade.

Our third Championship in six years made me again realise that we don't put enough emphasis on winning the league. To me that's what a coach dreams of. And at the end of the season if you finish in top place you should win the championship. That should be it in my opinion! They do it in football and it always used to be good enough in rugby league. But now it seems all we want to do is finish near the top so we can make a few more pounds out of these 'knock-out' games! Winning the league should be made more of. It should be the ultimate goal for every club. It should really mean something. In Australia they even call the winners of the league the 'minor premiers'. That's a bad name in my opinion, almost an insult, because there's nothing 'minor' about what they've achieved...

We returned to Wembley again in 1986 - for another 'dream' final as far I as I was concerned - against Castleford. But what a lot of people forget is that in the period from the Challenge Cup semi-final replay to the final, the injuries we sustained were horrendous...

We'd lost half the pack in the run-up to Wembley. Then Gavin Miller pulled a hamstring in the dressing room before the match - and we'd nobody else really - we'd gone as far as we could. That year, although I'd taken two young forwards, Paul Speckman and Paul Fletcher down with us, it was just for the experience. We started the match with Gordon Smith and John Lydiat on the bench.

The result was a bit ironic because we'd played Castleford in the Yorkshire Cup Final that year as well, at Headingley, and had beaten them 22-18. Sadly there was to be no repeat.

Not many Leeds' fans thought we should have been in the Wembley final at all, of course. Looking back, I'd probably have to agree that our luck was in for the first semi-final at Elland Road. We got away with that one! After we had 'Harko' sent off anything could have happened. But David Laws then scored that 'try' when everyone in the ground, apart from the officials 'suspected' he never got the ball down properly. It's incidents like that one, which win you Cups and Championships though, and as they say, over a season those debatable decisions even themselves out. That day our luck was in. There were plenty of other times when it wasn't!

The replay was a totally different story. Again the match was at Elland Road, on the following Thursday night - with our second half performance as near to perfection as anything I'd seen!

You don't have to play in a match for it to be memorable. And the replay when we defeated Leeds 17-0, was probably 'the game' that gave me the greatest pleasure as a coach! But it wasn't the result - or what it meant to the club that was so special - but the way we achieved it...

It had been 0-0 at half-time. But in the second half we applied the pressure, just kept things going and did the things that we planned we would do - and it just happened. Everything just fell into place. It was a virtually perfect performance. The way we achieved the win and how we went about the job couldn't be faulted.

The previous Saturday we may have been lucky - but there was nothing fortunate about our display in the replay - it was a truly stunning team performance. The Rovers' fans behind the posts sang and chanted for fifteen or twenty minutes after the game had ended. And if they hadn't been ushered to the exits by the stewards I dare say they'd have been there all night long. The players all realised they'd produced something very special. And any supporter who knew the first thing about rugby league appreciated they'd witnessed a remarkable performance at Elland Road that night. A performance I'd definitely class as my most satisfying moment as a coach...

But between that unforgettable night and Wembley, we'd lost players like Phil Hogan and Chris Burton with broken arms - and a number of others were carrying niggling injuries. One of the best kept secrets about that final for instance concerned Mike Smith, who had a problem right up to when he ran out onto the field at Wembley. Just before the kick-off I was given a much bigger problem to solve. Whether or not to select Gavin Miller?

Some people have pointed the finger at me since for selecting him, because it was later confirmed that he'd also been carrying an injury. But when I picked the team that day there wasn't any doubt in my mind, Gavin had to play! He'd been playing out of his skin. At that time he'd been the 'man of the season' in Australia and then won the 'Man Of Steel' over here. So for those seasons he had been the best player in the world, he'd been voted the top player in both hemispheres.

But at Wembley, less than an hour before our biggest game of the season, Gavin then 'tweaked' his hamstring in the dressing room. He was limbering up and it just went. It was funny because I'd thought he was 'kidding' at first. He used to be a bit of a joker at times. But unfortunately that wasn't one of them - Gavin's injury was the final straw. The build-up had become just one problem after another! Gavin had trained well, done everything that we'd asked of him and the team sheet had even been given in to the officials, so I couldn't have changed things anyway. And even if I could have taken his name off the list, it would have been difficult to put somebody else in. Not only that, leaving him out would have undoubtedly given Castleford a major boost!

That was the other thing I had to consider. All of a sudden we were in the dressing room preparing to play in a Wembley Challenge Cup Final and I was contemplating the fact that the best player in the world might not be available to play for us. Worse than that, in the next dressing room the opposition would soon see that Gavin Miller's name was not on the team-sheet. I decided there wasn't an option - Gavin had to play!

Gavin didn't have a poor game but he didn't perhaps impose himself like he usually did. The really disappointing thing about the match though was that despite all of our problems, it was still one that we could have won. We admittedly didn't play well but we still had the opportunity to snatch victory when John Lydiat scored a try in the very last minute. But John Dorahy couldn't add the touchline conversion and the game ended 15-14 in Castleford's favour.

John Dorahy was a great thinker about the game. He was always talking to you and getting things out of you. He wanted more knowledge about the game all the time - that's the type of lad he was - even then, I knew he wanted to go back to Australia and become a coach out there.

The day before the final I'd gone to Wembley to have a look at the pitch with the lads. I walked round and then stood with John Dorahy on the touchline and I remember him asking, 'What happens if I get a goal kick from here? There's not much room to walk back to take it, is there?'

He was right. There was hardly any room at all! I told him he would have to get his timing right.

I couldn't believe it when only twenty-four hours later, 'tin-lid' - John Lydiat - scored a try a minute from the end of the final. And John Dorahy had to take his conversion attempt from the exact place where we'd stood and talked the day before. History tells us that JD missed the goal and we lost the game. But I know we could have won it.

I'd be the first to admit some of the lads didn't played to their potential that day and things certainly didn't go for us. We did some very uncharacteristic things that we wouldn't normally have done and there were players who were usually unflappable, giving stupid penalties away. I suppose that was down to a bit of frustration creeping into our game. But having said all that we could still have won it in the last minute with that conversion. And although the record books will show Castleford as the Cup winners of 1986, when it came down to it, we were actually only one kick away from lifting the trophy. But that's life. We'd taken part in another Wembley final and it was a great day out for the club and the supporters. We could have won - but we didn't...

CHAPTER TWENTY-ONE
IT'S A SUPERMARKET NOW!

CRAVEN PARK - THE END OF AN ERA

It was the end of an era when the old Craven Park closed its' gates for the final time on April 9 1989. The day will live forever, not only for me but also for the thousands of supporters who had watched Rovers there since the ground had opened in the 1920s.

Back in 1922 Craven Park became the club's eighth ground. The opening game on September 2 ended in a 0-3 defeat against Wakefield Trinity. Just over a month later 22,282 fans watched Rovers play Hull. It remains a record attendance for the ground to this day - and one that will now obviously stand forever. The games were two of the first milestones for Rovers' new home. And in the following sixty-seven years, hundreds more tales of triumph and despair followed, each cherished by the rugby loving supporters who witnessed them...

It wasn't surprising therefore, that in 1989, like the fans of numerous clubs who have changed grounds in the last few years, some Rovers' followers were far from happy at having to leave 'their spiritual home'. Some didn't 'take' to the new Craven Park at all and I know of certain individuals who actually stopped going to support Rovers altogether. I'd have to say though, if you're a true fan, I think you'd follow your team wherever they played.

The last match at the old Craven Park was of course a highly emotional occasion. It proved a very heart wrenching day for everybody. The game against Widnes was televised later that evening on Yorkshire Television's 'Scrum Down' programme. And I still have a video of the programme containing the final shot where the gates of Craven Park swing shut for the final time.

The match against Widnes, who'd just been crowned as the League Champions couldn't have saved us from relegation, whatever the result. I brought a lot of the young lads in to play against Widnes to gain valuable experience. And as so often happens with one-off games - they all gave great performances. Some people of course asked, why hadn't I done it earlier. I replied I knew that the youngsters could play like they did but I also knew they couldn't play like that and keep it going week after week - it was a one-off display! I'd been trying to save the club - and the only way to do that was with the experienced players. It was the experienced players that would have got us through if anyone could. The kids were all right but after a couple of games they would have broken down. The system of 'blooding' the younger players had worked in previous seasons. We had introduced them, a couple in at a time - given them a game or two, then dropped them out - then when they were ready again, brought them back. With a good quality squad we could use that system very successfully. But we got to the stage when we didn't have the luxury of being able to do that. There wasn't enough young players coming through the system. And as soon as players became 'big' enough - if you want to put it like that - they were in!

There was nothing at stake but nearly eight thousand fans went to see the last game at Craven Park before the bulldozers moved in to do their work. We led at one stage in the second half, 13-6. But eventually went down 13-16. The result wasn't the important factor though. The youngsters had played well again and things looked far from all doom and gloom for the following year - albeit in the second division.

After the game I was hoisted shoulder high by the fans and paraded in front of the east stand. A few moments later, as their chants rang out in the background, I left the field close to tears...

Another Rovers' stalwart, long-serving Secretary, Ron Turner, also watched the end of an era that afternoon. Ron was a man who rarely showed his feelings, although he was passionate about rugby league and totally dedicated to Rovers. And our departure from the old Craven Park obviously proved a very emotional time for him.

Ron had started working at the club at the beginning of the 1969-70 season and became something of a fixture at Craven Park. He hailed from Cumbria and did a hell of a lot for Rovers. And like me he went through it all - the good times - and the bad ones. He was still there when I left the club in 1991. And didn't leave until the new millennium after giving Rovers over thirty years of conscientious service. He was always there! He seemed to be at the ground on Holderness Road and then the new one on Preston Road, twenty-four hours a day. No matter what time you arrived he was always in his office. He just got on with his job - and believe it or not he enjoyed it! You wouldn't have always thought so to look at him, but he loved the place and he loved everything about rugby league. Some of the players called him 'Scattercash'. I don't know why, a touch of irony I suspect! As he handed the lads their wages, you'd have often thought it was his own money he was giving out...

The new Craven Park had a lot to live up to. But sadly, despite the amount of money spent on it, the fact remains to this day that it never did! And it simply proved that there's no point in having a good stadium if you don't have good players and a successful team to play in it!

After all, the last twenty years at the old ground had been packed with classic matches - and memories of Cup winning teams, championship winning sides and some of the best players to ever wear the famous red and white jersey of Hull K.R. All that however was achieved from within a ground that was literally falling down around us!

The new Craven Park should have been and still could be an excellent facility for the east of the City. But it would have to have considerable investment to bring it up to the standard it deserves. The stadium never appeared fully finished. And the open ends and dog-racing and speedway tracks around the playing area have always been a problem with achieving an intimate atmosphere like the old ground had.

The demolition of Craven Park coincided fairly closely with the end of Rovers' glory days of the eighties. And it was significant that when the curtain fell there, it was also the time when Rovers were again relegated from the elite division.

The site of the old ground is now a supermarket. And anybody who isn't twenty or more will probably not even remember when the bustling crowds used to fill Holderness Road and cram into the ground to see a club, that at the time was undoubtedly the biggest name in rugby league...

I was at the new Craven Park for two years. I'd signed a contract that would keep me at the club until the end of the 1990-91 season. But I told the Rovers' board in October 1990 of my intention to leave when my contract was up. I saw Colin and told him I'd be leaving - and why - but I'd signed a contract and was determined to see it out. I wasn't going to start crying about it. I'd see it through - because that's the way I am. Although I always felt a little bitter against that statement that I would have money to spend, when now of course everyone knows I didn't get any. I knew it was going to be bloody hard work but in life you've got to take the good with the bad. When we first moved to the ground we were in the Second Division. But we had some fantastic support nonetheless.

The new stadium was officially opened on Sunday 24 September 1989. The first ever match on the ground was a Second Division game against Trafford Borough and with no disrespect to that club it was hardly the 'opener' that many fans had hoped for. Teams such as Halifax, Whitehaven and Oldham were also in the division and any of them it was felt would have provided more attractive opposition for our debut game in our new home. But maybe the opposition didn't really matter!

A capacity crowd of 8,500 turned out to be part of the occasion - they'd probably have done the same if we'd been playing the local school team - and saw us demolish Trafford Borough, 48-8. And when you look down the teamsheet for that opening encounter it wasn't difficult to see why.

The backs included George Fairbairn, Garry Clark, Mike Fletcher and Greg Austin - the half-backs were Wayne Parker and David Bishop - and the forwards boasted players such as Zook Ema, Tony Botica, Paul Lyman and Mike Smith. Aussie International Bryan Niebling and Andy Thompson were on the bench. And Paul Fletcher, Des Harrison and Anthony Sullivan were just three of the other players in the squad who didn't play that day. I think you'd have to agree it was a pretty good line-up for a Second Division side. It ultimately proved to be far too good for that division, running up scores of over half a century on ten occasions.

In the middle of March we beat Whitehaven 92-10. Greg Austin, Tony

Sullivan and David Bishop all scored hat-tricks and Mike Fletcher kicked fourteen goals. Not surprisingly with results like that we walked away with the title and were promoted back into the top flight at the first attempt. I'm proud to say I left the club in a good position, back in the first division...

Training nights, I found were always one of the most 'eventful' parts of coaching. In all the years I was coach at Rovers, I used to send the lads on long distance runs. I suppose they've been on hundreds of them in that time. But long distance runs were not the most popular part of training for some players. And if I made a list of those players, there's no doubt whose name would be at the top - John Millington!

At the old Craven Park there were some large sliding doors at the front of the ground on the West stand side. From the changing rooms to the doors was about thirty yards at the most. I never knew whether Millo set off quickly at the front of the group or simply 'disappeared' somewhere between the changing rooms and those green doors! What I do know is that in all those years that I set them off and watched them run past the doors - I can't remember 'Millo' passing me once. I'm certain he never did a full run in his life. But he always used his head. He never came back in too early - he was always about fourth or fifth from the end - and he always arrived back looking as if he'd done a good work-out.

So one day I said to John Moore, tell the players the route and then set them off. We knew that 'Millo' would be off like a shot! So John told them the route and sure enough 'Millo' was off! Once he'd gone I stopped the rest of them and said, Come on lads, let's go and have a game of touch football on the pitch. About forty-five minutes later 'Millo' re-appeared, saw us all playing touch on the pitch and came over to join us.

'What's going on?' he inquired. I told him we'd decided not to have a run that night, but to have a game of touch instead, but he'd already gone. John's reply started along the lines of: 'You little bastard, I'll get you back for that.' And various other expletives followed. But as far as I know he never completed a run in his life. And he never got me back either...

One of the runs I used to send them on quite often was to turn right out of Craven Park and run up Holderness Road towards Bilton, right round Ganstead Golf Course and then back. Some of them I know, including Phil Lowe, Ged Dunn and Dave Hall, they didn't think I knew but they used to take money with them and get on the bus for part of the way. I knew it from an early stage when I followed them on a Lambretta and stood and watched them from across the road but they didn't know it was me. I'd borrowed one of the lad's scooters and actually watched them get on the bus. They were brilliant at finding ways to make life easier and I suppose in a way I admired them for using their heads. It was something that I had to put down to experience.

'Millo' might have done the same, although I admit I never saw him. On other nights I'm sure he cut through the gardens on Hedon Road, he might have gone anywhere to have avoided those runs. He might not even have left the ground. I never found out how he did it until earlier this year when he finally divulged his secret!

182

'As soon as we went out road running - I used to vanish!' admitted 'Millo'. 'I used to know all the short cuts in east Hull. So when we set off on a ten mile road run I used to be in front of everybody. And it was the one thing that Roger could never weigh up - but I never hid - it was just because I knew all the shorts cuts.

I went on a run one night, the route was down Holderness Road, then along Saltshouse Road, through to Sutton and back again. I started at the front, but then worked my way to near the back as I usually did. I ran down Holderness Road and I got to the drain and thought I'll just cut down here. I thought that will cut the corner off. Then I'd rejoin the rest of the players as they went past...

At the other end, I was just climbing over the wall that led to the drain when I saw Roger stood behind a tree. He was having a little smoke but his bike wheel was sticking out. So I just hung back a bit. Steve Hartley went by, Allan Agar went by, David Hall went by and Peter Muscroft went by. And I thought I'll just join in behind them. Roger then stepped out and said, 'Well done Steve Hartley, well done Allan Agar, well done David Hall, well done Peter Muscroft... and well done John Millington. John Millington!!! How the hell did you get there?'

But I never caught the bus like some of them did. It was usually 'Lowey' and Ged Dunn, and they'd go round the route and sneak off at the other end and rejoin the rest of us!

I remember we were sitting in the dressing-room one night before we went out training and Roger said, 'Right we've had a complaint from a lady about people cutting through her garden and trampling all her flowers down. He was looking at me when he said it. He said, It's got to stop! I'm going to say no more - everyone knows who has done it. Now off you go!'

And as I was going out the door I said to him, If that woman gets in touch again Roger, tell her she's a lying b*****d, because I always go down the path!'

'Millo' was a non-stop joker and great to have around. And although it wasn't very often that I made him laugh, he was always very amused at one of the things I used to do. I probably still do it today - I don't know - I didn't realise I did it before! After a shower I used to get dried and the first things I put on before anything else were my socks and shoes. That always tickled Millo. Socks and shoes even before my trousers - although I probably didn't do it when we used to wear 'drainpipes'.

But I know I wasn't the only one with a strange dressing-room habit. A lot of players had their own little idiosyncrasies that they performed in the dressing room. Little quirks that they had to do. They didn't always tell you about them of course - but they thought that if they changed them, then it would change how they played on the day. That's how superstitious some of them were. I wasn't superstitious but some of the players had amazing little rituals! They wanted to be third in line when we ran out or they had to be fourth or fifth. Or they couldn't go out before a certain other player because the only time they had before we'd lost the match. It got really crazy at times. One day they might have done something and then had a

great game, so they had to repeat it in the hope they'd play as well again!
Len Casey was another player who you wouldn't describe as 'the keenest of trainers'. I recall when he turned up for one training session pretending to have a leg injury. But it was obvious he was feigning the injury as he didn't want to do the long distance run we had planned. I knew he didn't want to do it - he was always a 'short distance' man. I told Len to just sit down for a couple of minutes and wait for me. I'd get the players on their way and we'd do something different. He sat down and I went over to Frank Parker and asked him if he still had his fold-up bike at the ground. He said he had. I gave him my car keys and told him to put the bike in the boot. He went and put the bike in the boot and came back with the keys and said, 'Roger, there's something I should tell you.'
Len was obviously listening to what was going on, so I interrupted Frank and ended his intended warning in mid sentence!
Don't worry, I told Frank, you can tell me when you get back.
And before he could speak again I shouted, Come on lads, out you go, and I sent them off on their run. I then turned to Casey and said, come on Len let's go and have a drive round, we can see how the lads do on their run.
We set off and drove out into the countryside, stopping just short of Hornsea! We got out of the car and I told a puzzled looking Len to open the boot. There's a bike in there I said to him, put it together and I'll see you back at Craven Park. Well you should have seen the look on his face. I watched him put the bike together and set off on the ten or eleven mile journey back to Craven Park. What I didn't know when I left Len in the middle of nowhere was that Frank Parker was going to tell me that one of the pedals was 'knackered'. So on every revolution, when the left pedal got to the top, the chain slipped and the pedal crashed noisily to the bottom. It must have looked like poor Len was limping all the way back to Hull...
I remember another session when we were working on a 'set' move. It was simple enough - or so I thought. Roy Holdstock had to take the ball up, hit the line, settle it in for us and pass the ball to Len. All Casey had to do was be the pivot and pass the ball to the supporting player. Well we must have tried the move nine or ten times - but Len couldn't get it right - it didn't work once. In the end Casey just walked up, tapped me on the shoulder and said, 'Roger, can I take the ball up please?'
Len was a smashing kid to work with though - and a great mate. But he was the one person I'd never room with. He was absolutely terrible! 'Watkie' always found him OK to share with apparently - but I don't know why...
We've all heard the jokes about the guy with short arms and deep pockets - well that's Casey! Someone told me recently about a trick that Len pulled when he had his pub in Brough. It sums him up perfectly. He invited about thirty people over to his pub to watch a top rugby league match on the big screen. 'Bring your wives and we'll all enjoy it together - and at half-time I'll put a buffet on,' said Len.
But as soon as the match was into the second half and the buffet had all gone, Len said to one of his bar staff, 'Nip round and get a 'fiver' apiece off everybody will you?' That's classic Casey...

CHAPTER TWENTY-TWO
IT WASN'T
ROCKET SCIENCE
THE COACHING ROLLERCOASTER...

Memorable performances during my last couple of seasons at Rovers, I'd have to say, were few and far between. But there was one particular match against Hull in my very last season at the club that I remember with a great deal of satisfaction.

Surprise results happened on a regular basis in derby matches. And my last-ever derby at Craven Park as Rovers' coach produced another unexpected scoreline. Brian Smith was in charge at Hull, they won the Premiership that season and were near the top when they came to Craven Park on New Year's Day 1991. Nobody gave us a chance of winning that day. Nobody thought we'd get anywhere near them - we didn't have a hope in hell! But everyone was proved wrong again - Mike and Paul Fletcher and Paul Lyman scored tries - and we beat them 20-8.

That's what derby matches were all about...

It never seemed to matter whether Hull was at the bottom of the league and we were near the top or the other way round, when the two teams met, anything could happen - and usually did! The formbook was very often turned upside-down. And that was the thought I usually took into a derby match. It didn't matter where the two teams were in the table - it was all down to what happened on the day.

There are two other derbies which stick in my mind from my coaching days - both of them for the superb way the team performed.

The first of them was at Craven Park on October 7 1984. We were getting beaten 16-2 at half time. But we turned it around in the second half and took Hull apart. They only scored one point after the break and we finished up winning 26-17. Mike Smith was the star that day.

The other one was actually played on a soccer ground, the 1985 John Player Final at Boothferry Park. It was January 26 and there was still a lot of snow on the pitch. But it was a very entertaining match. And although the final score was only 12-0 to us there was a lot of good football played that day.

There obviously weren't many derby matches from my 'playing days' that I'd rank alongside the 1980 Wembley final. Most of them tended to be very dour affairs. But there's one incident that always stands out to me from those games which happened when we played Hull in the first round of the Challenge Cup in 1978. It had nothing to do with either entertaining football or superb performances however...

The match was at the Boulevard on February 26. Colin Tyrer who'd joined the club from Wigan, kicked two goals for us but was then sent off for flattening Hull's scrum-half, Keith Hepworth. When I asked Colin what he'd done it for, he replied it was because 'Heppy' had 'done' him in the Castleford versus Wigan Wembley Cup Final, eight years earlier.

Who said rugby league players don't have good memories?

Colin had been led off the Wembley pitch with blood pouring from a mouth injury that afternoon in 1970 following Hepworth's late challenge on him. It was an incident that many thought changed the course of the Cup final. Colin was an accurate goal-kicker - one of the best in the game. He'd already kicked Wigan into a first minute lead but after his departure they didn't score again. My pal Bill Francis, the Wigan centre, took over the kicking duties but missed a relatively easy penalty attempt. And after that Wigan kicked for touch numerous times when they were awarded further penalties, where Tyrer, had he still been on the pitch, would surely have put more points on the scoreboard. But Colin wasn't able to return and although an X-ray later revealed no broken bones, he did have to undergo extensive dental work. Cliff Hill came on for Colin and wrote his name in the record books as the first-ever substitute to be used in a Challenge Cup Final. And following one of the most controversial finals seen at Wembley, the Cup finally went to my old club Castleford by 7 points to 2.

But at the Boulevard, Colin was back in the dressing room earlier than planned for a different reason. Hull went on to beat us 9-7 and we were out of the Cup at the first round stage. I remember thinking, as Colin walked off, what a time to do something like that - right in the middle of a match!

I shouldn't have been surprised I suppose, derby games were always unpredictable...

Apart from that terrific New Year's Day victory, in complete contrast, my final season also produced what I'd have to describe as the worst day of my coaching life.

It was my very final game in charge on March 31 1991 at Sheffield. I was disgusted that a team could just lay down like that and die! I remember Bryan Niebling and a couple of others playing their socks off but people around him were just going through the motions. And in all my time at Rovers that was probably the most inept display I witnessed. I know we'd had some good hidings in the past, but the way that match unfolded was embarrassing. It was my last match in charge and to end my days at Rovers with a performance like that, I suppose I took it as a personal insult. But that's what it felt like to me...

I think that's what made me think I'd made the right choice to finish. My priority that year had been to ensure we maintained our first division status. That's all I was bothered about. It was hard but we did it. And achieving that had probably got to some of the kids - they maybe thought their job was over. But as I far as I saw it, I expected them to go out that day and play - and to enjoy themselves - there was no pressure on them. But the 62-16 scoreline, I thought was a disgrace!

Those two matches from my last year at Rovers, in a way summed-up my entire coaching career. The game of rugby league, like most sports, had a habit of producing unexpected highs and bitterly disappointing lows. As a coach, it was one of the things I'd learned to accept and cope with over the years. Another was the fact that you can talk until you're blue in the face about this, that and the other. But at the end of the day, no matter what happens on the pitch, the buck always stops with you. And when I watched last year's World Club Challenge - and other games like it - I just asked myself, who'd be a coach?

I'd done the same things at Craven Park as the Rhinos' coach Tony Smith - I knew how he felt. I'd planned things to the final detail and worked a certain way all through the week. Everything's gone well, let's keep that for Sunday, you tell your players. But once they go out there on that pitch, they are their own bosses. And if they're not thinking about what they are doing, and not doing the things we'd planned, there's only one person who takes the stick from the supporters - the coach. It's always happened that way and I suppose it happens even more so, these days.

When I'd first started coaching, I didn't have any difficulty being a player-coach. The only problem that I remember was that whilst I was on the pitch taking part in the game, I didn't see an overall picture. Fortunately I always had a good assistant on the bench in John Moore - he always managed to get the messages out to us and probably I should have given him a lot more powers. I should have said, don't worry about what you're doing John, if you're convinced it's right, do it. Because John was a marvellous tactician, he could read a game and see what was wanted. I should have given him more responsibility especially when I was playing full-time, because when I was in the 'front-line' things certainly appeared differently.

As a coach I first worked out how I wanted to do things, how I wanted the team to play the game. I insisted on strict discipline at training, that was always a big ask of mine - I insisted the lads got their fitness right.

But I also made training as interesting as possible. There's nothing worse than players getting bored with their training routines. And nothing more off-putting for them than to arrive at training, knowing exactly what they were going to do in the session.

Moulding the players into being a 'happy family' was important. But that wasn't always as simple to do as it sounded. Helping players with their off-field problems as well as their on-field ones was one of the trickiest aspects of being a coach that I encountered.

Players could appear as a 'happy family' at Craven Park but when they went home to their own families I didn't know if Joe Bloggs was going home to have another row with his wife or if he'd be sleeping on the settee! It was things like that, which I had to take into consideration. And problems such as those that the fans never even thought about...

The fans in the stand are all entitled to their opinion of course. Unlike some people, I'm a firm believer that just because they haven't played the game doesn't mean they can't have a valid opinion. But today I think the coaches often get blamed for a lot of things that are just not their responsibility.

It's true you certainly get more stick when things go wrong and the team plays badly, than you get praise when they go right and the team plays well. And no matter how well you do there's always somebody who is not satisfied. I remember when we won at Wembley for the first time in the history of the club. We arrived back at Craven Park on the Sunday and a bloke came up to me and said he wanted to win it again the following year. Now I'm all for ambition but I thought, isn't it amazing, we've just won the Cup for the first time in our lives but instead of enjoying the win and celebrating, he was already thinking about the following year! I suppose you just can't cater for people like that...

When I started coaching full-time, the methods that I used were a combination of everything I'd learnt from all over the place. What I'd been brought up with. What I'd learnt in Australia and even what I'd read in books. I remember when Allan Agar went back to Featherstone and coached them to a Wembley win against Hull in 1982-83 they paid for him to make a trip out to Australia and Allan asked me if I'd like to go with him. I paid my own way out and we had a fortnight out there together. I remember one day while we were there, we were browsing around a sports store in Eastern Suburbs and found this book on different training methods. There were pages and pages of different ideas. One used a ten by ten grid. Another called 'heavy hands' was adapted from cross-country skiing. It was obvious there was a great deal we could do to make training far more interesting and less regimented.

Rovers then sent me over to the States for ten days to study the training methods of the Chicago Bears. When we got back we had some tackle bags made and introduced tackling and scrummaging machines. It just made things a little different so the players weren't coming down to training every time and doing exactly the same thing. I know there were times when I trained and without being disrespectful to anyone who trained me, I found I'd go to training and I'd know exactly what was going to happen. I knew I would do my warm-up, I'd do some laps around the field, which were totally boring, and I'd do my sprints. At Rovers we wanted to make things a bit different. I know some nights, it's taken us more than three-quarters of an hour to set something up for the lads to do in training - to make it more interesting. It might have been just a silly thing, an exercise here, then a tackle over there, just to create a kind of little merry-go-round for them. You were still doing the same basic exercises but in a different and more entertaining way.

The best part about having a good squad of players, is when you got them into a rhythm, they virtually coached themselves. They knew what the sort of pattern we wanted was. And at that time the reason we were so successful was because there were so many players in that team who were thinkers. Players like Dave Watkinson, Mike Smith, Mark Broadhurst and Gary Prohm. They knew what the gameplan was - and they knew what their role in it was. That's what the team was about. It wasn't 'rocket science' I know - but they knew we were going to put the opposition in a corner - and basically knock 'seven bells' out of them! Then we'd just wait for them to make a mistake, or in the worst scenario they'd put in a kick, and we'd pick the ball up on the halfway line. And from that position, with the players that we had, we'd every chance of scoring every time we had the ball in our hands. All we did was draw the opposition in and then spread the ball wide - and it worked and it worked, over and over again. Then we'd bring our own kicking game into it...

It sounds very basic - and it was. But much better coaches than I have usually insisted that rugby league is a very simple game. I'd agree with that. And when you've got thirteen players who can play it well - it's even simpler! But I'd also add, it's often when a coach tries to qualify why he's there at all, that the problems start!

I took ideas for training from everywhere. I was lucky that I have a friend, Rod Johnson, who played professional soccer with Leeds United, Rotherham and Doncaster. I went with him on a few occasions to their training sessions at Doncaster when Lawrie McMenemy was manager there. We were on strike at the pit, which wasn't unusual at that time. So I trained with Doncaster for a few days because I had a Great Britain match the following weekend. And just seeing the different training methods that they used was a very interesting and enlightening experience. I also trained with Rod and the lads when he managed football teams around the Kippax area. And the ideas I got from him were amazing - I just picked up more and more different ideas wherever I went. I'd take the ideas that I wanted and I'd throw away those I didn't. I think that's one thing we did well at Rovers. John Edson, Johnny Moore, Ged Dunn and I made sure that we varied the training as much as possible. We tried to make it as enjoyable as we could. Obviously there were times when it couldn't be enjoyable for everyone, because at the end of the day a lot of hard work had to be done. There was no getting away from that. But if you can do the hard work in different ways it helps tremendously.

I can remember one of the many times when I looked after 'The Zetland' and a lad came in. I knew he coached one of the junior sides, the under tens or under twelves. He looked a bit down and I said, what's wrong with you? 'I've had a terrible training session,' he said.

What with the under tens? I inquired, you should be enjoying that!

'I know I should,' he said. How did you start the session off? I asked.

'Well, when we'd all got together, I told them we were going to start off by doing four laps of the field first.'

I thought no wonder he was having problems. I think you were wrong there mate. I told him. All you want to be doing with those under tens, is to throw a ball in the middle of them and let them enjoy themselves.

To me at that level it's not about winning, it's simply about learning the basics of the game. How to play the game, how to pass a ball properly and to have a good concept of the rules. There's enough competition later on when they get to fifteen and sixteen, when they want to start winning. But at the age of nine and ten all they should be doing is going out on the field, playing rugby and enjoying themselves. That's what we did when we were kids. It might have been thirty a side and we refereed ourselves, but we loved it! We must have done because we went back night after night, to do it all over again! And there were never any problems or punch-ups because one of us made the wrong decision or anything like that - we just got on with the game...

The one thing I feel most proud of about my coaching days was a general thing. It was the way I helped to transform a club, that in many ways was struggling, into a good, professional club. During the early eighties there's no doubt in my mind that we became a club with professional and go-ahead ideas that most other clubs could only dream about having.

After we'd won at Wembley, the club under Johnny Moore, John Edson, Ged Dunn and I became a top, professional outfit. During the first half of the 1980s it was a satisfying and enjoyable time to be at Craven Park. The players knew exactly what they had to do. And when they came to training, they knew that it would be different and interesting every time. That's part of the satisfaction I got out of coaching. To ensure that the kids remained focused and that they were always progressing and learning new things. It was like when I used to work at the pit. I used to get up some mornings and think, bloody hell have I got to go down that pit again? So what did I do? I got out! It's no good getting up in a morning like that. You've got to get up and want to do something.

The satisfaction I got at Rovers was also seeing the younger players starting to 'come through' from 'Eddo' and progress into the first team. Players like Tony Sullivan. And when they reached a certain level, they didn't just stop, but went on still further to the heady heights of representative and international football. As far as I was concerned, that's what coaching was about! And I've got to thank people like John, Ged and Johnny and the directors for giving me the opportunity to do it...

My last five years at Rovers were far more turbulent times. Some of them were great - but some of them were hell!

During that time I can remember the Rovers' Chairman, Malcolm West, ringing me up. My contract was up for renewal and Malcolm wanted to talk about a new one. Castleford had already been in touch. I was looking after Colin's pub, The Zetland Arms at the time and remember the conversation very well. Castleford had just parted company with their coach and before they appointed Darryl Van de Velde, David Poulter rang me and said, 'We'd like you to come to Castleford and be our coach.'

I said thanks very much Dave, I'm very honoured but I've got a meeting with my Chairman tomorrow and I'm going to sit down and talk about a new contract with him.

It was a time when big changes were taking place. Rovers were leaving their

Holderness Road ground to go to 'New Craven Park' on Preston Road. I was told that after the move I would have 'a million pounds' to spend on new players. A lot of the current squad were getting old together and there were quite a few 'in the twilight of their careers'. They'd been a marvellous set of players but your legs and your brain only go on for so long.

The other problem we had was that we didn't have the amount of good youngsters coming through like we'd had in previous years, so the team definitely needed some money spending on it. When my Chairman told me that after the move to the new ground he would have a million pounds for me to spend, what was I going to do? I wasn't going to turn my back on that! I said fair enough. The rest as they say is history. And history of course shows us it didn't quite turn out that way...

There was a lot of hard work and a lot of pain. I know we went down into the Second Division for one year but we came straight back up again. It's not as easy to do that these days, because I think the gap has got too wide now. But we were very lucky. We came back up into the first division and the season I retired, we retained that status and I left the club in the top flight. That was a priority. But if you think about setting off on a new season and your main priority is to stay up - it's bloody hard work! There wasn't a lot of enjoyment in it as far as I was concerned. To me rugby league was about enjoying yourself. But all of a sudden I was faced with a job where I wasn't doing that. And I've always said if you're not enjoying getting up to go to work, you might as well not go! And that's what it came to at the end. I haven't said that to many people but it really did get to that point. It became something that I realised I didn't want to do any longer. Where it had been a pleasure to get into the car and come to Craven Park, it was now getting to be hard work. And in the end I had to sit down and have a word with myself. I thought, was this going to finish up making me ill? And if the answer to that was yes, I might as well call it a day and get out there and then. There was a lot of soul-searching for two or three months before I finally decided that was exactly what I had to do.

It was very upsetting because I had a lot of very good friends in Hull. The people of Hull were just like the people of Castleford. I'd always thought the only difference was they were fishermen and sailors - and we were miners. But they had a very similar mentality and I knew it would be a tremendous wrench for me to leave. In the end it turned out to be even more traumatic than I'd imagined, not just for me but for Carol and Kay as well. Kay had been more or less brought up there. From being a baby she was always across in Hull with her mum...

I can honestly say of all the lads that I coached for fourteen years at Craven Park I never really had a problem with any of them. They were all great lads who got on with their job. Life was naturally more difficult near the end because we weren't as good a team by then. And there wasn't the money about that there had been in the earlier days when we could go out and sign the good players that we needed. It's true to say that virtually anyone who we wanted to bring to Craven Park we succeeded in getting there. All the overseas lads we signed were also all marvellous kids. They all came and just got on with the job. They all joined in perfectly with the lads that were already at the club - and there was never a hint of any animosity between any of them. They just got on with life and playing for Hull K.R.

There were some good years and I'll admit some that weren't quite so good. It was a pleasure to be a part of such a tremendous club most of the time but of course there were also days when I realised things could have been better! I suppose I'd have to say the problem I had with David Bishop was one of those times. But I've no problem at all talking about him...

We played a game at Oldham and he got himself in trouble and had to appear before the disciplinary committee. I took him along to the meeting, spoke for him on his behalf and he got off - job done! I didn't think the incident was as bad as people made out. And although Charlie McAllister received a broken jaw in the incident even he spoke up for David afterwards.

We stopped at my house on the way home from Leeds and had some tea and then carried on to Hull for training. I had a lot to think about. We were playing Widnes at the weekend and I thought about what would be best for David. He'd had a lot to deal with that week, he'd had the press on his back, and I decided that the best way to ease him back into things was to play him at substitute the following Sunday. He was playing at fullback at the time and I intended to bring David Lightfoot in at number one and play David off the bench. I could then use him as an impact player and could put him anywhere I wanted to on the pitch. Because when David was on the field he only went one way and that was forward! So that's what I did. But when we got to training and I told him he went ballistic!

There was only one way I could deal with the way he'd reacted. I'd just had enough. I said David if you aren't going to accept that, then go in, go away from the ground, I don't want you here. And basically that's all that happened. But of course it was then blown out of all proportion. And then it came down to a principle that there was no way he was going to play at Rovers again whilst I was there. And the board asked me over and over again during the following weeks about having him back.

But I said no! I said look, I'm finishing at the end of the season anyway, if you want him back now pay me up and I'll go. Or if you don't want to do that - he's banned and that's it! And I insist to this day that I never had any problems with David. All I wanted him to do was come and play for Rovers, and play under my rules. That's all I ever wanted - and that's all I want to say about the matter. I honestly don't feel it warrants any more than that. It wasn't a big deal as far as I was concerned.

David had a load of potential, but what he came out with on that night at training - and after all I'd done for him - there was no way that I'd have had him back in any team that I was running. I'd stuck by him and he treated me like he did. But these things happen - it's life, I suppose - and you have to get on with it!

He returned to play for Rovers the following season when I'd left and George Fairbairn had taken over as coach. But that's another story...

CHAPTER TWENTY-THREE
YOU MUST
BE JOKING!

I know I've said it on more than one occasion in previous chapters, that hindsight can be a wonderful thing. I'd like to say it again. And add in no uncertain terms, that joining Halifax was a total mistake!

When I finished at Rovers I told myself that I would have twelve months out of the game. That would give me the chance to see what opportunities came up, both in and away from rugby league. But that idea didn't last five minutes - when Halifax came in for me straight away - and I agreed to become their new coach.

It was a vastly different set-up at Thrum Hall and a totally contrasting regime to what I'd been accustomed to at Rovers. I don't think I attended more than five board meetings in the twenty-five years I was at Rovers. But I went to one every week at Halifax!

The Chairman at Halifax was a multi-millionaire. And I could sign anybody I wanted to as long as he suggested it.

Don't get me wrong, they were nice enough people. But some of the opinions I got from the board were abysmal and I thought I've got this every Monday. I couldn't do with it...

At Rovers players used to come to talk to me, I was the first port of call. And there was no point in them going upstairs because the directors wouldn't talk to them, unless they'd already discussed whatever their problem was with me first.

But at Halifax it was all totally different to what I'd known in the past. The players would go straight to the directors and I'd be stood there like an idiot, not knowing what was going on. It was little things like that, which I didn't like.

Even at my initial interview I admit things didn't seem quite right and I thought to myself on more than one occasion, 'What am I doing here?'

They asked my opinion about the Halifax team that had just gained promotion from the second division. And what my thoughts were about where it would finish in the first division?

I told them that if they didn't invest in new players they'd go straight back down. My reasoning was simple. I'd recently left Rovers where they'd just completed a difficult first season back in the top division. They'd struggled but they'd survived! And they had a better squad of players than Halifax... If you go into the new season without strengthening the squad, you'll go straight down again! I said.

'Right, OK!' was their immediate reaction.

My assessment of the situation seemed to be what they wanted to hear and I got the job. They brought in a number of new players such as Karl Harrison from Hull, Mark Preston from Wigan and an old mate of mine from Rovers, Paul Harkin was signed from Leeds. And the club had a relatively successful first year and finished seventh. We beat Leeds at Headingley, which they hadn't done for years and years. But it turned out to be a bridge too far however in the Premiership! We went to St Helens and got murdered, 52-6. After that they said, 'Right, let's start again.'

They brought a few more players in but it started getting tricky then. And it came as no surprise to me that it wasn't long before I was sacked...

I'd coached at the very top level with Hull K.R. and won every trophy the game had to offer. But in 1994 I tasted the other side of coaching when I joined new club, Ryedale York, for their challenge in the second division.

How I went for it, especially after my experiences at Halifax, I'll never know. It was my friend, Razza (Pete Astbury) who put the idea to me in the first place. He was the lad who had broken my leg when I was thirteen, he played for one school and I played for another.

He later played professionally for Leeds and Bradford. He said Ray Batten who he'd played with at Leeds and was still good friends with, had just been on the telephone. Ray was now a director at York - and wanted to know if I'd be interested in taking over as coach?

Again I said I was - and again I got the job. And again it was never right! The problems were probably a lot to do with me. I'd been at Rovers who were a very professional outfit. But all of a sudden, at these other clubs, everything seemed so different and the way they operated was so alien to what I was used to.

They'd been under a certain coach for so many years that it was all 'done by numbers'. And I couldn't do with that. It was all, when this happens, we play the ball like this, and when this happens, we play the ball like that! First we do this and then we do that. It was all so regimented. I couldn't get into that. It wasn't my way. I'd always given my teams a general play and let them get on with it. But it went on and on and on!

I suppose I knew from day one that I wasn't destined for a long career at York. And the next thing that happened proved me right.

I was meant to meet the Chairman in his local pub one night. He wasn't there but I knew what was going to happen. The strange thing was that it upset Peter more than it did me. I remember asking him, Peter what are you so upset for? You knew this would happen and so did I - it's all 'player power' here.

The York experience had been short-lived. I'd joined them in June and was gone by December!

But the time I had there, coupled with my spell at Halifax, made me realise something that I'd never truly appreciated before. They emphasised just how lucky I'd been at Rovers. To get a club like Hull K.R. and to have a set of players and directors to work with like I had - it had been almost perfect... After those two experiences you probably won't be surprised to hear that I wouldn't dream of going back into coaching now. But I still take an interest in things. I still talk to the kids who play the game. And I also watch 'live' games at Castleford and Super League matches on television. Rugby League is still a very important part of my life.

And after coaching at the highest level for so many years, I can't deny that I sometimes have to smile - and sometimes cry - at some of the things I see. There are definitely times when I watch the game and think, they'd never have done that if I'd been coaching them!

They talk about modern day coaches, they're full time professionals. But there are times when I look at that screen or out onto the pitch and I think - that player doesn't even know what he should be doing in that part of the field. I can see it! There are other times when a team 'have won the game' but a player is still trying to force a pass to somebody. And you see it over and over again. A forced pass, the player knocks it on and the opposition scores 'a quick try' in the last couple of minutes to win the match. It's things like that which make me think, they can't be coaching them.

You see it even at International level. Last Year, the Tri-Nations Final promised so much but ultimately produced the same old story. When it came to the match that mattered Great Britain were once again blown away by a breathtaking Aussie display. Britain had played so well in the competition's 'league' games and had finished at the top of the table, beating the Aussies fairly comfortably 24-12 on the way. Many fans once again believed this at last might be the opportunity for us to beat the Aussies in a series for the first time since 1970. But as so often before, all that hope and expectation disappeared in another shattering defeat in the final, after the Aussies raced into a half-time lead of 38-0.

The British lads just seemed to freeze on the day. Adrian Morley said they'd played the occasion and not the game. But whatever the reason for such a turnaround, on the night at Elland Road when it mattered most, they couldn't repeat their previous display. They stood off the Aussies, missed tackles and made more mistakes than in all their previous games put together. Worst of all our kicking game was wretched. Yet the Aussie lad, Brett Kimmorley, all he did was put our players into a situation where they had to make a decision about that ball on the pitch. But their blokes were never put under that pressure. It's hard to believe our kickers are being coached...

Up to the final, everyone in the squad had played well and it was our kicking game that was our biggest problem. But then we also let ourselves down in little parts of the game where we should have kept thinking. And in my opinion it took Brian Noble too long to play his best team! He kept Danny McGuire out for the first match. He wasn't confident enough to play him - but I think he should have been in from the start...

I really got mad after the first match they played but although Great Britain lost, it wasn't anything to do with what happened on the pitch. I was in the club at home when Britain were just beaten in the last minute. I went to the toilet and this bloke in there said to me,

'Fitness again, that's what beat us, lack of fitness!'.

Fitness! I said, that was the last thing that cost us the game, they were more tired than we were. If you were suggesting about 'know-how' or intensity I'd agree with you. But fitness - you're having a laugh!

The Aussies won because they played for the full eighty minutes. We lost because we 'switched-off' for the last few seconds - it was as simple as that! Every player should remember ten seconds is a long time in rugby league...

HALL OF FAME
November 25 2000
Pictured at
Old Trafford with
Hall Of Fame
members, from
left: Neil Fox,
Vince Karalius,
Alex Murphy, Tom
Van Vollenhoven
and Billy Boston

Left: The other
Roger Millward
Stand

CHAPTER TWENTY-FOUR
ROGER TODAY-
LOOKING BACK...

The one thing that never fails to amaze me is that I haven't been forgotten. I didn't just finish playing the game and within a year or two, people forgot all about me. It's the exact opposite in fact.

After I was awarded the MBE in 1983 I thought my days of receiving awards would come to an end. But they didn't!

I continued to receive 'honours' long after my playing and coaching days were over. And it's a marvellous feeling to think that what I've done and what I've achieved in rugby league hasn't been forgotten.

An example of that was the award that the Lions introduced recently, The Tom Mitchell Award. On November 1 1998 I was voted the first winner of the trophy as 'Lion Of The Year'. The new annual award was inaugurated to commemorate the name of the manager of the 1958 Lions.

It was introduced to recognise one of the all-time greats each year and having represented Great Britain twenty-nine times between 1966 and 1978 it was felt appropriate that I should be the first recipient. And I was naturally very honoured to receive it.

Another honour that I found particularly humbling was when I was selected as one of the 'Immortals' team. The name was given to the side, chosen by a panel of judges which in their opinion constituted the best Great Britain X111 of all time. The team was selected in 1995 and promoted by "Open Rugby' magazine as part of the game's centenary celebrations. I thought it was interesting to note that apart from Ellery Hanley, I was the most 'modern' player to make the side.

The team selected was: 1 Jim Sullivan, 2 Billy Boston, 3 Harold Wagstaff, 4 Neil Fox, 5 Mick Sullivan, 6 Roger Millward, 7 Alex Murphy, 8 Alan Prescott, 9 Joe Egan, 10 Brian McTigue, 11 Martin Hodgson, 12 Dick Huddart, 13 Ellery Hanley.

It's flattering to think that people must still think I did a reasonable job because they still remember me and what I achieved. It's also nice that I can go to places like Bridlington and people still recognise me and come up to talk to me. I often think it's remarkable that they even remember who I am.

I've had a couple of problems since I finished playing rugby league. The most serious was a heart attack in May 1995. I was working for a construction firm at the time. It wasn't the best job I've ever had. Three brothers ran the company and I was the transport manager. They thought a 'tachodisc' was a Mexican dinner - which was about how near they got to filling one in correctly! But that was part of my job to ensure that they did. If not, I'd have had the police on my back! Needless to say, I always thought it was a fairly pressurised job and I suppose my attack was just a culmination of things that came to a head.

It was a Wednesday when I first felt a bit under the weather. I got this ache in my chest but I didn't do anything about it. The following day it was a bit worse so I took some 'Gaviscon'. On the Saturday night we went out to celebrate my son-in-law, John, grandmother's birthday at Whitwood.

We were having dinner and again I didn't feel too well and I said to Carol I'd have to go out. I went and got myself a gin and tonic and sat on the landing outside the dining room and had a drink. Carol came out to see how I was and I said I thought we'd better go home. I went to bed, but had to get up early on the Sunday morning - it was starting then.

It was about five o'clock and I just got on the settee and lay there. I got into a position where I felt as comfortable as I could. Carol came down a little later, I think it was about seven o'clock by then, and I said, Carol, you'd better ring for the ambulance or the emergency doctor.

'Don't you think we should wait for an hour or so? It's a bit early for a Sunday morning,' she replied as cooly as you like. It sounds funny now but I can assure you it wasn't at the time! There I was, lying on the sofa with the pain getting worse and worse - and she was worried about the time! I think my reply might have been in the negative.

The doctor finally arrived and told me to start with a spray. He said he didn't think it had been a heart attack but he sent me to the hospital for tests. The doctors there however confirmed that it had been a heart attack and I had three months off work.

I was on tablets to start with - I was taking five a day. But now it's down to just an aspirin every day - and watch the cholesterol! When I went back to the construction company, I was luckily made redundant - what a relief that was! I applied for the vacancy at the local school, which had come up in the meantime and I started at Royd's in December 1996...

A lot of my spare time, especially during the run-up to the pantomime season, is taken up helping 'front of house' with the Kippax Amateur Operatic Society. Carol and Kay are performers in the Society and a few years ago, I remember the Christmas production of 'Little Red Riding Hood' at the Castleford Civic Society turned into a real family affair. Kay played the title role, whilst her husband, John, played the big, bad wolf. And to complete the family quartet, Carol was in the chorus and I worked 'front of house'. It was a great success, like every production they put on. Every show seemed memorable in its' own way. But there's one that I remember more than all the rest because it had a particularly painful ending for me...

I've had trouble with my fingers and thumbs for as long as I can remember. But never in my wildest dreams did I think working in 'amateur dramatics' or moving a grand piano would help to resolve the problem. However in May 2000 that's exactly what happened. In the hall where Carol and Kay perform, there's a grand piano on the stage. And before they put a show on the piano has to be moved out of the way. I and the other guys move it down onto the main floor of the hall and then after the Saturday show we clear up the auditorium, put the chairs away, and put the piano back in place. The piano is extremely heavy and requires at least ten pairs of hands to lift it back onto the stage. It is something which has been done countless times over the years. But on this particular occasion we were all around it lifting it back onto the stage when the leg suddenly broke and the whole thing collapsed. Fortunately it landed on the edge of the stage. But unfortunately there was something between the bottom of the piano and the edge of the stage - it was my thumb!

What made me laugh, or at least it made me laugh a long time afterwards, was that I'd immediately shouted out that I'd lost my thumb, or words to that effect. Mark Waters ran off to get a bucket of ice and somebody else went to phone for an ambulance. But Vic, Kay's father in-law, had taken my outburst literally and had actually gone to look on the floor for my thumb! And it got worse! I'd previously seen a specialist about the problems I'd been having with my hands and he'd diagnosed that four of my fingertips were cancerous. It had begun when my nails started to go discoloured. It was awful and it got embarrassing at times - when I was out for dinner or at lunch with somebody - at one point I even started to wear gloves. And when I went to the hospital to have the 'trapped' thumb attended to, they decided to operate on my fingers at the same time. So the final result was cancer - four, grand piano - one!

My fingers can still be a source of embarrassment even now, although for a totally different reason, especially when I'm stood at the bar with some money in my hand. And all of a sudden the change drops through the little gap where the top of my finger should be.

But it's also had its' benefits because when I play golf, I don't slice the ball any more! Honestly, I've now got a perfect swing. And if I'd have known before how much the operation would improve my golf handicap, I'd have had it done twenty years ago!

Another honour followed in 2000 when along with Vince Karalius and Tom Van Vollenhoven I was inducted into Rugby League's Hall Of Fame. The three of us were chosen by a panel of statisticians, archivists and journalists for inclusion from a list of over thirty outstanding players voted for by the public. We joined the original Hall Of Fame members: Harold Wagstaff, Billy Boston, Albert Rosenfield, Jonty Parkin, Jim Sullivan, Gus Risman, Brian Bevan, Alex Murphy and Neil Fox.

At my induction I remember pointing out that I thought we had a lack of good British halfbacks. And that some teams were even using loose forwards in the stand-off role. Apart from Sean Long at St Helens, Richard Horne at Hull and the two lads at Leeds, that's basically still true today. Halfbacks have a very reduced influence in the game in 2005. And although today's game is very fast and very physical, I wonder what's happened to all the craft and guile? Britain always produced small, nuggety halfbacks who could organise a team.

I'm just getting more and more worried that we are losing all the players with guile. They just don't seem to be brought up with any craft at all these days. When I signed for Castleford we had eight halfbacks on the books. Where are these types of players now? They only seem to produce them in Australia these days. Britain desperately needs to develop more of its' own creative stand-offs and scrum-halves - and allow them to do their own thing. Don't get me wrong there are some marvellous and very skilful players in the game. But every time the majority of them get to within ten yards of the line now, all they seem to do is kick the ball...

Throughout my career I've often been asked who I thought were the best players I'd ever played with. And which players I'd choose in my 'best-ever' Rovers' team. So I wasn't too surprised when the questions cropped up again whilst I was compiling this autobiography. I've always tried my best to avoid making such decisions. But this time there appeared to be no way out. The only stipulation was that I was naturally allowed to name myself as stand-off. Here are my answers - and a few more besides...

Choosing a definitive list of names I quickly found was virtually impossible. I'd no sooner decided on one player than I'd think yes, but what about 'so and so'? But having had time to deliberate over the many possible contenders, I've come up with the following Rovers' team. In my view it represents the best seventeen players that I either played with or coached during my career at Craven Park. I'm certain it's one which would give any side a run for its' money! My 'Best-Ever' team would be: 1 George Fairbairn, 2 Chris Young, 3 Mike Smith, 4 Alan Burwell, 5 Clive Sullivan, 6 Me, 7 Allan Agar, 8 Mark Broadhurst, 9 David Watkinson, 10 Brian Lockwood, 11 Phil Lowe, 12 Paul Rose, 13 Len Casey. Subs: 14 Gary Prohm, 15 Johnny Moore, 16 Bill Holliday, 17 Gavin Miller.

Choosing the best three players that I've played with or against was also an incredibly difficult task. But after much thought I came up with the following: The best back, I'd chose Cronulla's Stevie Rogers. Steve played a total of 199 games in two spells with Cronulla, 1973 to 1982 and then 1985. Stevie was a tremendous centre. His son, Matt, also played for the Kangaroos and is now in the Wallabies' squad. He's a super player as well and one day he might be as good as his dad. The best halfback, I'd have to say Alex Murphy. And the best forward - probably the most difficult one to choose - but it would have to be Malcolm Reilly. Malcolm came from the same village that I live in now, Kippax. He's always been a tremendous competitor and a marvellous player.

My favourite game ever? There are two - I can never split them. The Third Test at the Sydney Cricket Ground - July 4 1970 when we won the Ashes - and Wembley 1980 when I finally lifted the Challenge Cup. They both still mean so much to me.

Who was the hardest tackler I played against? The hardest tackler I've ever come up against and there have been plenty, was a lad called Dennis Manteit. The match was back in 1967, a Test match against Australia on October 21 at Headingley. Dennis was in the second row for the Aussies and I was playing at stand-off for Great Britain. I'd started the game pretty well when all of a sudden something hit me. All I remember thinking was, what the hell was that? I imagined the feeling was pretty similar to what being hit by a double-decker bus must be like. It was in fact Dennis.

The hardest tackle I suffered? - for obvious reasons it has to be the one by Terry Major at Workington.

I was also once asked if Paul Woods had been someone who I found difficult to play against. After all said the questioner 'Didn't he nearly take your head off in the International match at Craven Park?' Yes, he 'nearly' did, I replied... But 'nearlys' of course, didn't count.

My favourite and least favourite ground?

I never liked playing at Workington very much although not for the reason you might suspect. It was always difficult to win at Derwent Park - we had many a good hiding up there - but it was tough at a lot of places. The problem about playing at Workington was the travelling to get there in the first place. And it was even worse making the long journey back, especially when you'd lost, that was the hardest bit. Worse still was when we had to go for a mid-week match. You have to realise that Workington on a Wednesday night is not the most attractive place to be. Especially as I was often knackered even before I'd set off on the long trip to Cumbria. If I'd been on day shifts, they didn't finish until a quarter past one! So I'd miss one shift as I had to be on the bus by eleven o'clock in the morning in Tadcaster. Then we'd make the long trek there and back - and I didn't get home until about two in the morning. That of course meant I'd miss the next day's shift as well. So I'd played one game of rugby but missed two shifts at the pit. No wonder the boss used to go crazy with me...

We did have some good matches up there as well I suppose - but they're always a lot more difficult to remember! Whitehaven was never a favourite ground either. That was where we had to get changed in a very strange looking building and the pitch was very open to the elements.

The places I used to love playing at were the big grounds like Wigan, St Helens and Leeds. I always remembered the big grounds and the stands all round them from when I was a kid.

Does size matter? It's a question I must have been asked a hundred times over the years. And after what I achieved in the game I'd obviously have to answer with a definite, No!

I would admit that there were not that many players of my size around in my era, or after it come to that. I suppose only Tommy Bishop and Steve Nash spring to mind. Today there's Rob Burrow at Leeds and Stacey Jones isn't a giant but after those two there are not many more in the top flight. I think I was probably the smallest player to play International football but I don't think I ever appeared in the 'Guinness Book of Records' or anywhere like that to prove the fact.

But although it seems to be the motto that the bigger they are in Super

League these days the better, it's still true that they still can't handle these little 'uns running round. It was the same when I played against the Aussies, they couldn't lay a finger on me most of the time. I'm obviously biased but I'd always say that if you're good enough, you're big enough!

I can't remember my size being a problem. Many people thought my lack of height and weight would be a major drawback to me, in what appeared on the surface to be a sport where size, power and brute strength, at least to the untrained eye, were the major requirements.

Those who knew the game better realised this was far from the case and if anything I'd have to say that my size actually presented me with far more plusses than minuses.

I may have had more problems if it had been true that size always equalled strength and ability. That the bigger a player was, the better he was. Fortunately for me however, in the case of a number of opponents I faced, that maxim was certainly not true.

A lot of players, especially forwards may have been five, six or seven stones heavier than me but that never caused me a problem - at least no more than it would any other player who tried to stop them. My tackling technique I know was a sound one. And like numerous other players who may have lacked a bit of height, such as Tommy Bishop, Steve Nash and Keith Hepworth, I don't recall having too much difficulty in usually being able to bring, even the biggest forwards, to an abrupt halt.

But I also know for a fact that somebody like Peter Fox wouldn't have signed me because he preferred big players. He liked skilful players as well don't get me wrong and thought the world of John Holmes. 'Holmesy' was big and skilful, but I wasn't Peter's type of player.

That was his opinion and I respected it. Peter and I are still very good friends today - and we still have our own different opinions...

I've always had a more open mind however about size. If a player had the skill and they had the brain that was enough for me! Although I'll admit there were naturally times that I'd wished they had the size as well.

And when Rovers were at the top, I'd have to agree we were a bloody big side at that time. When you think of Paul Rose and Phil Lowe and then Roy Holdstock who was a six-footer and Watkie who wasn't far off and Mark Broadhurst in the front row. Gary Prohm and Mike Smith in the centres - and Steve Hubbard was a huge man for a winger - so we weren't a small side by any stretch of the imagination...

One of the trickiest questions people ask me is, was it easier for you to become a successful coach because you'd been a great player?

I can assure you, that's a very difficult one to reply to without sounding 'big-headed'.

The simple answer is, no! I don't think you have to have been a good player to become a good coach - and vice versa. The fact that you may have reached the top as a player doesn't mean you'll repeat that success if you take up coaching. We can all name some great players who never did anything as coaches. And we can all name great coaches who had either very limited success or none at all as a player. It's often difficult for a good player to become a good coach. As a player, you may have played at the top level but whilst you are in that position you will probably never have blamed yourself for anything. You're so one eyed when you're a player. But when you get to be a coach you've got to look at things differently. You are going to get beaten. Somebody is going to drop a goal against you in the last minute. Somebody is going to make a mistake that costs you the game. And it's how you handle those situations...

Another question that I'm continually asked is, how do I think the top players of yester-year would fare in today's game? I always reply with the same answer - I think the vast majority of the top players of my era, myself included, would be all right in today's Super League. Not now of course - I haven't got the fingers for it!

It's very difficult to cross the years and say what you'd be like playing rugby today. But I'm sure the players who I played with and against - and the ones I watched when I was just a little lad - the great players - I'm sure they would all make the transition to today's game without a lot of problems. There's no two ways about that in my mind. There's a lot to be said about Super League players of today. But equally there's a lot to be said about what we had in my day - I thought we were pretty skilful.

The game is definitely a lot different today. But personally I think the ten metre rule is one of the things that's ruining it. In my opinion it's taken all the skill out of the game. I was watching a match recently and wondered if we had changed the rules. I wondered if it was now compulsory to kick on the sixth tackle.

Don't take that the wrong way - I still think it's a great game - and I think the marketing and the promotional side is fantastic - that's one thing that's hard to fault. But although I still love the game and always will, I think that at times it gets very predictable.

And the Super League 'set-up' is totally loaded at the moment. You can have one good year and as a result, be 'penalised' the following year, with more games against the top sides. Or you can have a poor season and then be 'rewarded' for it, with 'easier' matches the following year. But playing the same team three times in a season is a load of rubbish. The only purpose it serves is to help the teams who finish in the bottom half of the league, have a better chance of finishing in the top five the following year.

But if you think about it seriously, what do we want? I think most people want to see a twenty-six or twenty-eight match season. Well why don't we just have fourteen or fifteen teams in the top division, all playing each other home and away each season. Is that too easy a concept? Then you would have the chance to introduce a proper State of Origin - Yorkshire v Lancashire fixture - with some credibility. Lets face it, it's a bit 'Mickey Mouse' at the moment, isn't it? It's getting to be like the old County matches where everyone cried off the day before and the match was played between two weakened sides. Again when I first played there was usually only one way to play for Great Britain and that was to play for Yorkshire, Lancashire or Cumberland first - and I think we should go back to that.

Those league games coupled with the County matches would make up a perfect fixture list. They do it in Australia with the State Of Origin and they are a fantastic success and provide their test squads. In fact it's one of the few things we haven't copied. But the Aussies watch the Origin matches in their thousands...

CHAPTER TWENTY-FIVE
I'VE LOVED EVERY MINUTE

The definition of 'Friend' reads as follows - 'A person with whom one enjoys mutual affection and regard; one who is not an enemy.'
It's a simple statement but one that means so much - life would be very lonely without them.
I am a very lucky person, I've played this great game of Rugby League and because of my involvement in the game, I've made many friends all over the world. It would be remiss of me to say that all my friends are from Rugby League, for this is certainly not true.
Probably the reason I'm putting pen to paper at this particular time is the fact that these friends away from Rugby League have played a major part in my life in more ways than one. And I want to say thank you to them for giving me the privilege of being part of their lives.
Friends - where do you start to acknowledge these people that have been part of your life? And where do you finish? I think I had better apologise now because I'm sure to miss someone!
I'm glad this computer has a 'spell check', I've used some big words...

In my time as coach at Rovers I took up golf after being introduced to the game by Frank Myler on the 1970 tour. I found that it was a great game and pastime to take my mind off the everyday demands of my coaching duties. Every Wednesday, which was my official day off, supposedly, a gang of us would get together and play golf. Rovers never even attempted to get in touch with me on a Wednesday!
We had some great times culminating in our once a year, three day golfing holiday, to places like Southport, Bridlington, Scarborough and St. Anne's - never mind the expense! The lads also went abroad to play but I could never go with them because it was during the rugby season. Among the group were Alan Preece and Brian Rowe who both played professional rugby league in the sixties...
Others in the group were my local landlords, Harry Britten and George Horner. The three of us once took Malcolm Reilly to play at our local club, Garforth. It was evident that Malcolm had never played golf before. On the

second tee Malcolm teed his ball up and was preparing to give it everything he'd got. Looking up he noticed that the group in front were still on the fairway.

'Is it safe to hit it?' he asked.

'Yes,' replied George. 'Them in front are safe, it's us at the back and side of you that are in danger.' Malcolm's game has come a long way since then...

I love to get out on the golf course - I used to be a member at Garforth for years and years. And although I don't play a great deal now because of work commitments, I always try to play in the Celebrity Golf Days for Charity and thank people like John Helm, the TV Sports Presenter and other organisers for inviting me...

My two local hostelries now are the 'Central Club' in Kippax and the 'New Inn' (Doddies) at Great Preston, a little village next to Kippax. Harry, Malcolm and I are regular visitors to the club on a Friday night during the Super League season. It's a rugby league orientated establishment and the banter between the lads is second to none. No matter whom you support you always get a hard time. And if you're a 'Rhino', as Harry is, you just tend to get a little more. The 'New Inn' is a predominantly soccer pub, especially Leeds United although other clubs, namely Liverpool and Newcastle have representatives. It's one of those pubs in which you feel very much at home, no matter who you are - and the mentality of the clientele can be assessed by the following couple of tales...

Not that long ago Hull K.R. named a stand after me and within a couple of hours of it being in the newspapers I called in the pub for a drink. As I walked in the door there was an A4 size photograph pinned up on the bar. The photograph was of the bus shelter outside the pub but our local computer wizard, Mick Clay, had superimposed the line 'The Roger Millward Stand' on the front of the shelter, that had everybody in stitches for a few days.

The 25th Year Reunion earlier this year, for all the Rovers' players who had taken part in the 1980 Wembley Cup Final against Hull F.C. reminds me of another 'Tale from Doddies'...

To promote this event the Hull Daily Mail had carried a photograph of me holding the cup up at a reception on our return home from Wembley.

Young Steven, the landlord's son had somehow got hold of this picture. And when I walked into the pub, there again pinned to the bar, was the picture with the captions 'Bet he couldn't do that now?' and 'Who is he anyway?'.

I can remember the Kippax Amateur Operatic Society presenting a cabaret at the Civic Centre, which included a meal, with waiter service to the tables. Carol asked if I would be prepared to act as a waiter. This was of course pre-summer 2000. It was a wonderful night and I really enjoyed being a waiter until on taking an order at this particular table, a man, I refuse to call him a gentleman, took pleasure in telling me, 'How the mighty have fallen'. He really must have thought that I was doing waiter service for a living - but it was his attitude that really got to me. And he may have had some other thoughts about my skills as a waiter when I 'accidentally' spilt two pints over him later in the evening...

During my days at Rovers I also worked as an electrician in the mining industry. I actually worked at the pit, Wheldale Colliery, just up the road from the Castleford ground.

It was known affectionately as the 'Sunshine Pit' because every time the sun came out we went on strike. But talk about camaraderie, here was a set of men performing probably the hardest work in the world and looking out for each other at the same time. The laughs we had at work during that time in the mining industry were great...

I can remember playing Widnes in the floodlight cup, a competition that was played on a Tuesday night. I was on nights, my shift started at 10 p.m. and finished at 05.15 a.m. the next day. Hull was a good fifty-five miles from Castleford. We were still on the 'old path' to Hull - not the M62 - and it was probably a run of at least an hour and twenty minutes at that time of night.

It was a really good game and we beat Widnes, a good result for us as Widnes was the 'Cup Kings' at the time. I finished the game and left Hull immediately after changing.

The next morning the 'electrical' boss was at work at 5.15 a.m. - which we thought was a little unusual...

'You did well last night Roger,' he said. Which I thought was a bit funny, as he wasn't usually a rugby fan. Yes, we played well and everything seemed to go for us, I replied.

'No Roger, not the result of the game, I was watching you on television at 9.00 p.m. and you had clocked-on for 10.00 p.m.' he exclaimed. Deathly silence followed. My friend Allen Williams and I had been rumbled.

'Just be careful,' he said.

The one thing that stood out to me during my early years of playing rugby for Castleford and working in the pit was the fact that most, if not all of the miners I worked with were big supporters of the club. They actually paid to come and see me play rugby. They knew what the game was all about. And if you hadn't had a good game on Saturday you soon got to know about it at 6 a.m. on a Monday morning in the cage taking us to the pit bottom. They didn't take any prisoners - they said it as they saw it. This was another way of learning how to keep your feet on the ground. The cage on a Monday morning decided at what stage your career in Rugby League had reached. In my opinion it was a good and honest yardstick for a young lad of sixteen or seventeen years of age. To be judged and given the nod by my mining colleagues meant a great deal to me and all the other budding young rugby league players - and there were plenty of them in the mining industry at the time...

Winning the Challenge Cup in 1980 was obviously the highlight of my career. The victory brought prestige to both the club and the city. It also provided the catalyst for a 'rare piece of publicity' for the game of rugby league on national television. Although in the end I'm not sure that the BBC got exactly what it expected...

I remember Clive Sullivan had starred on 'This Is Your Life' after we'd won the World Cup in 1972. But I finally got my chance of stardom, when just after the 1980 final, I appeared with the rest of the Rovers' lads on 'That's Life' with Esther Rantzen.

They had a feature on her show about a woman from Leeds and her little lad who had a rugby ball that he kept kicking around the house. The ball knocked all the ornaments and things off the mantlepiece, so they decided to bring him over to Hull to give him a proper day's training with a top rugby league team. And so they asked us if we'd be willing to do it.

They were filming all day for what turned out to be about a three-minute slot on the television on the Saturday night.

I remember the bloke who always seemed a bit effeminate, although I'm not sure if he was, came to do the interviewing and I'm sure 'Millo' ended up throwing him in the bath at the end of the filming. The little lad went through some training drills with us. It showed you him passing and kicking the ball and me tying his bootlaces to start with. And when we were all getting in the bath at the end for the last shot, I'm sure John threw the reporter in, microphone and all!

I was also always invited to the 'Sports Personality Of The Year' at the BBC and more often than not used to finish up with Bill Beaumont. That was the time that rugby league and rugby union were always supposedly at loggerheads with each other. But as far as the players from both codes were concerned you would never have known it. They all got on very well. I used to go to the show most years and invariably ended up chatting with the union lads, like Bill and Steve Smith and they were real good kids. I know Bill liked most sports and watched a lot of rugby league.

But I remember when Malcolm Reilly and myself were at Kirkstall Road. We'd been to watch the Leeds Rugby Union side playing and we were in the clubhouse after the match when this bloke came over and asked us to leave. I can't imagine anything so petty as that happening these days, especially at Leeds. But I recall I just looked at Malcolm, thinking to myself, Oh Malcolm don't 'go off'! Fortunately for everybody he didn't - he just 'left quietly'.

As well as touring with Great Britain as a player I also had the pleasure, along with Peter Fox and other rugby league personalities of leading Supporters' trips to Australia. These were actually set up by Brian Smelt, a good friend and businessman in Hull. The pleasure we got from fronting those trips was marvellous - and some of the tales we returned with were even better...

On one trip in particular, most of the party had travelled down to Gatwick Airport on the day before our departure. The rest of the party were due at about 10 a.m. the next morning. We had decided over dinner that night that we would greet the rest of the party as they arrived and instead of removing their cases from the bus we would leave them on board and add our cases to them. We would then invite the people into the hotel for breakfast whilst we, the leaders, took the bus to Gatwick and checked in all the baggage.

The bus arrived on time and we set about our task of loading the baggage, which took us about forty-five minutes. We were just about to set off when

Brian Smelt came out of the hotel with one of the supporters. Dennis was his name and he asked us, 'Have any of you found a watch?'

'No,' we replied.

'Dennis had lost an expensive watch and he thinks it might be on the bus near his luggage,' explained Brian.

No more to do, we unloaded the bus to where Dennis' luggage was - but alas there was no sign of the watch. We then re-loaded all the cases back onto the bus and set off to Gatwick to check them in.

On our arrival back at the hotel I was met by Brian and Dennis. Dennis had a big smile on his face.

'Roger, I've found my watch,' he announced.

Oh, that's good Dennis, I said, where did you find it?

'It was on my arm. While I was asleep on the journey down, it must have slipped up my arm and I couldn't see it because of my coat'.

This had all the makings of being a memorable trip, I thought to myself!

I later discovered during our stay in Sydney, that unfortunately Dennis had been mugged one night on his way back to the hotel. And yes, you've guessed it - they took the watch!

Also during our stay in Sydney we arranged for the party to attend a league game at North Sydney. We purchased the tickets and handed them out, all that was left to do was for the party to make their own way across to the ground, which was only about three miles away across the Sydney Harbour Bridge... only?

An hour or so before kick-off, Brian, Peter and I came out of our hotel. There was four of our party standing at the bus stop, obviously waiting for a bus and looking totally bewildered.

'What number bus do we need Roger?' one of them asked. I thought, how the hell do I know, I'm a visitor here the same as you. I'm sorry I haven't a clue, I said very diplomatically. We're getting a taxi, I continued. It's only $2 door to door - and if you want to know, the taxi rank is there, next to the bus stop...

At breakfast one morning I sat on a table with a couple of gentlemen that were touring with us. As I sat down with my cornflakes, one of the gentlemen got up to get his breakfast. As the first one left the table, the other one said to me,

'Roger, John's a great bloke and I enjoy his company but I don't like sleeping with him.'

Sleeping with him? I asked. 'Yes there's only one double bed in our room and we've slept together for the last couple of nights,' he declared.

What room are you in? I inquired. But then deciding to find out what was going on, I said, come on, let's go and have a look!

We left the breakfast table and went straight to their bedroom. On entering the room Harry said 'Look! I told you there's only one bed.'

Yes, there was only one bed, but to the left of it was a fold-away single bed, which during the daytime, was made up as a settee. The look of embarrassment on his face when I explained it to him was priceless. But they enjoyed the rest of their tour I might add, sleeping separately...

Reminiscing about those trips to Australia reminds me of the friendships I made, that have carried on to this day. I honestly cannot remember anyone not enjoying the trips - it was just a pleasure to be there with them...

Over the past few years we have had many a good weekend in Bridlington with our friends, Carol and Eric Ingham. Eric and I usually go out to watch the game on a Friday night, usually at the 'Greyhound' pub and the girls come along later. From there we usually carry on down to 'Rags' Restaurant which is owned by my old touring partner, Les Dyl. From there we invariably finish up in the 'Brunswick', where there's usually a 'turn' on.

I recall one particular night, the singer asked if there was anyone in the pub who would volunteer to back him as he sang 'Under the Boardwalk'. Eric and I looked at each other and decided - this was after a couple of drinks, I might add - that it would be us that would back him. Looking round I thought, nobody knows me in here. So up we got, ready to do our thing! The singer set the music but just before it started he turned to us and said very loudly, 'Wow! I never thought I would be having Roger Millward backing me on stage!'

I wish I could have seen my face as he uttered the words. The girls were in stitches - and we also got a rollicking from the singer because we missed one of the 'under the board walks'. But I think that on the whole he was happy with our performance...

Recently I've made several trips to Hull to discuss certain things regarding this autobiography. I would like to take this opportunity of thanking Lee Chester and his dad, Dave, and all the regulars of 'The Embassy Club' on Hedon Road for making me feel, once again, at home. Thank you, it is much appreciated...

I've enjoyed telling my story. Remembering the traumatic and the poignant. The light-hearted, the uplifting and the humorous. The memorable victories and the heartbreaking defeats. The friendships I've made and the friends I've lost. The times of elation and the moments of despair - that combine to make up this account of my life in rugby league...

And my only hope, if you're reading this book and have got to this stage, is that you've enjoyed reading it...

I also enjoyed my time in 'the greatest game'. But when people ask me, 'would you like to be playing now with all this money in the game?' I can honestly reply, No!

I loved every minute of my life in rugby league, when it was my time. This is now the time for other people. We have some great players playing today and all I would say to them is, enjoy yourselves! Don't forget you're a long time out of the game when you've retired. Don't miss out on your destiny. And never forget the people who love you - the supporters!

Roger Millward 2005

Pictured in 2005 with my family, grandson Charlie, son-in-law John, daughter Kay and wife Carol

CAREER RECORD
REPRESENTATIVE HONOURS:
GREAT BRITAIN TEST APPEARANCES (28 + 1 SUB)

1966
Mar 5   Great Britain 4 v France 8 at Wigan (Only appearance as a Castleford player)
1967
Oct 21   Great Britain 16 v Australia 11 at Leeds
Nov 3   Great Britain 11 v Australia 17 at White City, London
Dec 9   Great Britain 3 v Australia 11 at Swinton
1968
Feb 11   Great Britain 22 v France 13 at Paris
Mar 2   Great Britain 19 v France 8 at Bradford
1968   **WORLD CUP**
May 25   Great Britain 10 v Australia 25 at Sydney (World Cup)
June 2   Great Britain 2 v France 7 at Auckland (World Cup)
June 8   Great Britain 38 v New Zealand 14 at Sydney (World Cup)
1970
June 20   Great Britain 28 v Australia 7 at Sydney
July 4   Great Britain 21 v Australia 17 at Sydney
July 11   Great Britain 19 v New Zealand 15 at Auckland
July 19   Great Britain 23 v New Zealand 9 at Christchurch
July 25   Great Britain 33 v New Zealand 16 at Auckland
1971
Mar 17   Great Britain 24 v France 2 at St Helens
Sept 25   Great Britain 13 v New Zealand 18 at Salford
Oct 16   Great Britain 14 v New Zealand 17 at Castleford
Nov 6   Great Britain 12 v New Zealand 3 at Leeds
1973
Dec 1   Great Britain 5 v Australia 15 at Warrington
1974
June 15   Great Britain 6 v Australia 12 at Brisbane
July 6   Great Britain 16 v Australia 11 at Sydney
July 20   Great Britain 18 v Australia 22 at Sydney (sub)

1977   WORLD CUP
June 5   Great Britain 23 v France 4 at Auckland (World Cup)
June 12   Great Britain 30 v New Zealand 12 at Christchurch (World Cup)
June 18   Great Britain 5 v Australia 19 at Brisbane (World Cup)
June 25   Great Britain 12 v Australia 13 at Sydney (World Cup)
1978
Oct 21   Great Britain 9 v Australia 15 at Wigan
Nov 5   Great Britain 18 v Australia 14 at Bradford
Nov 18   Great Britain 6 v Australia 23 at Leeds

          Roger did not play any Tests after 1978
1979   He was chosen for the 1979 Great Britain Tour of Australia and New Zealand but
          due to injury only played in 3 matches before being replaced by David Topliss
Match details:
1966
GREAT BRITAIN 4 v FRANCE 8 - March 5th Wigan (Only appearance as a Castleford player)
1 Ken Gowers, 2 Bill Burgess, 3 Geoff Shelton, 4 Alan Buckley, 5 John Stopford, **6 Roger
Millward,** 7 Alex Murphy, 8 Charlie Bott, 9 Bernard Prior, 10 Cliff Watson, 11 Bill Ramsey,
12 John Mantle, 13 Dave Robinson Sub: Bill Holliday Goals: Ken Gowers 2
Attendance: 14,004
1967
GREAT BRITAIN 16 v AUSTRALIA 11 - October 21st Leeds
1 Arthur Keegan, 2 Chris Young, 3 Ian Brooke, 4 Malcolm Price, 5 Alan Burwell, **6 Roger
Millward,** 7 Tommy Bishop, 8 Mick Clark, 9 Peter Flanagan, 10 Cliff Watson, 11 Bob Irving,
12 John Mantle, 13 Dave Robinson Tries: Chris Young, Roger Millward, Goals: Roger
Millward 3, Tommy Bishop, Bill Holliday Referee: Fred Lindop (Great Britain) Attendance:
22,293
GREAT BRITAIN 11 v AUSTRALIA 17 - November 3rd White City, London
1 Arthur Keegan, 2 Chris Young, 3 Ian Brooke, 4 Neil Fox, 5 Bill Francis, **6 Roger Millward,**
7 Tommy Bishop, 8 Bill Holliday, 9 Peter Flanagan, 10 Cliff Watson, 11 Bob Irving, 12 John
Mantle, 13 Frank Foster Tries: Tommy Bishop Goals: Neil Fox 3, Tommy Bishop
 Attendance: 17,445
GREAT BRITAIN 3 v AUSTRALIA 11 - December 9th Swinton
1 Arthur Keegan, 2 Chris Young, 3 Ian Brooke, 4 Malcolm Price, 5 Gary Jordan, **6 Roger
Millward,** 7 Tommy Bishop, 8 Bill Holliday, 9 Peter Flanagan, 10 Cliff Watson, 11 Bob
Irving, 12 Bob Valentine, 13 Dave Robinson Try: Malcolm Price Attendance: 13,615
1968
GREAT BRITAIN 22 v FRANCE 13 - February 11th Paris
1 Bev Risman, 2 Chris Young, 3 Ian Brooke, 4 Neil Fox, 5 Alan Burwell, **6 Roger Millward,**
7 Tommy Bishop, 8 Mick Clark, 9 Peter Flanagan, 10 Cliff Watson, 11 Ray French, 12 Arnie
Morgan, 13 Charlie Renilson Tries: Bev Risman 2, Alan Burwell, Roger Millward Goals: Bev
Risman 5 Attendance: 8,000
GREAT BRITAIN 19 v FRANCE 8 - March 2nd Bradford
1 Bev Risman, 2 Chris Young, 3 Ian Brooke, 4 Neil Fox, 5 Alan Burwell, **6 Roger Millward,**
 7 Tommy Bishop, 8 Mick Clark, 9 Peter Flanagan, 10 Cliff Watson, 11 Ray French, 12 Arnie
Morgan, 13 Charlie Renilson Tries: Chris Young, Alan Burwell 2, Roger Millward, Arnie
Morgan Goals: Bev Risman 2 Attendance: 14,196
1968 WORLD CUP IN AUSTRALIA & NEW ZEALAND
GREAT BRITAIN SQUAD: Bev Risman-Captain (Leeds), Kevin Ashcroft (Leigh), John
Atkinson (Leeds), Tommy Bishop (St Helens), Ian Brooke (Wakefield Trinity), Alan Burwell
(Hull Kingston Rovers), Mick Clark (Leeds), Derek Edwards (Castleford), Peter Flanagan
(Hull Kingston Rovers), Ray French (Widnes), Bob Haigh (Wakefield Trinity), **Roger
Millward (Hull Kingston Rovers),** Arnold Morgan (Featherstone Rovers), Charlie Renilson
(Halifax), Mick Shoebottom (Leeds), Clive Sullivan (Hull), John Warlow (St Helens),
Cliff Watson (St Helens), Chris Young (Hull Kingston Rovers).
Manager: Bill Fallowfield (RL Secretary) Coach: Colin Hutton (Hull Kingston Rovers)
GREAT BRITAIN 10 v AUSTRALIA 25 - Saturday May 25th 1968 Sydney
1 Bev Risman (c), 2 Ian Brooke, 3 Mick Shoebottom, 4 Alan Burwell, 5 Clive Sullivan,
6 Roger Millward, 7 Tommy Bishop, 8 Mick Clark, 9 Kevin Ashcroft, 10 Cliff Watson,
11 Ray French, 12 Bob Haigh, 13 Charlie Renilson. Tries: Ian Brooke, Clive Sullivan.
Goals: Bev Risman 2 Referee: John Percival (New Zealand) Attendance: 62,256

212

GREAT BRITAIN 2 v FRANCE 7 - Sunday June 2nd 1968 Auckland
1 Bev Risman (c), 2 Clive Sullivan, 3 Ian Brooke, 4 Alan Burwell, 5 John Atkinson, **6 Roger Millward,** 7 Tommy Bishop, 8 Mick Clark, 9 Peter Flanagan, 10 Cliff Watson, 11 Arnie Morgan, 12 Bob Haigh, 13 Charlie Renilson. Sub: John Warlow. Goal: Bev Risman
Referee: Col Pearce (Australia) Attendance: 15,760
GREAT BRITAIN 38 v NEW ZEALAND 14 - Saturday June 8th 1968 Sydney
1 Bev Risman (c), 2 Clive Sullivan, 3 Ian Brooke, 4 Alan Burwell, 5 John Atkinson, **6 Roger Millward,** 7 Tommy Bishop, 8 Mick Clark, 9 Peter Flanagan, 10 John Warlow, 11 Ray French, 12 Arnold Morgan, 13 Charlie Renilson. Subs: Mick Shoebottom, Cliff Watson.
Tries: Clive Sullivan 3, Alan Burwell 2, Ian Brooke, Arnie Morgan, Mick Shoebottom
Goals: Bev Risman 7 Referee: Col Pearce (Australia). Attendance: 14,105
World Cup Final
AUSTRALIA 20 v FRANCE 2 - Monday June 10th 1968 Sydney
Referee: J Percival (New Zealand). Attendance: 54,290.

1970 TOUR OF AUSTRALIA AND NEW ZEALAND
GREAT BRITAIN SQUAD:
Frank Myler-Captain (St Helens) John Atkinson (Leeds) Dave Chisnall (Leigh) Ray Dutton (Widnes) Derek Edwards (Castleford) Tony Fisher (Bradford Northern) Peter Flanagan (Hull Kingston Rovers) Alan Hardisty (Castleford) Keith Hepworth (Castleford) Chris Hesketh (Salford) Syd Hynes (Leeds) Bob Irving (Oldham) Doug Laughton (Wigan) Phil Lowe (Hull Kingston Rovers) Roger Millward (Hull Kingston Rovers) Terry Price (Bradford Northern) Malcolm Reilly (Castleford) Dave Robinson (Wigan) Barry Seabourne (Leeds) Mick Shoebottom (Leeds) Alan Smith (Leeds) Clive Sullivan (Hull) Jimmy Thompson (Featherstone Rovers) Johnny Ward (Salford) Cliff Watson (St Helens) Manager: J. Harding (Leigh) Coach: Johnny Whiteley (Hull)
GREAT BRITAIN 28 v AUSTRALIA 7 - June 20th 1970 Sydney
1 Derek Edwards, 2 Alan Smith, 3 Syd Hynes, 4 Frank Myler, 5 John Atkinson, **6 Roger Millward,** 7 Keith Hepworth, 8 Dennis Hartley, 9 Tony Fisher, 10 Cliff Watson, 11 Doug Laughton, 12 Jimmy Thompson, 13 Malcolm Reilly Sub: Mick Shoebottom for Edwards
Tries: Roger Millward 2, John Atkinson, Tony Fisher Goals: Roger Millward 7 Syd Hynes
Referee: Don Lancashire Attendance: 60,962
GREAT BRITAIN 21 v AUSTRALIA 17 - July 4th 1970 Sydney
1 Mick Shoebottom, 2 Alan Smith, 3 Syd Hynes, 4 Frank Myler, 5 John Atkinson, **6 Roger Millward,** 7 Keith Hepworth, 8 Dennis Hartley, 9 Tony Fisher, 10 Cliff Watson, 11 Doug Laughton, 12 Jimmy Thompson, 13 Malcolm Reilly Tries: Syd Hynes, John Atkinson 2, Roger Millward, Dennis Hartley Goals: Roger Millward 3
Referee: Don Lancashire Attendance: 61,258
GREAT BRITAIN 19 v NEW ZEALAND 15 - July 11th 1970 Auckland
1 Mick Shoebottom, 2 Alan Smith, 3 Syd Hynes, 4 Frank Myler, 5 John Atkinson, **6 Roger Millward,** 7 Barry Seabourne, 8 Dennis Hartley, 9 Tony Fisher, 10 Cliff Watson, 11 Doug Laughton, 12 Jimmy Thompson, 13 Malcolm Reilly Tries: Syd Hynes, John Atkinson, Roger Millward, Doug Laughton 2 Goals: Syd Hynes 2
Referee: J Percival (New Zealand) Attendance: 15,948
GREAT BRITAIN 23 v NEW ZEALAND 9 - July 19th 1970 Christchurch
1 Ray Dutton, 2 Alan Smith, 3 Syd Hynes, 4 Frank Myler, 5 John Atkinson, **6 Roger Millward,** 7 Keith Hepworth, 8 Dennis Hartley, 9 Tony Fisher, 10 Cliff Watson, 11 Doug Laughton, 12 Jimmy Thompson, 13 Malcolm Reilly Tries: Frank Myler, Roger Millward 2, Malcolm Reilly Goals: Ray Dutton 4 Attendance: 8,600
GREAT BRITAIN 33 v NEW ZEALAND 16 - July 25th 1970 Auckland
1 Ray Dutton, 2 Alan Smith, 3 Chris Hesketh, 4 Frank Myler, 5 John Atkinson, **6 Roger Millward,** 7 Keith Hepworth, 8 Cliff Watson, 9 Tony Fisher, 10 Johnny Ward, 11 Bob Irving, 12 Phil Lowe, 13 Malcolm Reilly Sub: Syd Hynes Tries: Alan Smith, Chris Hesketh, Keith Hepworth, Cliff Watson, Phil Lowe 2, Syd Hynes Goals: Ray Dutton 5, Roger Millward
Attendance: 13,137
1971
GREAT BRITAIN 24 v FRANCE 2 - March 17th 1971 St Helens
1 Derek Whitehead, 2 Alan Smith, 3 Chris Hesketh, 4 Billy Benyon, 5 John Atkinson, 6 Roger Millward, 7 Steve Nash, 8 John Warlow, 9 Tony Fisher, 10 Cliff Watson, 11 John Mantle, 12 Jimmy Thompson, 13 Doug Laughton Subs: 14 David Watkins, 15 Mike Coulman Tries: Derek Whitehead, Alan Smith, Billy Benyon, Roger Millward 2, Jimmy

Thompson Goals: Whitehead 3
1971
GREAT BRITAIN 13 v NEW ZEALAND 18 - September 25th 1971 Salford
1 Derek Whitehead, 2 Les Jones, 3 Billy Benyon, 4 Chris Hesketh, 5 Clive Sullivan, **6 Roger Millward,** 7 Steve Nash, 8 John Warlow, 9 Tony Karalius, 10 David Jeanes, 11 Bill Ashurst, 12 Mike Coulman, 13 John Mantle Tries: Billy Benyon, Chris Hesketh, Bill Ashurst Goals: Derek Whitehead
GREAT BRITAIN 14 v NEW ZEALAND 17 - October 16th 1971 Castleford
1 Derek Edwards, 2 Clive Sullivan, 3 David Watkins, 4 Chris Hesketh, 5 Joe Walsh, **6 Roger Millward,** 7 Alex Murphy, 8 Mick Harrison, 9 Tony Karalius, 10 Mike Coulman, 11 Colin Dixon, 12 John Mantle, 13 Bob Haigh Subs: 14 Billy Benyon, 15 Mike Stephenson Tries: Clive Sullivan, Joe Walsh, Roger Millward, Mike Coulman Goal: David Watkins
GREAT BRITAIN 12 v NEW ZEALAND 3 - November 6th 1971 Leeds
1 Derek Edwards, 2 Clive Sullivan, 3 Chris Hesketh, 4 John Holmes, 5 John Atkinson, **6 Roger Millward,** 7 Ken Loxton, 8 Mick Harrison, 9 Tony Karalius, 10 David Jeanes, 11 Bob Irving, 12 George Nicholls, 13 Terry Halmshaw Sub: Dennis O'Neill Tries: John Atkinson Goals: John Holmes 2, 2dg
1973
GREAT BRITAIN 5 v AUSTRALIA 15 - December 1st Warrington
1 Paul Charlton, 2 Alan Smith, 3 Syd Hynes, 4 Chris Hesketh, 5 Clive Sullivan, 6 David Eckersley, **7 Roger Millward,** 8 Terry Clawson, 9 Colin Clarke, 10 Mick Harrison, 11 George Nicholls, 12 Phil Lowe, 13 Doug Laughton Subs: 14 David Watkins, 15 Colin Dixon Try: Roger Millward Goal: Roger Millward Attendance: 10,019
1974 TOUR OF AUSTRALIA AND NEW ZEALAND
GREAT BRITAIN 6 v AUSTRALIA 12 - June 15th Brisbane
1 Paul Charlton, 2 David Redfearn, 3 David Watkins, 4 Chris Hesketh, 5 John Bevan, **6 Roger Millward,** 7 Steve Nash, 8 Terry Clawson, 9 Keith Bridges, 10 Jim Mills, 11 Colin Dixon, 12 Jimmy Thompson, 13 George Nicholls Subs: 14 David Eckersley, 15 John Gray Goals: Terry Clawson 2, David Watkins Attendance: 30,280
GREAT BRITAIN 16 v AUSTRALIA 11 - July 6th Sydney
1 Paul Charlton, 2 Les Dyl, 3 David Eckersley, 4 Chris Hesketh, **5 Roger Millward,** 6 Ken Gill, 7 Steve Nash, 8 Jim Mills, 9 John Gray, 10 Jimmy Thompson, 11 Colin Dixon, 12 Eric Chisnall, 13 George Nicholls Sub: Steve Norton Tries: Ken Gill, Colin Dixon, Eric Chisnall Goals: John Gray 3, 1dg Attendance: 48,006
GREAT BRITAIN 18 v AUSTRALIA 22 - July 20th Sydney (sub)
1 Paul Charlton, 2 Maurice Richards, 3 Les Dyl, 4 Chris Hesketh, 5 John Bevan, 6 Ken Gill, 7 Steve Nash, 8 Terry Clawson, 9 John Gray, 10 Jimmy Thompson, 11 Colin Dixon, 12 Eric Chisnall, 13 George Nicholls Subs: **14 Roger Millward,** 15 Paul Rose Tries: Maurice Richards, Les Dyl Goals: John Gray 6 Attendance: 48,006
1977 WORLD CUP IN AUSTRALIA AND NEW ZEALAND
GREAT BRITAIN SQUAD:
Roger Millward-Captain (Hull Kingston Rovers) Eddie Bowman (Workington Town) Len Casey (Hull Kingston Rovers) Les Dyl (Leeds) Keith Elwell (Widnes) George Fairbairn (Wigan) Keith Fielding (Salford) Bill Francis (Wigan) Ken Gill (Salford) Alan Hodkinson (Rochdale Hornets) Phil Hogan (Barrow) John Holmes (Leeds) Sammy Lloyd (Castleford) Steve Nash (Salford) George Nicholls (St Helens) Steve Pitchford (Leeds) Peter Smith (Featherstone Rovers) Jimmy Thompson (Featherstone Rovers) David Ward (Leeds) Stuart Wright (Widnes) Manager: Reg Parker (Blackpool Borough) Coach: David Watkins (Salford)
GREAT BRITAIN 23 v FRANCE 4 - June 5th 1977 Auckland
1 George Fairbairn, 2 Keith Fielding, 3 John Holmes, 4 Les Dyl, 5 Stuart Wright, **6 Roger Millward,** 7 Steve Nash, 8 Jimmy Thompson, 9 David Ward, 10 Steve Pitchford, 11 Eddie Bowman, 12 George Nicholls, 13 Phil Hogan Subs: 14 Ken Gill, 15 Len Casey Tries: Les Dyl, Stuart Wright, Roger Millward, Goals: George Fairbairn 7 Attendance: 10,000
GREAT BRITAIN 30 v NEW ZEALAND 12 - June 12th 1977 Christchurch
1 George Fairbairn, 2 Stuart Wright, 3 John Holmes, 4 Les Dyl, 5 Bill Francis, **6 Roger Millward,** 7 Steve Nash, 8 Jimmy Thompson, 9 David Ward, 10 Steve Pitchford, 11 Eddie Bowman, 12 George Nicholls, 13 Phil Hogan Sub: 15 Len Casey Tries: Stuart Wright 2, Roger Millward, Eddie Bowman, George Nicholls, Phil Hogan Goals: George Fairbairn 6 Attendance: 7,000
GREAT BRITAIN 5 v AUSTRALIA 19 - June 18th 1977 Brisbane

1 George Fairbairn, 2 Stuart Wright, 3 Bill Francis, 4 Les Dyl, 5 Keith Fielding, **6 Roger Millward,** 7 Steve Nash, 8 Jimmy Thompson, 9 David Ward, 10 Steve Pitchford, 11 Eddie Bowman, 12 George Nicholls, 13 Phil Hogan Subs: 14 John Holmes, 15 Peter Smith Try: Roger Millward, Goal: George Fairbairn. Attendance: 27,000

GREAT BRITAIN 12 v AUSTRALIA 13 - June 25th 1977 Sydney
1 George Fairbairn, 2 Stuart Wright, 3 John Holmes, 4 Les Dyl, 5 Bill Francis, **6 Roger Millward,** 7 Steve Nash, 8 Jimmy Thompson, 9 Keith Elwell, 10 Steve Pitchford, 11 Eddie Bowman, 12 Len Casey, 13 Phil Hogan Subs: 14 Ken Gill, 15 Peter Smith Tries: Steve Pitchford, Ken Gill Goals: George Fairbairn 3. Attendance: 24,400

1978

GREAT BRITAIN 9 v AUSTRALIA 15 - October 21st 1978 Wigan
1 George Fairbairn, 2 Stuart Wright, 3 Eric Hughes, 4 Eddie Cunningham, 5 John Bevan, **6 Roger Millward,** 7 Steve Nash, 8 Jimmy Thompson, 9 David Ward, 10 Paul Rose, 11 George Nicholls, 12 Len Casey, 13 Steve Norton Subs: 14 John Holmes, 15 Phil Hogan Try: John Bevan Goal: George Fairbairn. Attendance: 17,644

GREAT BRITAIN 18 v AUSTRALIA 14 - November 5th 1978 Bradford
1 George Fairbairn, 2 Stuart Wright, 3 John Joyner, 4 Les Dyl, 5 John Atkinson, **6 Roger Millward,** 7 Steve Nash, 8 Jim Mills, 9 Tony Fisher, 10 Brian Lockwood, 11 George Nicholls, 12 Phil Lowe, 13 Steve Norton Subs: 14 John Holmes, 15 Paul Rose Tries: Stuart Wright 2, Goals: George Fairbairn 6. Attendance: 26,447

GREAT BRITAIN 6 v AUSTRALIA 23 - November 18th 1978 Leeds
1 George Fairbairn, 2 Stuart Wright, 3 John Joyner, 4 John Bevan, 5 John Atkinson, **6 Roger Millward,** 7 Steve Nash, 8 Jim Mills, 9 Tony Fisher, 10 Vince Farrar, 11 George Nicholls, 12 Phil Lowe, 13 Steve Norton Subs: 14 John Holmes, 15 Paul Rose Tries: John Bevan, Roger Millward. Attendance: 29,627

1979 GREAT BRITAIN TOUR OF AUSTRALIA & NEW ZEALAND
Doug Laughton-Captain (Widnes) Mick Adams (Widnes) Len Casey (Bradford Northern) Steve Evans (Featherstone Rovers) Peter Glynn (St Helens) Jeff Grayshon (Bradford Northern) Phil Hogan (Hull Kingston Rovers) John Holmes (Leeds) Eric Hughes (Widnes) Mel James (St Helens) John Joyner (Castleford) Graham Liptrot (St Helens) Brian Lockwood (Hull Kingston Rovers) Tommy Martyn (Warrington) Roy Mathias (St Helens) Jim Mills (Widnes) **Roger Millward (Hull Kingston Rovers)** Keith Mumby (Bradford Northern) Steve Nash (Salford) George Nicholls (St Helens) Steve Norton (Hull) Alan Redfearn (Bradford Northen) Trevor Skerrett (Wakefield Trinity) Mike Smith (Hull Kingston Rovers) Gary Stephens (Castleford) Charlie Stone (Hull) David Ward (Leeds) David Watkinson (Hull Kingston Rovers) John Woods (Leigh)
Replacements during tour: J. Burke (Wakefield Trinity) for Mills George Fairbairn (Wigan) for Martyn David Topliss (Wakefield Trinity) for Millward
(Roger didn't play in any Test Matches on this tour due to injury.)

PLAYING FOR GREAT BRITAIN
Roger scored 17 tries in Test and World Cup matches during his Great Britain career, making him sixth in the all-time try-scores' list
Roger scored 20 points (two tries and seven goals) against Australia at Sydney on June 20 1970, to equal Lewis Jones' record against the Aussies set in 1954
Roger made a total of 29 appearances for Great Britain between 1966 and 1978
His Great Britain career lasted for 12 years and 9 months
Roger was the youngest player ever chosen for Great Britain (18 years 37 days) when he was a non-playing substitute for the Second Test against New Zealand at Bradford on October 23 1965.
Roger is one of only six players who have made three full tours, 1970, 1974 and 1979 for Great Britain. The others are Jonty Parkin - 1920, 1924 and 1928. Jim Sullivan - 1924, 1928 and 1932. Joe Thompson - 1924, 1928 and 1932. Gus Risman - 1932, 1936 and 1946. Brian Edgar - 1958, 1962 and 1966.

ENGLAND TEST APPEARANCES (3 + 1 SUB) & 13
1969/70 EUROPEAN CHAMPIONSHIP
1969
Oct 18   England 40 v Wales 23 at Leeds
Oct 25   England 11 v France 11 at Wigan

1970
Feb 24   England 26 v Wales 7 at Leeds (substitute)
Mar 15   France 14 v England 9 at Toulouse
1975   EUROPEAN CHAMPIONSHIP
Jan 9   England 11 v France 9 (Captain) at Perpignan
Feb 25   England 12 v Wales 8 (Captain) at Salford
1975   WORLD CHAMPIONSHIP
Mar 16   England 20 v France 2 (Captain) at Leeds
June 10   England 7 v Wales 12 (Captain) at Brisbane
June 28   Australia 10 v England 10 (Captain) at Sydney
Sept 20   England 22 v Wales 16 (Captain) at Warrington
Oct 11   England 48 v France 2 (Captain) at Bordeaux
Oct 25   England 27 v New Zealand 12 (Captain) at Bradford
Nov 1   England 16 v Australia 13 (Captain) at Wigan
1977   EUROPEAN CHAMPIONSHIP
Jan 29   England 2 v Wales 6 (Captain) at Leeds
Mar 20   England 15 v France 28 (Captain) at Carcassone
1978   EUROPEAN CHAMPIONSHIP
Mar 5   England 13 v France 11 (Captain) at Toulouse
May 28   England 60 v Wales 13 (Captain) at St Helens

Roger made 3 appearances plus one as a substitute for England in the 1969-70 European Championship. He also made another 13 appearances for England after the reintroduction of European and World Championship matches in 1975.
Roger played in three World Cups - for Great Britain in 1968 and 1977, and for England in 1975
Match details:
1969-70 EUROPEAN CHAMPIONSHIP
ENGLAND 40 v WALES 23 - October 18th 1969 Leeds
1 Arthur Keegan, 2 Bill Burgess, 3 Syd Hynes, 4 Chris Hesketh, 5 John Atkinson,
6 Roger Millward, 7 Alex Murphy, 8 John Stephens, 9 Peter Flanagan, 10 Johnny Ward,
11 Dave Robinson, 12 Bob Haigh, 13 Ray Batten Subs: 14 Mick Shoebottom, 15 Cliff Watson
Tries: Syd Hynes 2, Ray Batten 2, Alex Murphy, Cliff Watson, Bob Haigh, Roger Millward
Goals: Roger Millward 7, Alex Murphy 1 drop goal. Referee: Eric Clay (Leeds)
ENGLAND 11 V FRANCE 11 - October 25th 1969 Wigan
1 Arthur Keegan, 2 Bill Burgess, 3 Syd Hynes, 4 Chris Hesketh, 5 John Atkinson,
6 Roger Millward, 7 Alex Murphy, 8 John Stephens, 9 Peter Flanagan, 10 Johnny Ward,
11 Cliff Watson, 12 Bob Haigh, 13 Ray Batten Subs: 14 Mick Shoebottom, 15 Jimmy
Thompson Tries: John Atkinson, Syd Hynes, Bill Burgess Goals: Roger Millward
Referee: Georges Jameau (Marseilles) Attendance: 4,568
1970
ENGLAND 26 v WALES 7 - February 24th 1970 Leeds
1 Ray Dutton, 2 Alan Smith, 3 Syd Hynes, 4 Billy Benyon, 5 John Atkinson,
6 Mick Shoebotton, 7 Barry Seabourne, 8 Malcolm Dixon, 9 Peter Flanagan, 10 Cliff Watson,
11 Phil Lowe 12 Bob Haigh, 13 Malcolm Reilly Subs: **14 Roger Millward,** 15 John Stephens
Tries: Syd Hynes 2, John Atkinson 2, Mick Shoebottom, Phil Lowe Goals: Ray Dutton 4
Referee: R.L. Thomas (Oldham) Attendance: 9,393
ENGLAND 9 v FRANCE 14 - March 15th 1970 Toulouse
1 Ray Dutton, 2 Alan Smith, 3 Syd Hynes, **4 Roger Millward,** 5 John Atkinson, 6 Mick
Shoebotton, 7 Barry Seabourne, 8 John Stephens, 9 Peter Flanagan, 10 Johnny Ward, 11 Phil
Lowe 12 Jimmy Thompson, 13 Malcolm Reilly Subs: 14 Chris Hesketh, 15 Brian Lockwood
Try: Alan Smith Goals: Ray Dutton 3
Referee: Billy Thompson (Huddersfield) Attendance: 10,000
1975 EUROPEAN CHAMPIONSHIP
ENGLAND 11 v FRANCE 9 - January 19th 1975 Perpignan
1 Martin Murphy (Oldham) 2 Keith Fielding (Salford) 3 John Walsh (St Helens) 4 Les Dyl
(Leeds) 5 David Redfearn (Bradford Northern) 6 David Topliss (Wakefield Trinity)
7 Roger Millward-Captain (Hull Kingston Rovers) 8 Mick Coulman (Salford 9 John Gray
(Wigan) 10 John Millington (Hull Kingston Rovers) 11 John Cunningham (Barrow) 12 Eric
Chisnall (St Helens) 13 George Nicholls (St Helens) 14 David Eckersley (St Helens) for
Fielding (Half time) 15 Mick Morgan (Wakefield Trinity) for Millington (76)

Tries: Fielding, Dyl, Murphy. Goal: Gray Referee: M. Caillol (France) Attendance: 7,950

ENGLAND 12 v WALES 8 - February 25th 1975 Salford

1 Les Sheard (Wakefield Trinity) 2 Ged Dunn (Hull Kingston Rovers) 3 Derek Noonan (Warrington) 4 Les Dyl (Leeds) 5 John Atkinson (Leeds) 6 Ken Gill (Salford) **7 Roger Millward-Captain (Hull Kingston Rovers)** 8 Mick Coulman (Salford) 9 John Gray (Wigan) 10 Phil Jackson (Bradford Northern) 11 Tommy Martyn (Warrington) 12 John Cunningham (Barrow) 13 Mick Morgan (Wakefield Trinity) 14 David Topliss (Wakefield Trinity) 15 David Chisnall (Warrington) for Morgan (64) Tries: Noonan, Atkinson Goals: Gray (3) Referee: Stan Wall (Leigh) Attendance: 8,494

1975 WORLD CHAMPIONSHIPS - Played on home and away basis

ENGLAND SQUAD: Roger Millward-Captain (Hull Kingston Rovers), Mick Adams (Widnes), John Atkinson (Leeds), Keith Bridges (Featherstone Rovers), Paul Charlton (Salford), Dave Chisnall (St Helens), Eric Chisnall (St Helens), Phil Cookson (Leeds), Mike Coulman (Salford), Ged Dunn (Hull Kingston Rovers), Les Dyl (Leeds), Dave Eckersley (St Helens), George Fairbairn (Wigan), Keith Fielding (Salford), Colin Forsyth (Bradford Northern), Ken Gill (Salford), Parry Gordon (Warrington), John Gray (Wigan), Brian Hogan (Wigan), John Holmes (Leeds), Eric Hughes (Widnes), Bob Irving (Wigan), Jeff Grayshon (Dewsbury), Phil Jackson (Bradford Northern), Tommy Martyn (Warrington), Mick Morgan (Wakefield Trinity), Steve Nash (Featherstone Rovers), George Nicholls (St Helens), Derek Noonan (Warrington), Steve Norton (Castleford), Barry Philbin (Warrington), Dave Redfearn (Bradford Northern), Jimmy Thompson (Featherstone Rovers), John Walsh (St Helens), Stuart Wright (Wigan). Manager: William Oxley (Barrow) Coach: Alex Murphy (Warrington)

ENGLAND 20 v FRANCE 2 - March 16th 1975 Leeds

1 Paul Charlton 2 Keith Fielding 3 Derek Noonan 4 Les Dyl 5 John Atkinson 6 Ken Gill **7 Roger Millward-Captain** 8 Dave Chisnall 9 John Gray 10 Phil Jackson 11 Tommy Martyn 12 George Nicholls 13 Barry Philbin Subs: 14 John Walsh 15 Mick Morgan for Philbin (Half time) Tries: Fielding (2) Millward, Morgan Goals: Gray (4) Referee: K. Page (Australia) replaced by H. Hunt (Prestbury) after 27 minutes due to illness. Attendance: 10,842

ENGLAND SQUAD FOR THE AUSTRALASIAN SECTION

Roger Millward-Captain (Hull Kingston Rovers) John Atkinson (Leeds) Keith Bridges (Featherstone Rovers) Dave Chisnall (Warrington) Eric Chisnall (St Helens) Phil Cookson (Leeds) Mike Coulman (Salford) Ged Dunn (Hull Kingston Rovers) Les Dyl (Leeds) George Fairbairn (Wigan) Keith Fielding (Salford) Ken Gill (Salford) Parry Gordon (Warrington) Tommy Martyn (Warrington) Mick Morgan (Wakefield Trinity) Steve Nash (Featherstone Rovers) George Nicholls (St Helens) Derek Noonan (Warrington) Steve Norton (Castleford) John Walsh (St Helens) Manager: William Oxley (Barrow)

Coach: Alex Murphy (Warrington)

ENGLAND 7 v WALES 12 - June 10th 1975 Brisbane

1 George Fairbairn 2 Keith Fielding 3 Derek Noonan 4 Les Dyl 5 John Atkinson **6 Roger Millward-Captain** 7 Steve Nash 8 Dave Chisnall 9 Mick Morgan 10 Mick Coulman 11 Eric Chisnall 12 George Nicholls 13 Steve Norton Subs: 14 Ken Gill for Millward (78) 15 Tommy Martin for Coulman (51) Tries: Martin Goals: Fairbairn (2) Referee: J. Lancashire (Australia) Attendance: 6,000

ENGLAND 10 v AUSTRALIA 10 - June 28th 1975 Sydney

1 George Fairbairn 2 Keith Fielding 3 John Walsh 4 Les Dyl 5 Ged Dunn **6 Roger Millward-Captain** 7 Steve Nash 8 Mick Coulman 9 Keith Bridges 10 Mick Morgan 11 George Nicholls 12 Phil Cookson 13 Steve Norton Subs: 14 Ken Gill for Millward (60) 15 Eric Chisnall for Cookson (65) Tries: Dunn, Gill Goals: Fairbairn (2) Referee: John Percival (New Zealand) Attendance: 33,858

ENGLAND 22 v WALES 16 - September 20th 1975 Warrington

1 George Fairbairn 2 Keith Fielding 3 Eric Hughes 4 John Holmes 5 John Atkinson 6 Ken Gill **7 Roger Millward-Captain** 8 Brian Hogan 9 Keith Bridges 10 Colin Forsyth 11 Jeff Grayshon 12 Bob Irving 13 Steve Norton Subs: 14 David Eckersley for Holmes (43) 15 George Nicholls for Gill (63) Tries: Fielding, Holmes, Hughes Goals: Fairbairn (6) Bridges (dg) Referee: M. Caillol (France) Attendance: 5,034

ENGLAND 48 v FRANCE 2 - October 11th 1975 Bordeaux

1 George Fairbairn 2 Keith Fielding 3 Eric Hughes 4 John Holmes 5 Ged Dunn 6 Ken Gill **7 Roger Millward-Captain** 8 Brian Hogan 9 Keith Bridges 10 Colin Forsyth 11 Jeff Grayshon 12 Bob Irving 13 Steve Norton Subs: 14 David Eckersley for Norton 15 George Nicholls for Hogan Tries: Fielding (4) Dunn (2) Holmes (2) Hogan, Hughes, Forsyth, Gill

GLORY DAYS
Premiership Winners - 1980-1981

Division One Champions and Premiership Winners
1983-84

Goals: Fairbairn (4) Millward (2)
Referee: John Percival (New Zealand) Attendance: 1,581
ENGLAND 27 v NEW ZEALAND 12 - October 25th 1975 Bradford
1 George Fairbairn 2 Stuart Wright 3 Eric Hughes 4 John Holmes 5 Ged Dunn 6 Ken Gill 7
Roger Millward-Captain 8 Brian Hogan 9 Keith Bridges 10 Colin Forsyth 11 Jeff Grayshon
12 Mick Adams 13 Steve Norton Subs: 14 Les Dyl for Wright (52) 15 George Nicholls for
Adams (39) Tries: Gill (3) Norton, Wright, Hughes, Dunn Goals: Fairbairn (3)
Referee: A. Lacaze (France) Attendance: 5,507
ENGLAND 16 v AUSTRALIA 13 - November 1st 1975 Wigan
1 George Fairbairn 2 Ged Dunn 3 John Holmes 4 Les Dyl 5 David Redfearn 6 Ken Gill
7 Roger Millward-Captain 8 Brian Hogan 9 Keith Bridges 10 Jimmy Thompson 11 Jeff
Grayshon 12 Bob Irving 13 Steve Norton Subs: 14 Eric Hughes for Redfearn (Half time) 15
Mick Adams for Bridges (39) Tries: Grayshon, Holmes Goals: Fairbairn (5)
Referee: John Percival (New Zealand) Attendance: 9,393
1977 - EUROPEAN CHAMPIONSHIP
ENGLAND 2 v WALES 6 - January 29th 1977 Leeds
1 George Fairbairn (Wigan) 2 Stuart Wright (Widnes) 3 John Holmes (Leeds) 4 Les Dyl
(Leeds) 5 Les Jones (St Helens) 6 Ken Gill (Salford) **7 Roger Millward-Captain (Hull
Kingston Rovers)** 8 Brian Hogan (Wigan) 9 Keith Bridges (Featherstone Rovers) 10 Jimmy
Thompson (Featherstone Rovers) 11 Jeff Grayshon (Dewsbury) 12 Les Gorley (Workington
Town) 13 Doug Laughton (Widnes) 14 David Eckersley (Widnes) for Gill (38)
15 Malcolm Reilly (Castleford) for Gorley (Half time) Goal: Fairbairn
Referee: Billy Thompson (Huddersfield) Attendance: 6,472
ENGLAND 15 v FRANCE 28 - March 20th 1977 Carcassone
1 George Fairbairn (Wigan) 2 Ged Dunn (Hull Kingston Rovers) 3 Eric Hughes (Widnes) 4
Les Dyl (Leeds) 5 David Smith (Leeds) 6 Ken Gill (Salford) **7 Roger Millward-Captain
(Hull Kingston Rovers)** 8 Mick Coulman (Salford) 9 David Ward (Leeds) 10 Vince Farrar
(Featherstone Rovers) 11 Phil Lowe (Hull Kingston Rovers) 12 Paul Rose (Hull Kingston
Rovers) 13 Steve Norton (Castleford) 14 John Holmes (Leeds) for Millward (58) 15 George
Nicholls (St Helens) for Ward (Half time) Tries: Lowe, Nicholls, Smith Goals: Fairbairn (3)
Referee: M. Masse (France) Attendance: 12,000
1978 - EUROPEAN CHAMPIONSHIP
ENGLAND 13 v FRANCE 11 - March 5th 1978 Toulouse
1 George Fairbairn (Wigan) 2 Stuart Wright (Widnes) 3 Eric Hughes (Widnes) 4 Les Dyl
(Leeds) 5 John Atkinson (Leeds) **6 Roger Millward-Captain (Hull Kingston Rovers)** 7
Steve Nash (Salford) 8 Mick Harrison (Leeds) 9 Keith Elwell (Widnes) 10 George Nicholls
(St Helens) 11 Phil Lowe (Hull Kingston Rovers) 12 Mick Adams (Widnes) 13 Len Casey
(Hull Kingston Rovers) 14 John Holmes (Leeds) for Millward (39) 15 Jimmy Thompson
(Bradford Northern) Tries: Hughes (2) Holmes
Goals: Fairbairn (2) Referee: F. Escande (France) Attendance: 6,000
ENGLAND 60 v WALES 13 - May 28th 1978 St Helens
1 Geoff Pimblett (St Helens) 2 Stuart Wright (Widnes) 3 Eric Hughes (Widnes)
4 Les Dyl (Leeds) 5 John Atkinson (Leeds) **6 Roger Millward-Captain (Hull Kingston
Rovers)** 7 Steve Nash (Salford) 8 Mick Harrison (Leeds) 9 Keith Elwell (Widnes) 10 George
Nicholls (St Helens) 11 Paul Rose (Hull Kingston Rovers)
12 Len Casey (Hull Kingston Rovers) 13 Steve Norton (Hull) 14 David Eckersley (Widnes)
for Millward (Half time) 15 Jimmy Thompson (Bradford Northern) for Nicholls (Half time)
Tries: Wright (4) Atkinson (2) Hughes (2) Norton, Dyl, Casey, Nash, Pimblett
Goals: Pimblett (9) Referee: Fred Lindop (Wakefield) Attendance: 9,759

**Roger played for the England team which won The European Championship in 1969-70,
1975 and 1978.**

CAREER APPEARANCES

	Apps	Tries	Goals	Points
Castleford	34+6	16	5	118
Hull K.R.	400+7	207	617	1,825
Yorkshire	12	8	22	68
Great Britain	28+1	17	15	81
England	16+1	3	10	29

INDEX

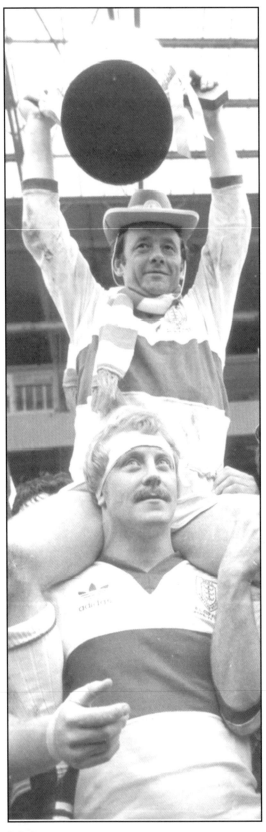

HULL KINGSTON ROVERS' CAREER RECORD

AS A PLAYER
Aug 1966 - Oct 1980

YORKSHIRE CUP WINNERS
1966-67, 1967-68, 1971-72, 1974-75,
Beaten Finalists
1975-76

AS A PLAYER COACH
March 1977 - Oct 1980

BBC2 FLOODLIT CUP WINNERS
1977-78
Beaten Finalists - 1979-80

DIVISION ONE CHAMPIONSHIP
1978-79

RL CUP WINNERS
1980

AS A COACH
Oct 1980 - May 1991

RL Cup Beaten Finalists
1980-81, 1985-86

PREMIERSHIP WINNERS
1980-81, 1983-84
Beaten Finalists - 1984-85

DIVISION ONE CHAMPIONSHIP
1983-84, 1984-85

REGAL TROPHY WINNERS
1984/85
Beaten Finalists - 1981-82, 1985-86

YORKSHIRE CUP WINNERS
1985-86
Beaten Finalists - 1980-81, 1984-85

Charity Shield Beaten Finalists
1985-86

DIVISION TWO CHAMPIONS
1989-90

Second Division Premiership
Beaten Finalists - 1989-90